Teaching Honesty in a Populist Era

Teaching Honesty in a Populist Era

Emphasizing Truth in the Education of Citizens

Sarah M. Stitzlein

OXFORD
UNIVERSITY PRESS

OXFORD
UNIVERSITY PRESS

Oxford University Press is a department of the University of Oxford.
It furthers the University's objective of excellence in research, scholarship,
and education by publishing worldwide. Oxford is a registered trade mark of
Oxford University Press in the UK and in certain other countries.

Published in the United States of America by Oxford University Press
198 Madison Avenue, New York, NY 10016, United States of America.

Library of Congress Control Number: 2024940143

9780197775882 (hardback)
9780197853788 (paperback)

DOI: 10.1093/9780197775912.001.0001

Paperback Printed by Marquis Book Printing, Canada

The manufacturer's authorized representative in the EU for product safety is
Oxford University Press España S.A. of Parque Empresarial San Fernando de Henares,
Avenida de Castilla, 2 – 28830 Madrid (www.oup.es/en or product.safety@oup.com).
OUP España S.A. also acts as importer into Spain of products made by the manufacturer.

Contents

Acknowledgments

This book benefited from helpful conversations with participants in the 2023 Philosophy of Education Society Conference, the 2022 Ohio Valley Philosophy of Education Society Conference, the 2023 Conflict and Controversy in the Classroom Conference in Amsterdam, and the 2023 John Dewey and his Legacy Conference at the Center for Dewey Studies. I am also indebted to the following for their feedback and assistance with developing aspects of this book: Kathleen Knight Abowitz, Veli-Mikko Kauppi, Tony Laden, Rebecca Taylor, Paula McAvoy, Terri Wilson, Amy Shuffelton, Ben Kotzee, Nicholas Burbules, Maddie Charles-Carlin, Danny Foster, Barrett Smith, and Katie Sellers. I am grateful for financial support from the National Endowment for the Humanities, the University of Cincinnati Arts, Humanities, and Social Sciences Grant, and the Niehoff Center for Film & Media Studies Research and Creative Fellowship. Thank you to the following journals, which granted permission to print significantly revised and expanded versions of earlier articles.

Sarah M. Stitzlein, "Political Dissent and Citizenship Education During Times of Populism and Youth Activism," *Theory and Research in Education* 20, no. 3 (2022): 217–236.

Sarah M. Stitzlein, "Teaching Honesty and Improving Democracy in the Post-Truth Era," *Educational Theory* 73, no. 1 (2023): 51–73.

Sarah M. Stitzlein, "Divisive Concepts in Classrooms: A Call to Inquiry," *Studies in Philosophy and Education* 41 (2022): 595–612.

Sarah M. Stitzlein, "Populist Challenges to Truth and Democracy Met with Pragmatism Alternatives in Citizenship Education," *Educational Theory* 74, no. 5 (2024).

1

Honesty and Democracy

Honesty matters. Seeking and telling the truth impacts our ability to thrive in the world, physically, socially, and politically. Whenever we, as citizens, face a problem, must reach a decision, or must figure out how to live together, we ask the key civic question: "What should we do?"[1] We try to answer this question by engaging in civic reasoning, which can include gathering information and deliberating among positive courses of action. Our ability to find or form satisfactory answers to this civic question depends on our propensity to honestly determine and share the truth.

Worrisome recent events, propagated by those on both the Right and the Left, demonstrate obstacles to good civic reasoning posed in a post-truth setting. This includes examples such as the discrediting of the U.S. voting system (Republican Donald Trump and Democrat Stacey Abrams) or widespread refusal of COVID-19 vaccination (Republican sceptics of the CDC and Democrat anti-vaxxers). In such a context, "objective facts are less influential in shaping political debate or public opinion than appeals to emotion and personal belief."[2] This post-truth setting also entails increasing polarization in how we disagree over what counts as facts, distrust formerly trusted sources of information (science, journalism), consume information, and circulate misinformation (inaccurate information that does not intend to mislead others) and disinformation (inaccurate information that is shared purposely to mislead others). Additionally, on the heels of complex and sometimes conflicting reports on the source of the pandemic and the role of Russia in U.S. elections, citizens increasingly question the potential partisan bias of the National Institutes of Health, Federal Bureau of Investigation (Mueller and Durham Reports), and other longstanding democratic institutions meant to uphold objective health and legal inquiry.

This is not to say that lies, partisanship, conspiracies, and favoring personal opinion are new phenomena, nor that truth is a thing of the past, for no such golden era of political life ever existed. Rather, it is to suggest that, across the political spectrum, the way we establish, regard, and share truth has changed in recent years. It is to emphasize that failing to sufficiently shore up the role of

Teaching Honesty in a Populist Era. Sarah M. Stitzlein, Oxford University Press. © Oxford University Press 2024.
DOI: 10.1093/9780197775912.003.0001

truth and honesty may further jeopardize the well-being of our democracies and the citizens who compose them.[3]

These struggles are exacerbated by several recent phenomena. One example is that we live in a time when there is more information known and readily available to us than ever before, and yet we struggle to sift through that information, especially when it is shared through unvetted social media, conflicts with information we see elsewhere, or contradicts our personal views. There is an array of ways that people might respond to this confusing abundance: some hand it over to the experts to sort out, others retreat in confusion, some boldly take a stand, and still others accuse their partisan rivals of lying, thereby discrediting some of the available options.[4] Further, recent developments in artificial intelligence throw into doubt the source and accuracy of circulating information and how it might best be employed. A second example entails the recent spread of populism, where truth arises from the common sense of "the people," intentionally bucking the knowledge of expert "elites." Within populism, information is sometimes wielded to achieve political ends or shape political narratives. And, as a final example, conspiracy theories have become dramatically more widespread, with "over half of the American population consistently endorsing some kind of conspiratorial narrative about a current political event or phenomenon."[5] Exemplifying the weaving together of the growing phenomena of populism and conspiracy theories, "two in five Americans say that it is definitely or probably true that . . . there is a single group of people who secretly control events and rule the world together." The proportion of people who agree with this statement increased dramatically between 2021 and 2022.[6] This lends some credence to President Barack Obama's declaration just weeks before the attack on the Capitol, facilitated by QAnon and other conspiracy theorists, that conspiracy theories are "the biggest threat to democracy."[7]

Additionally, the value of honesty itself seems to be declining, as indicated by polling data regarding the personal practices of both citizens and their leaders. One survey, for example, reveals that about one-fifth of American respondents did not think it was important to share only accurate information on social media.[8] Another poll showed significant declines in the percentage of people who believe it is extremely important for the president to be honest.[9] Relatedly, it seems that some political leaders have been rewarded for dishonesty. For example, President Trump's rise was partially supported by the attention he received for his false allegations that President Obama was not born in the United States and therefore not a citizen eligible for the presidency. In another example, former Representative George Santos seems to have earned his position by lying about his qualifications, including his background, education, and work experience, leaving constituents struggling to figure out whether their chosen leader was still worthy of their trust, even as some top national leaders defended him.[10] Still other examples come from Democrats, including Senator Richard Blumenthal, who won over some voters by touting his service on the ground in Vietnam, while he actually served stateside after multiple deferments. Despite seemingly declining commitments to honesty, citizens on both sides of the aisle continue to be frustrated with the dishonesty they detect in their opponents and are incensed by the hypocrisy of those opponents pointing fingers back without acknowledging such problematic behavior in their own ranks.

In recent years, some philosophers and educational scholars have begun to respond to the changes in our post-truth world, proposing ways to understand and respond to them educationally. Sarit Barzilai and Clark Chinn have categorized four primary lenses through which scholars have approached this task. The first, which they title "not knowing how to know," attributes most of the problems that have arisen lately to the inability of citizens to deal with digital information well, especially when it relates to matters of civics and science. As a result, scholars in this camp call for increased media and scientific literacy. The second, which they call "fallible ways of knowing," is focused on how cognitive limitations and biases distort quality reasoning. They call for teaching about the impact of intellectual shortcomings and epistemic vigilance. The third, which they call "not caring about truth (enough)," holds that our current problems result from citizens being insufficiently concerned with truth as an aim. In response, they believe educators should emphasize intellectual virtues and a deep commitment to truth. The final lens, which they title "disagreeing about how to know," claims that there is a loss of shared epistemology. Educators, then, should help students discuss those differences and, ultimately, reestablish the "epistemic authority of science."[11] Whereas most scholars have taken up just one of these lenses, I follow Barzilai and Chinn in believing that "an affective educational response to the post-truth condition must ultimately take all four lenses into account."[12] Missing from their categorization of the field, however, is the explicit role of honesty. In hopes of offering a broader and more useful solution than the narrower ideas proposed within each lens regarding truth, I emphasize honesty across each domain and situate all of the domains within our difficult social and political context.

When we lose sight of the importance of honesty, or even when we retain our appreciation for honesty but are unable to agree upon trusted evidence or authorities, we hinder our ability to function as a society. We hamper our ability to solve pressing problems such as controlling the spread of disease, managing immigration, ensuring fair elections, limiting drug smuggling, and more. To better enable young citizens to successfully engage the fundamental civic question "What should we do?," we must foreground the role of honesty within education. Currently, schools in the United States pay far too little attention to honesty. Going forward, I argue, they must demonstrate what honesty means and why honesty matters. Schools should affirm the value of honest leaders and nurture the habits of young citizens to seek and tell the truth themselves.

Book Overview

In this book, I respond to recent struggles, especially those related to the rise of populism, that have dramatically changed the role of honesty and truth in civic and political life.[13] I argue that honesty is a key component of a well-functioning democracy. Honesty, when viewed morally, is concerned with good character. When viewed epistemologically, it's concerned with being accurate. When viewed civically, it's concerned with how we trust each other and fruitfully live together. We value all of those in a democracy. Honesty fosters the sorts of behaviors and relationships between citizens that enable civic reasoning as we solve shared problems and figure out how to live together. I seek to clarify the relationships between honesty, truth, trust, and healthy democratic living from a pragmatist perspective. By "pragmatist" here, I am referring to a philosophical tradition, rather than a political pragmatism that might emphasize what is practical (pragmatic), instrumental, or expedient in a situation. Situating citizenship education within that pragmatist framework, I will describe how we might better cultivate honesty, thereby reviving democratic life, especially our ability to engage in civic reasoning well.

In this book I ask: *what* is honesty, *how* is it connected to truth, *why* are both important to and at risk in democracies today, and *how* should we teach them in schools? I take up some recent struggles in democracies, especially as evidenced in populist upheavals, to suggest how improved citizen practices of honesty might revive democracy. I build on populist calls for democracy to better reflect the will of the people, while also pushing back on the potential harms of populism that stem from emphasizing political dichotomies, devaluing experts, and diminishing the role of inquiry in determining truth.[14]

Chapter 2 introduces typical understandings of what honesty is and how it is connected to truth. I describe common accounts of honesty as a virtue and of truth as a correspondence between what we say or believe and an actual state of affairs that exists objectively. I show how populism, in particular, presents an alternative account of what honesty is and operates with a post-truth understanding that debunks the existence of an objective account of reality. I pause to define populism and show how it gives rise to problematic ways of understanding and practicing honesty. Then I introduce pragmatism as an alternative that captures some of the more democratizing elements of populism, while heading off some of its more worrisome tendencies to de-value honesty. I explain how pragmatists determine truth as "what works" to bring about flourishing for oneself and others, then use that to build a new understanding of honesty as truth-seeking and truth-telling that is richly social and civic in its approach and goals. I show how adopting such a pragmatist view of honesty and truth may help us tackle some of the difficulties faced by democracies today.

A recent poll found that 38 percent of ordinary citizens and 57 percent of citizenship education specialists believe that schools should be developing an informed community.[15] Clearly, being able to assess and use information appropriately, including in the service of one's community, is at the heart of fulfilling this aim. Yet, Chapter 3 exposes significant shortcomings in current education, where honesty and truth are rarely discussed. Some commentators have raised concerns with post-truth and have argued that we need to fight it by arming students with more facts and media literacy skills to enable them to sort out fact from fiction. While I appreciate their concern with post-truth and their turn to schools to address it, I argue that those approaches are often naive and shortsighted insofar as they do not develop more long-lasting commitments to or practices of honesty. Moreover, rather than simply labeling some statements fact and others fiction (and then condemning and discarding the latter), our schools need to wrestle with why some fictions are upheld and how citizens should interpret and respond to them.[16] Aiming to address that missing component in the development of good citizens, I explain how a pragmatist might cultivate habits of honesty. Rather than a virtues- or character-based education for honesty, a habits approach reflects a deeply social understanding of democracy and provides civic, rather than primarily moral, motivations for being honest. I then turn to schools to describe how they might form communities of inquiry that employ the key civic question, "What should we do?", in order to build the proclivity to seek and tell the truth. I describe how schools can nurture this disposition as students take up real and pressing problems in the world around them.

I situate my calls to teach honesty within *citizenship education*. I want to distinguish this term slightly from the related terms *civics education* and *education for democracy*. Typically, civics courses focus on how governments work and the rights and responsibilities of citizens within them. They contain a heavy dose of history and law, and they are frequently geared toward building patriotism and loyalty among youth. Citizenship education is broader, taking up matters of how one lives in local, national, and global contexts. It goes beyond a focus on government to also consider other spaces where people interact in civic or political ways, such as in clubs or religious organizations. Whereas civics education tends to employ a *civil* notion of citizenship that emphasizes legal status, citizenship education is more likely to emphasize a *civic* notion of citizenship, concerned with what citizens *do*—how they engage in practices of citizenship (like civic reasoning) rather than getting bogged down by who counts as a legal citizen.[17] Citizenship education is most explicit in courses related to the humanities and social studies (history, economics, geography), but it certainly extends across the curriculum. For example, discussions in a science class about environmental concerns relate to how one develops a sense of responsibility to care for one's natural resources. Finally, education for democracy is the most encompassing in how it understands the realm of the citizen. It goes beyond just school-based learning to include civic society and other environments where aspects of democracy can be learned and practiced.

Given that I am concerned with what and how we teach honesty in schools as a key location for developing citizens, I focus this book on citizenship education. Schools are the most overt place where we learn about citizenship and how to be citizens, where instruction in citizenship is often more explicit than in our communities or civic lives. That is not to say, however, that the suggestions I offer here should be confined to traditional classroom spaces; they certainly can be employed elsewhere. That is also not to say that students are merely citizens-in-the-making while in school; they are already capable of many aspects of citizenship, and some students frequently demonstrate those aspects in and outside of schools. Finally, I recognize that *citizenship education* is a largely Anglo-American term, and that some other places in the world may capture the content and spirit of citizenship education with other terms, like *Bildung*. My intention here is to be inclusive of those understandings, even as I employ this term.

Chapters 4 and 5 attend to two particular contexts in schools and communities that demonstrate the need for teaching honesty. Chapter 4 responds to an uptick in political dissent in recent years, especially among youth and populists. While dissent is a valuable component of ensuring quality life within a democracy, dissent cannot be done well if it does not emphasize truth-telling or truth-seeking as citizens navigate conflicting beliefs, practices, and policies. This chapter showcases how pragmatist classroom inquiry works against populist dichotomous groupings of "the people" versus "the elite," because such dichotomies prevent us from functioning smoothly together. Epistemic blind spots result when we are unable to see a situation from a competing perspective and are unwilling to attend to dissenting views raised by "the other side." Building on philosophies of agonism, I describe how students should learn to engage as adversaries rather than as enemies, even when starting from places of conflict that are common in our world today. Philosophers such as Chantal Mouffe argue that we need to "transform antagonism into agonism," a more productive way of using disagreement to improve democratic life.[18] Within an antagonistic view, those who disagree with us are seen as moral enemies or competitors that we seek to destroy. This view seems increasingly widespread, even seeping into our language, as growing numbers of both Democrats and Republicans describe members of the other party as "enemies."[19] But within an agonistic view, those who disagree with us are seen as adversaries, where we recognize that we share some common ground with them as citizens committed to principles of democracy. Rather than annihilate them or their views, we must learn how to live with them and even engage with them in ways that may change our own stances. Pragmatists remind us that "if disagreement matters, then we have no choice but to see ourselves as abiding by the norm of truth and taking ourselves to aim at truth."[20] Quality dissent and civic interaction take disagreement seriously because it reveals that one perspective may be more justified or more mistaken than another.[21] Disagreement helps us sort out which is worth following in order to improve our lives.

Chapter 5 responds to a rash of recent legislation that seeks to curb the discussion of controversial issues in schools, especially those perceived to be divisive because they entail aspects of race, gender, and sexuality, and the oppression that may relate to each. Whereas many educators have been quick to call for classroom discussion of contentious issues, I reveal limitations of such an approach. For example, classroom discussion tends to emphasize asserting one's personal stance and giving reasons for it. While these are important skills to learn for democratic life, discussions do not adequately investigate the problem to thoroughly understand it or consider how best to address it. Moreover, classroom discussions, especially in the form of debates, may privilege dominant speakers, overlook minority viewpoints, fail to attend to the affective dimensions of controversial issues, and may exacerbate polarized views. In light of those concerns, I show how pragmatist inquiry, which often includes discussion, avoids some of the shortfalls of *only* doing discussion and goes further in helping students not just learn about divisive issues but also engage them in more richly democratic ways. Within such inquiries, honesty is essential in both what we teach and how we teach it. Without honest accounts of even potentially divisive subjects, students will not come to fully understand those issues, how to navigate them with fellow citizens, or how to solve problems that arise from them. This approach recenters honesty in order to heal and improve democracy.

In sum, this book offers an improved path forward within our schools by detailing how to cultivate habits of truth-seeking and truth-telling. Such honesty will better enable citizens to navigate our difficult political moment while also increasing the likelihood that citizens can craft long-term solutions for democratic life together.

What I Bring to the Table

I arrive as someone who is deeply concerned with the civic and political struggles we face in our society. Professionally, I work as a philosopher of education, and I employ political philosophy to respond to changes in democracy and recommend potential solutions through education. I grew up on a livestock farm in the Midwest, where practical, hands-on, commonsense knowledge was celebrated by my Republican family. My family also valued K-12 education, and although many members were suspicious of political bias in universities, some pursued college degrees, usually in agriculture or education. That value was perhaps best reflected by my grandmother, father, two sisters, cousins, and nephew all choosing to become teachers, some in rural areas and others more recently in small towns and suburbia. Although I considered becoming a full-time K–12 teacher while an undergraduate and have spent many years since volunteering in schools, I decided then to continue my journey through to receiving a Ph.D., focusing on more theoretical aspects of education. I left the countryside to teach at a large urban university, complete with heftier title and paycheck. As a result, in the eyes of many of my family members I shifted from the people to the elite.

Across that trajectory, my political affiliation began to change. That was provoked, in part, because of a significant matter related to truth in our country's history: the decision to go to war in 2003 based on the assertion that Iraq had weapons of mass destruction. Truth and honesty mattered because real lives were on the line. A spouse of a soldier at the time, I found myself doubting the evidence presented by Republican secretary of state Colin Powell, yet feeling patriotically compelled to support my husband and all of those serving our country, a feeling magnified by the experience of 9/11. I struggled to know whom to trust and what to believe. As the body counts on all sides of the war on terror grew, my husband was presented with an ultimatum designed to lure him into agreeing to longer military service. As weapons of mass destruction were not located, my dissatisfaction with Republican leadership grew and

I began to publicly dissent against the war. While I retained a deep commitment to loving my country and other core values from the Right, I moved increasingly toward the Left, and now find myself aligned with Democrats on most issues.

I sit down at the table these days with my Libertarian husband, my traditionally conservative father, and my son, who even at a young age is becoming quite vocal in his political views, especially regarding matters of equity and justice. We sometimes strain to find common ground. We struggle to know which evidence, people, and institutions to trust as we try to figure out which vaccines we should take, how to make sense of conflicting reports about the security of our country's borders, and how to answer other pressing questions. Whereas many Americans today increasingly live in families and neighborhoods that are aligned politically, and are surrounded by like-minded peers in workplace and social media environments, I've had to learn to navigate between and across borders regularly. I am grateful for that because it has not only helped me be a citizen better equipped for the challenges of our polarized country today but also rendered me better prepared to approach this book with those people—rural farmers, middle-class teachers, loyal soldiers, and urban academics—all in mind as people whom I love and trust.

It may come as no surprise, then, that I end up endorsing a more pragmatist account of truth and honesty, one that may work better in an array of settings. But make no mistake: this is not an approach that, in an effort to appeal to all, leaves no one satisfied and replicates the status quo. The proposal I offer aims to be more inclusive and requires substantial changes to the way that we educate citizens, including teaching them how to dissent and how to engage with controversial issues. I invite you to join me in considering those proposals and I hope you will remain open as I consider claims and concerns across the political spectrum.

My Audience and What They Can Take Away from the Table

I aim to speak here primarily to other philosophers of education, but not only to them. Philosophers of education are centrally concerned with the aims of education. One of the most long-standing aims is that of educating for democracy, preparing citizens who can perpetuate and improve our political system. This book takes up this aim and considers it anew in light of shifts in our political environment, including how citizens assess and wield information to achieve civic and political outcomes, including how we affirm our affiliation with like-minded others. It offers philosophers of education new fodder for consideration in terms of both the ends and means of how we do democratic education when democracy itself is struggling. Currently practicing and future teachers enrolled in teacher education may benefit from learning about this long-standing and changing aim, including how they can foreground it in their daily classroom practices.

Scholars of other disciplines, including political philosophers and curriculum theorists, may also be interested in how I describe the shifting political environment and the theories offered to explain it, as well as the resulting changes to schooling that I argue should follow from it. These might be developed into curricular and pedagogical practices that may serve current social studies educators as well as the educators in universities who prepare teachers. Pragmatist philosophers may take interest in how I employ key ideas from that tradition to shed light on political life today, including providing a unique lens on recent psychological and sociological phenomena that are posing significant problems to democratic ways of life and how habits of democracy might help us craft a path forward. Pragmatism has recently enjoyed renewed interest, and this project offers a new domain in which pragmatist thinking can be employed. I introduce philosophical ideas in a scholarly way that aims to convey some nuance and sophistication, though I do not go into great detail into matters of epistemology and metaphysics that might interest some scholars in other subfields of philosophy, as it goes beyond the scope and intention of my more applied focus on schooling here.

I aim to be accessible, using language and tone that invites more generalist audiences to the table also. This may include fellow citizens who are seeking ways to make sense of our recent struggles in democracy and wondering what they might do to contribute to a better future. I invite each of you to join me in this analysis and in the work ahead as we seek to repair and improve our democracy together.

Notes

1. Gideon Dishon and Sigal Ben-Porath, "Don't@ Me: Rethinking Digital Civility Online and in School," *Learning, Media and Technology* 43, no. 4 (2018): 434–450; William Galston, "Truth and Democracy: Theme and Variations," in *Truth and Democracy*, ed. Jeremy Elkins and Andrew Norris (Philadelphia: University of Pennsylvania Press, 2012), 130–145; Peter Levine, *What Should We Do? A Theory of Civic Life* (New York: Oxford University Press, 2022).

2. *Oxford English Dictionary Online*, s.v. "post-truth, adj.," accessed December 15, 2023. https://doi.org/10.1093/OED/7768605775.

3. To be clear, I do not subscribe to some sort of nostalgic view that holds that truth devoid of emotion or opinion ever led political life.

4. I'm drawing here on responses outlined by Jason Baehr in "Democracy, Information Technology, and Virtue Epistemology," in *Virtues, Democracy, and Online Media*, ed. Nancy Snow and Maria Silvia Vaccarezza (New York: Routledge, 2021), 5.

5. J. Eric Oliver and Thomas J. Wood, "Conspiracy Theories and the Paranoid Style(s) of Mass Opinion," *American Journal of Political Science* 58, no. 4 (2014): 952.

6. Taylor Orth, "Which Groups of Americans Are Most Likely to Believe Conspiracy Theories?," YouGov, March 30, 2022, https://today.yougov.com/topics/politics/articles-reports/2022/03/30/which-groups-americans-believe-conspiracies.

7. Barack Obama, "Why Obama Fears for Our Democracy," interview by Jeffrey Goldberg, *The Atlantic,* last modified November 19, 2020, https://www.theatlantic.com/ideas/arch ive/2020/11/why-obama-fearsfor-our-democracy/617087/.

8. Gordon Pennycook, Ziv Epstein, Mohsen Mosely, Antonio Arechar, Dean Eckles, and David Rand, "Understanding and Reducing the Spread of Misinformation Online," in NA-Advances in Consumer Research, vol. 48, ed. Jennifer Argo, Tina M. Lowrey, and Hope Jensen Schau. (Duluth, MN: Association for Consumer Research, 2020), 863–867.

9. Polling done by the Associated Press, Yahoo, and the *Washington Post* and cited in Jonathan Rauch, *The Constitution of Knowledge: A Defense of Truth* (Washington, DC: Brookings Institution Press, 2021), 173.

10. Jennifer McLogan, "Rep. George Santos' Constituents Feel Left in Limbo as Congressman Faces New Allegations," CBS News, last modified January 30, 2023, https://www.cbsn ews.com/newyork/news/rep-george-santos-constituents-feel-left-in-limbo-as-congress man-faces-new-allegations/; Kevin Freking, "Santos Steps Down from House Panels amid Ethics Issues," Associated Press, January 31, 2023, https://apnews.com/article/george-san tos-congress-house-committees-6e46e2badad39fb190d38105a800236f; Brian Mann, "Santos Took Office One Month Ago and His New York District Says He's Got to Go," NPR, February 5, 2023, https://www.npr.org/2023/02/04/1153843337/george-santos-new-york-district.

11. Sarit Barzilai and Clark A. Chinn, "A Review of Educational Responses to the 'Post-Truth' Condition: Four Lenses on 'Post-Truth' Problems," *Educational Psychologist* 55, no. 3 (2020): 111.

12. Barzilai and Chinn, "A Review of Educational Responses to the 'Post-Truth' Condition," 116.

13. Wendy Rahn, *Populism in the US: The Evolution of the Trump Constituency* (New York: Routledge, 2018); Jakob Schwörer, *The Growth of Populism in the Political Mainstream: The Contagion Effect of Populist Messages on Mainstream Parties' Communication* (Cham, Switzerland: Springer, 2021).

14. It is challenging to know how to write about populism and post-truth, in part because these labels are read as pejorative. The assumption is often that the audience is unsympathetic to them, and many people who endorse aspects of them would not choose those labels for themselves.

15. Jack Schneider, Eric Soto-Shed, and Karalyn McGovern, "Teaching Students to Be Skilled Citizens," *Kappan* 104, no. 8 (2023): 47–51.

16. Bianca Thoilliez, "'Making Education Possible Again': Pragmatist Experiments for a Troubled and Down-to-Earth Pedagogy," *Educational Theory* 72, no. 4 (2022): 1–17.

17. I draw these distinctions of "citizen" from James Tully, *Public Philosophy in a New Key*, 2nd ed. (Cambridge: Cambridge University Press, 2008).
18. Chantel Mouffe, *Deliberative Democracy or Agonistic Pluralism* (Vienna: Institute for Advanced Studies, 2000).
19. Phillip Bump, "Democrats Have Joined Republicans in Calling Their Opponents 'Enemies,'" *Washington Post*, August 1, 2022.
20. Cheryl Misak, "Making Disagreement Matter: Pragmatism and Deliberative Democracy," *Journal of Speculative Philosophy* 18, no. 1 (2004): 18.
21. Of course, there are some disagreements that are not a matter of truth, such as those of taste. One person may prefer chocolate ice cream and another vanilla ice cream. Here we can agree to disagree.

2

Honesty and the World Today

To respond to our post-truth era, the decreasing valuing of honesty, and the impact of both on democracy, we must first try to make sense of what honesty and truth mean and why they are significant. In this chapter, I will briefly consider dominant philosophical understandings of honesty, describe its relationship to truth and trust, and discuss its connection to democracy. I will introduce a pragmatist account of truth and honesty, explaining how it offers a unique lens for responding to recent struggles, especially those tied to populism, and envisioning improved alternatives.

Despite the seemingly increased importance of honesty in our world, few scholars have devoted much attention to it recently.[1] Those who have studied or theorized honesty typically describe it as a way in which we conduct our thinking that is carried out in action and is relatively stable across time. Many people see honesty as a virtue, a way of acting that is aligned with the good. Reflecting a virtue account, honesty is seen as a personal responsibility that drives thinking and actions. Because of the way that it is consistently enacted, it is often regarded as a trait demonstrating good character. It leads one to avoid not just lying but also related phenomena like misleading, cheating, and other forms of deception. Those who behave honestly do not intentionally lie or share false information, though they may be mistaken or inadvertently share false information. Where the intention is justified but the outcome is faulty, we call this an "honest mistake."

Philosopher Christian Miller and his research team are some of the few people studying honesty today. Miller defines honesty as "the virtue of being disposed, centrally and reliably and for good or virtuous motivating reasons, to not intentionally distorting the facts as the agent sees them."[2] He explains key aspects of honesty, including two that are concerned with veracity in communication. The first entails truthfulness. This means that a person cares about the truth and is disposed to reliably express it. The second is forthrightness. This means that a person is particularly open and complete when pursuing and sharing truth; they don't hide or hold back on disclosing important information.[3] Honesty means taking truth seriously, which encourages one to pursue and tell the truth.

Teaching Honesty in a Populist Era. Sarah M. Stitzlein, Oxford University Press. © Oxford University Press 2024.
DOI: 10.1093/9780197775912.003.0002

Honesty has related components of accuracy and sincerity, mostly notably laid out in the earlier work of esteemed ethicist Bernard Williams.[4] Accuracy is achieved when a person earnestly seeks valid truth claims to the best of that person's ability. Sincerity means being open and straightforward in telling what one believes to be the truth, without deceiving oneself or others. While my central focus in this book is on the aspects of honesty related to civic life, including matters of truth and the sharing of facts and information, these and other aspects of honesty work together to lead us to determine that an honest person keeps promises and follows the rules—components of honesty as trustworthiness that I will not describe here. While average folks may not describe honesty using such specific terminology, I believe it is fair to say that most would see truthfulness, accuracy, forthrightness, and sincerity as key features of honesty if they were offered up for consideration. Seeing them as well established and useful, I will employ them throughout this book, even as I seek to further clarify and build upon them to offer a definition of honesty in terms of pragmatist habits.

Miller's definition refers to distorting the facts "as the agent sees them." This caveat suggests that an account of honesty must take into consideration the facts that one shares and how they are determined, while recognizing that one may be mistaken and still be speaking and acting in good faith. Facts are a matter of truth. A long-standing view of truth is the correspondence theory, where a proposition corresponds directly with some clear state of affairs. In other words, a proposition matches some objective aspect of reality. That proposition (or its referent) would then be called a fact. For example, the claim "Russia is the largest country in area" is a reflection of an objective state of reality. To give an honest account is to be forthright, accurate, and sincere when proclaiming some proposition corresponds to the actual state of affairs. To honestly assert "Russia is the largest country in area" entails checking the accuracy of the claim relative to available records and measurement data, then sharing this statement without the intention to deceive. To display one's forthrightness about this claim, one might further provide the specific land area of Russia or a comparison between Russia's size and that of its closest rival in order to give a more complete account. Recognizing that one may have limited access to or may be mistaken about the objective world, Miller says that it is enough to not intentionally distort the facts one does have or share. Miller sides with a more subjective view regarding sharing the facts "as the agent sees them." The focus, then, is more on how one relates those facts to others in appropriate ways. I follow suit to an extent, but I situate my definition of honesty within a pragmatist notion of truth that works quite differently than a correspondence theory. Within that view, one must continually reassess facts and verify truth, setting a standard for community participation that pushes past being complacent with sharing what one believes to be the case.

Honesty clearly plays an important part in discussions of ethical behavior, including determining whether or not one is a good person. When viewed as a virtue, honesty must have good motivations behind it. On the other hand, some parents pay little attention to moral intentions and may simply warn their children, "You should never lie," to demand honesty and truth-telling. Yet, to get a fuller picture of honesty, we need to consider the social conditions that may lead one to lie, sometimes for justified reasons and sometimes for more problematically self-serving ones. Simply knowing that being honest is the right thing to do may not compel one to actually do it. To address this problem, some scholars of moral or character education have suggested developing a self-identity that will help to provide motivational force by making upright behavior key to one's self-understanding in such a way that behaving otherwise risks one's own identity.[5]

This initial account of honesty, reliant upon a moral, atomic self who enacts virtue—or even a separate account where one fulfills a duty (in the sense supported by Immanuel Kant)—seems rather contextually naive. It lacks a sufficient understanding of the self as social and as forming and being formed by the environment.[6] It focuses on the character of the individual herself, rather than how her behaviors shape others or the world around her. Notably, honesty is other-regarding. Honesty rarely stops simply with one person independently seeking or sharing the truth. Instead, honesty pushes us to consider relationships, trustworthiness, and the impact on those around us of the beliefs we assert. In this way, honesty supports both epistemic and civic endeavors, offering benefits to democratic communities. I will not constrain my discussion of honesty to the realm of moral virtue. Rather, I aim to bring honesty to bear on matters of civic life, where our concern is not just with the behavior of individuals but also with its impact on social and coordinated living. For when we enact honesty in democracy and civic reasoning, part of what we are doing is establishing or preserving just relations between citizens as we solve shared problems. We treat others as worthy of knowing the truth and using it to enrich their lives as we ask, "What should we do?"

Honesty takes on greater significance when located within an understanding of democracy as a social way of life aimed at solving shared problems, where individuals are interdependent and where they are mutually shaped by their interactions and transactions. When honesty is understood as functioning that way in democracy today, we come to see why urging someone to do "what's right," or even castigating liars for their moral shortcomings, is insufficient for producing sustainable honest behavior and the trusting relationships it bolsters. In other words, chiding by parents or teachers may not go far enough in heading off the temptation to lie or in confronting the conditions that encourage dishonesty. This situation is exacerbated by a political environment where dishonesty is seemingly on the rise and where some significant psychological and sociological phenomena work against honesty. As I will explain in this book, it is the pragmatist perspective, which emphasizes human relationships, social intelligence, and motivations for honesty based in civic inquiry, that brings a unique and educational perspective to more commonly held understandings of honesty.

Complications to Truth and Honesty from Populism

In 2016, the Oxford Dictionaries selected "post-truth" as the word of the year, and in 2017 the Cambridge Dictionary selected "populism."[7] These words did not just experience a brief spike in usage in those years, however; employment of these words and the phenomena they describe have continued to grow significantly. Yet, despite their increasing prominence and influence on democratic life—privileging emotion and opinion in battles between the people and the elite—discussions of truth and populism remain largely absent from American citizenship education.[8] In classrooms, students are more likely to learn about how liberal democracies are intended to function, as well as the historical figures and events that led to that democratic ideal. Too rarely do classes take up the far-from-ideal aspects of democracy that take place daily inside and outside of school walls, such as distrust of the media or lack of faith in government institutions. Citizenship education tends to promote the ideals of liberal democracy, while overlooking the ways in which democracy has fallen short of its promises—a key driver of populism.[9]

Discussions of truth—when it is overtly discussed at all—ignore how truth functions within populism, including in the related issues and pronouncements of famous populist leaders, such as "fake news" and "alternative facts" (the former was the American Dialect Society's 2017 Word and Euphemism of the Year).[10] Those phenomena, often framed in terms of deliberate distortion, are neither as novel nor as significant as post-truth, which "captures new conditions for public communication that signal the impossibility of truth as shared assessments about reality."[11] Because of the growth of these phenomena and the way they challenge philosophical and common understandings of truth and honesty, I take them up here.

Citizenship education tends to imply that truth, itemized as facts one holds and wields, is a tool for mastering the knowledge and skills required to achieve freedom and prosperity in a democracy—as if discovering one clear and accurate account will necessarily lead to good personal and democratic living. Yet truth, traditionally celebrated as the correspondence between a proposition and the objective reality it describes, has proven quite difficult to secure in many contexts. Indeed, we increasingly see citizens fighting over what is fact and what is not, sometimes in rather trivial ways, such as claims about the number of people attending President Trump's inauguration, but also in non-trivial examples, such as declarations that vaccines cause autism. Moreover, the aspiration of pursuing such a singular truth has failed to deliver its intended outcomes of freedom and prosperity. Frustrated by those results, many populists increasingly see democracy and their place in it quite differently than how members of the elite do.

I focus here on populism as a symptom of wider problems in liberal democracy rather than as their cause, though populism can certainly exacerbate those problems or provoke others.[12] I argue that citizenship education should more overtly take up some of these challenges to liberal democracy posed by populism. In this book, I provide pragmatist accounts of truth and inquiry to attend to some of the problems populism reveals and the kind of truth it favors. I put forward pragmatist visions of truth and democracy to build on the populist call for democracy to better reflect the demands of the people, while also trying to prevent the devaluing of experts and inquiry that populism too often champions.

Defining Populism

Describing "populism" as the 2017 Word of the Year may problematically give the impression that the word suddenly arrived on the scene at that point, perhaps due to contentious events around that time, like Brexit or the election of populist leaders in Europe, Latin America, and the United States. But populism has a long history, as well as a long record of being ridiculed by intellectuals and historians, largely for being seen as ignorant, emotional, or detrimental to democracy.[13] I wish to take populism seriously, recognizing it as a significant reflection of citizens' frustrations with traditional liberal democracy and being open to the dissenting views it expresses in good faith.

Populism has been described as an ideology, a discourse, a movement, a form of expression, and more.[14] Some political scientists and many media reporters invoke more comprehensive definitions of populism, reading onto it specific worldviews, such as preferences for authoritarian leaders, nationalism, or xenophobia.[15] These attributions, focused largely on the practices

and beliefs of certain populist leaders, overemphasize these problematic figures and their views. This leads critics to quickly write off populism or even
cast it as an evil endeavor led by buffoons. I focus instead on treating populism as a thin and rather vague ideology that is often expressed through
discourse.[16] Such a broad definition helps to explain how populism has
reappeared and re-formed across time and place. Divorcing populism from
specific leaders or thick ideologies containing particular policy positions,
such as socialism, enables us to better see the wide array of populist activities
and views across the political spectrum, encompassing both Left and Right
populisms.[17]

At the core of populism as a thin ideology is a vision of society as composed
of two homogeneous and antagonistic groups: the people and the elite. In this
"us versus them" scenario, populism holds that the will of the people should
trump the control of the elite because the people are seen as hardworking,
good, and pure, while the elite are viewed as those in the government,
media, economy, academy, or culture who are corrupt and power-hungry.[18]
Florida governor Ron DeSantis describes elites from his Right populist perspective: "These elites are 'progressives' who believe our country should be
managed by an exclusive cadre of 'experts' who wield authority through an
unaccountable and massive administrative state. They tend to view average
Americans with contempt, believe in the need for wholesale social engi-
neering of American society, and consider themselves entitled to wield power
over others."[19] Populists on the Left similarly highlight the far-reaching power
of the elites they describe, though they tend to be talking more about wealthy
corporate leaders who put financial interests over the well-being or wishes of
the poor or working class.

Many populists work to distinguish themselves from the elite. Employing
populist discourse to separate herself and people like her from what she
sees as an elitist Left, U.S. representative Marjorie Taylor Greene tweeted, "I
am being attacked by the godless left because I said I'm a proud Christian
Nationalist. These evil people are even calling me a Nazi because I proudly
love my country and my God. The left has shown us exactly who they are.
They hate America, they hate God, and they hate us."[20] Populism maps competing tribes in the world, sometimes using overt labels more specific and
pejorative than just "the elite," such as Left populist senator Bernie Sanders's
use of "the billionaire class." This discourse groups people distinctly and in
opposition to each other, shutting down the possibility for diversity within
groups, collaboration across them, or compromise between them.[21] To quote
an example from a campaign speech by President Trump, "The only important thing is the unification of the people because the other people don't mean

anything."[22] Additionally, because those seemingly typical citizens who disagree with the people threaten to expose the group as not the homogeneous cluster that populists envision, those questioning individuals are often characterized as self-interested and aligned with power-driven elites.[23]

Populism prioritizes the firsthand experience and direct expression of the people, unfiltered by aspects of democracy like the media or other institutions. These experiences and opinions are captured by the concept of "common sense." As such, populism often functions as a discourse, offering stories, performances, language, and rhetoric about each group and their claims. Through such discourse and performances, even those from elite families or backgrounds, including populist leaders like President Trump or other millionaires, can become seen as part of the people, especially if they seem to invoke and celebrate the common sense of the people or if they openly challenge the ways of the elite.[24]

These rhetorical tools and performances mobilize the affect of participants—their embodied, emotional reactions. These commonly include anger and resentment toward the elite but can also involve a sense of patriotism and belonging that makes populists feel good. Affect includes, yet goes beyond, individual feelings; it is "relational, political and embodied."[25] Those affective responses are tapped to provoke action. Sometimes they drive us to unite with other people, thereby deepening our connection and loyalty to those we see as like us, in part because they experience similar affective responses to the same stimuli. Sometimes they provoke political action, where we align with others to pursue power or shared interests. Populism builds upon, and sometimes may manipulate, our affect to shape our identities and assert our distinction from competing groups. Populism dictates that we may legitimately feel empathetic and other positive feelings for those like us and disdain and other negative feelings for those who are not.

Demonstrating how elites often wield more power to achieve their desired ends while the needs of the people too often go unfulfilled, populism reveals that democracy falls short of its promises of *e pluribus unum*, the pursuit of happiness, and justice for all. Instead, the populist map shows division, unfairness, and competition.[26] Explaining the appeal of populism today, Governor Ron DeSantis said, "The desirability of populism lies in what the populist impulse is trying to achieve . . . to counteract the failures of an unrepresentative ruling class with a more representative and successful government that represents a logical response by the people who bear the brunt of their failures."[27] Dissatisfied with the results of democracy, populists take issue with the procedures and institutions of democracy, including pointing fingers at the powerful people directing them.[28] Populism, then, tends to come to the fore during times of turmoil, where political trust is low and desire for change is high.[29]

In those moments, democracy is often seen as unresponsive to the demands of the people, and the motivations of leaders within democracy are seen with suspicion. Even though different segments of the people may have different demands, they become united by their shared experience of having been ignored or suppressed by the elite. U.S. president Trump tapped into that spirit during his inauguration speech, saying, "To all Americans in every city near and far, small and large, from mountain to mountain, from ocean to ocean, hear these words: You will never be ignored again. Your voice, your hopes, and your dreams will define our American destiny. And your courage and goodness and love will forever guide us along the way."[30] Feeling validated, many citizens were led to support Trump and take up his political causes.

Many people would not proclaim themselves to be populists, perhaps because some see the term as an insult aligning them with a group disparaged by political commentators and the press. And yet, many uphold key aspects of the thin ideology form of populism, celebrating common sense and pushing back against those they perceive as elites. Other people, however, embrace the label "populist," seeing it as an identity that emboldens them to political action on behalf of the people and against the liberal democracy and its leaders that have failed them. I focus here on both groups, attributing the label "populist" to those who uphold or perform the thin ideology just described.

In this book, I want to largely set aside political and ethical assessments about whether populism is good or bad for democracy,[31] though I will briefly touch on the topic here. Looking at populism in a favorable light, we see that it can reveal current problems with liberal democracy and empower citizens to demand change while also celebrating their voices and experiences. That said, populism may also derail valuable aspects of liberal democracy. Without describing them in detail, I will briefly list some of those problematic implications. First, the general will of the people may trample the rights of minorities traditionally protected by the principles and constitutions of liberal democracies. Second, populists' celebration of the common sense of the people may lead to skepticism toward or discrediting of otherwise trustworthy knowledge arising from government institutions or scientific organizations simply because it is viewed as elitist. Third, seeking to affirm the narratives of their political group and to question the knowledge and motives of elites, populists sometimes fall prey to false conspiracy theories about those in power or the knowledge they proclaim. Fourth, antagonism between the people and the elite may become so intractable that it is difficult to work across groups to ask the civic question about how to live together or construct policies for the public sphere.[32] Fifth, populism may reduce the sort of pluralist deliberation that is necessary for citizens to feel represented and, thereby, for liberal democracy to retain its political legitimacy.[33] Finally, while populism may be good at revealing that there are significant problems with liberal democracy, it often struggles to put forward alternatives to those problems, sometimes because it is hyperfocused on perpetuating conflict with the elite.[34]

I start with the recognition that populism is widespread and is growing in many regions of the world. That is not to say that we should swiftly or thoroughly celebrate populism simply because it exists or is increasing. But given its pervasiveness, we need to understand how it operates and how students can be best equipped to live in an increasingly populist world today, challenge it when necessary, and embrace it when warranted. Moreover, we need to understand how populism identifies aspects of democracy that are in serious need of attention or improvement. I follow Edda Sant in taking up what she calls "the reconstructive task" of education, where education can open new pathways for democratic life or mend old ones.[35]

It is important to recognize patterns that extend across the political spectrum of populism, Right and Left. We can learn more from the best of what populism has to offer and the worst of what it may cause by considering the full range. That said, Right populism has been far more widespread in recent years in the United States, my central country of concern. And Right populism has been more worrisomely active in practices that run counter to truth and honesty, perhaps most clearly evidenced in the January 6, 2021, attack on the Capitol and ongoing election denial. Because of these factors, you will see that I more often engage with examples from the Right. I do not want to frustrate or alienate my more Right-leaning readers by doing so, however. I hope to do so in a way that is fair, in part by avoiding discussion of particular ideologies endorsed by Right populists or the larger political agendas they may entail and by limiting my discussion to aspects of thin ideology. I will focus on aspects of populism only related to matters of truth and honesty, showing how they present epistemic and civic opportunities and roadblocks. Then I will put forward a pragmatist alternative that embraces some aspects of populism while heading off some of its pitfalls, including proclivities toward dishonesty, within the larger project of citizenship education.

Populist Understandings of Truth and Honesty

Many scholars focus more on the specific demands of populists, such as calls for changes to economically unjust systems. Instead, I look at how populists determine the truth of the empirical and moral claims that underlie those demands and whether they honestly share them with forthrightness, accuracy, and sincerity. Back-to-back Words of the Year, "populism" and "post-truth" have come to the foreground alongside each other. Importantly, though, populism has a long history and post-truth is not limited only to the realm of populism. Also, populism is not alone in its questioning of objective correspondence theories of truth. Some postmodernists, for example, have taken issue with the inability of language to capture truth or to do so in ways that are undistorted by power. They have been pedaling their views on truth long before the recent populist resurgence that has posed a serious challenge to liberal democracy. That said, there appears to be increasing adoption of post-truth among populists.

In a post-truth setting, "objective facts are less influential in shaping public opinion than appeals to emotion and personal belief."[36] Moreover, post-truth signals "the impossibility of truth as shared assessment about reality."[37] This goes well beyond the mere deceptions of fake news or lying leaders to suggest a larger critique of the concept of scientific, rationalist, objective truth that has long been invoked in liberal democracy. It suggests that even if an objective reality exists, we may not be able to agree about which propositions accurately correspond with that reality. Post-truth dethrones such objective truth and replaces it with an array of opinions, which are sometimes touted as "facts" as a way to claim authority and legitimacy for those views. Those opinions can spread widely in today's interconnected world, especially through social media, where there is no agreed-upon system for verifying them, and yet they amass affective emoji responses as they persuade others to adopt them. Or, as in the case of populist leader President Trump's alternative social media platform, intriguingly called Truth Social, opinions are "ReTruthed" as they are affirmed and shared with others. Their legitimacy as truth or fact comes not from being a reflection of reality but from being affirmed repeatedly, especially among those that one trusts and from within one's tribe.

For many populists, truth is not objective, nor is it a common good. Rather, truth, when situated in populist Manichean battles between the people and the elite, is viewed in terms of conflicting and constructed, yet indisputable, narratives to which members of competing political tribes loyally adhere.[38] These narratives help to explain the unjust outcomes of liberal democracy, where the elite obtain more power and wealth because of their supposed access to truth (through advanced degrees, high-tech knowledge, etc.). History shows that the marketplace of ideas in liberal democracy has been far from unbiased and that the institutions intended to protect the rights and well-being of citizens sometimes limit them or run counter to their desires.

Populist narratives, instead, uphold the knowledge of the people and casti-
gate the corrupt elite who devalue that knowledge as they maintain an unfair
system.

In the populist context, there is no clear truth to be grasped; rather, truth is
constructed and contested, and yet propositions are still declared to be truth
or lies. Populists invoke post-truth in how they see each group, the people
and the elites, as having a separate version of truth that arises from their
differing experiences, emotions, and opinions. In the words of political com-
munications scholar Silvio Waisbord, "The root of populism's opposition to
[a traditional notion of] truth is its binary vision of politics."[39] This binary
outlook suggests that a common, shared truth across the people and the elite
is impossible. Some populists fault liberal democracy for upholding the illu-
sion that truth, as some sort of shared common good, can even be found or
accepted. Truth cannot be divorced from politics; it is steeped in power. In
this regard, populists demonstrate that truth, in some objective sense where
truth reflects a reality that exists apart from politics, doesn't exist. Those further to the Right argue that truth certainly cannot be ferreted out through
fact-checking by the media or through accountability procedures overseen by
democratic institutions such as health or investigative organizations (especially the Federal Bureau of Investigation), which they believe are led by biased and morally suspect elites. For example, Governor DeSantis warns, "We
have seen institution after institution become thoroughly politicized. Many
are actively trying to impose an ideological agenda on society."[40] In another
example, conservative talk show radio host Rush Limbaugh "regularly rails
against 'a universe of lies' comprised of the 'four corners of deceit,' which are
the mainstream media, science, government, and academia. He bemoans 'the
corruption that exists between government and academia and science and the
media. Science has been corrupted. We know the media has been corrupted
for a long time. Academia has been corrupted. None of what they do is real.
It's all lies!' "[41]

While scholars like Waisbord may diagnose populism this way, it is likely
that populists themselves, if asked directly, would not argue that a shared
truth is impossible but, rather, would claim that there is one truth, they hold
it, and elites (especially media) fail to see that truth or intentionally distort it.
This perspective may be most obvious among Christian evangelical or funda-
mentalist populists, who proclaim one clear religious truth accessible through
certain beliefs and practices.[42] Part of what populists aim to do is to discredit
the elite (their political rivals) by casting them as corrupt. They then call for
law and order as well as clear Christian rules, while simultaneously wielding
seemingly objective rules to serve their ends.

Populism needs shared narratives among the people to unite them, espe-cially around their moral claims against the elite. The "facts" that compose those narratives "are subsidiary to narratives—to pre-determined visions of politics, the clash between popular and elite interests, and ideological visions of the world. As kernels of knowledge, facts are inseparable from power for they are produced according to epistemic premises grounded in relations of domination."[43] The people and their leaders construct those narratives that reaffirm the views of the people against the elite, whose narratives are seen as false, or, more often, pejoratively, as lies or "fake news." Populists seek to shore up their own positions, so they assert seeming facts that support the predetermined goals of their narrative.

I say "seeming" here because I am distinguishing the populist account of facts from the correspondence theory account where facts reflect objective realities about the world. Populist facts are not necessarily accurate reflections of the world; rather, they are endorsed because they are aligned with the overall political narrative and its goals. Proclaiming them to be true (and affirming them through activities like "ReTruthing" them on social media) lends epistemic and moral heft to those seeming facts and narratives, driving up affective and loyal responses to them. The need to further vilify the enemy and prove one's allegiance to the people may lead some populists to con-struct dishonest, inaccurate accounts or even false conspiracy theories about shadowy forces at play. This is not to say that populists do not care about truth, for clearly they do. They care, though not in the way that one committed to honesty cares. In part, populists care about truth because of what truth *does* for their tribe, including the way that asserting truths aligned with their reli-gious, political, or scientific views enables them to uphold their commitments and their tribal boundaries.

Given the relationship between truth and honesty, the components of hon-esty are dramatically reshaped within a populist framework. For populists, truth-telling emphasizes the sincere way in which one expresses or enhances the narrative of the people, regardless of the accuracy of the claims asserted or the deception they may cause. Being sincere demonstrates that one is aligned with the people. Philosopher Bernard Williams, who put forward one of the most significant modern accounts of truth, also emphasized the component of sincerity, which he saw as being open and straightforward in telling what one believes to be the truth, without deceiving oneself or others.[44] This notion of sincerity is aligned with the populists to the extent that it is a way of sharing what one believes to be the case, but the populist notion of sincerity is far less concerned with trying to prevent inaccuracy or deceptiveness. For populists, sincerity does not rely upon sophisticated reason or empirical data. Instead, sincerity grows out of one's personal experiences and sharing them in a way that produces an affective response in others, typically one that strengthens the divide between the people and the elite and nurtures one's identity within a particular tribe. It is our affective response that makes things *feel* true. Edda Sant connects sincerity back to the binary division, noting that "accuracy does not have primacy, sincerity does.

Knowledge is a matter of trust. And if academics are not to be trusted, neither is the knowledge they produce."[45] This is more so among Right populists, who tend to view people with advanced degrees as having been indoctrinated into elitist views over the course of their extended education.[46] Or academics may use "politically correct" language that is not straightforward, thereby giving the impression of insincerity. The speaker sounds calculating rather than candid and, therefore, is ultimately deemed dishonest.[47] While sincerity may affectively resonate with us, the proposition may not prove useful or—if it is inaccurate or deceptive—could even be harmful.

Populists emphasize personal experience as reliable knowledge, where the individual is the arbiter of truth. Liesbet van Zoonen aptly calls this an "I-pistemology."[48] Notably, populists don't emphasize taking in information from others to build knowledge or verify truth. Instead, their focus is on personal expression and assertion—pushing one's view outward. These assertions often disregard how one is connected to or interdependent on others for understanding and transacting with the world. This form of I-pistemology, then, stifles other key aspects of democracy, such as relationships of trust and exchange. Populism is not alone in derailing democracy in this way, for liberalism also has a tendency to celebrate forms of individualism and autonomous thinking that run counter to democracy as a social activity that involves listening and shared work. As I will explain, what we need instead is to emphasize the social connectivity of knowledge-building and truth validation in order to tie epistemology with democratization. Just Serrano-Zamora further adds, "More generally, if citizens' practices are oriented by an epistemology that puts special emphasis on epistemic interdependence and cooperation, we can expect that the interpretation of political norms and values will be more engaging and inclusive, since epistemic cooperation tends to disclose practice possibilities that deepen the values and reinforce the conditions that are necessary for the democratic project."[49] To revive democracy, we need to build epistemic communities.

In the next section, I will consider pragmatist theories of truth and democracy, explaining how they complement some aspects of populism while challenging others. I contend that populist truth is useful only if it actually works epistemically and civically to secure a better life for the people. Populist truth may be helpful in uniting groups politically, but it isn't civically useful if it doesn't ensure their ability to work together with other groups (or even in parallel with those groups) to achieve well-being. And that's where pragmatism may offer a better approach.

Pragmatist Honesty

I provide a brief overview here of a pragmatist account of honesty that builds most directly on the work of American pragmatist John Dewey and his ideas on truth, though it also draws on key ideas expressed by other founding pragmatists (Charles Peirce and William James) and their contemporaries.[50] It may be surprising to see pragmatism presented as a champion of truth, when many pragmatists in the past have given up the "quest for certainty" and turned instead to solidarity, flourishing, and other aims of shared social living. Richard Rorty, a neopragmatist, once scoffed that truth, in an objective, unconditional, and fixed sense, "is not the sort of thing one should expect to have a philosophically interesting theory about."[51] Critics such as Daniel Dennett have claimed that too many pragmatists undervalue truth. Others, including Bernard Williams, have argued that pragmatists

> encourage us to get beyond fussing about something called "the truth," and address ourselves just to technical and social benefits, solidarity, democracy, the discouragement of cruelty, and other laudable ends. It seems not to occur to them that even if the ideals of discovering and telling the truth were in themselves illusions, if the ideas of "the truth" were itself empty, those illusions might well play a vital part in our identifying and pursuing those objectives.[52]

Notably, even if a correspondence theory of truth is left behind, pragmatists must attend to how achieving their other aims may rely upon some form of truth. As Williams himself concludes, even if we set aside arguments over what the definition of truth is, we still must attend to the *value* of truth. For Dewey and many other pragmatists, truth is central to democracy, even if truth is not simply understood as mere correspondence to reality. Truth has epistemic value because it helps us better understand our environment, and it has civic value because it helps us work together to adapt to that environment or reconstruct it to secure our well-being within it. But for pragmatists, truth does not exist ready-made in the world, waiting for us to discover it; nor is it accessible only to those who have specialized training or credentials. Instead, truth is constructed and, as such, is often partial or temporary.

The January 2021 attack on the U.S. Capitol exposes just how much truth matters: democracy and lives are on the line when citizens struggle to discern truth or adhere to mis- or disinformation spread by their leaders and each other. Truth plays a significant role in achieving the aims pragmatists have long sought, even as they have distanced themselves from it, especially when truth is problematically conceived as a certainty arising from a correspondence to some objective state of affairs. Truth is significant for how it helps citizens make sense of and successfully traverse their world. Notably, pragmatists don't place some overarching value on truth as a grand epistemic aim on its own. Rather, pragmatists situate truth within democracy as a "way of life," where we are more concerned with how we live together. It is this civic thrust that shifts the focus from a conception of truth to an account of the importance of honesty as truth-seeking and truth-telling in a democracy.

Starting with Pragmatist Truth

Pragmatists are concerned with the concrete differences in our lived experiences that an idea being true will make. Pragmatists focus on the consequences of our beliefs to determine whether or not they are true. Ideas become true insofar as they "work" for us. They help us explain the world and make predictions about it. They fruitfully combine our experiences and lead us to further experiences that satisfy our needs. This is the pragmatist version of growth, where knowing or employing truth enables individuals to navigate smoothly from one situation to the next. Truth as "what works" is that which helps us traverse the world, avoid difficulties, and get out of problematic situations. We must test beliefs against the widest range of experiences as we can to see if they hold up. Those benefits, then, are not just for individuals; instead, a criterion for determining truth is demonstrating that it enables the flourishing of a community.

For William James, truth entails tracing and determining the practical consequences of an idea. James explains, "The truth of an idea is not a stagnant property inherent to it. Truth *happens* to an idea. It *becomes* true, is *made* true by events. Its verity *is* in fact an event, a process, the process namely of its verifying itself, its veri*fication*. Its validity is the process of its valid*ation*."[53] Dewey also points toward a more verificationist conception of truth, which he describes as "warranted assertibility."[54] Pragmatist truth is not disconnected from reality, for it is through empirical experimentation that we validate our hypotheses and verify their consequences. Pragmatists look to see whether what we deem to be true stands up to the evidence and is affirmed through our experiences. Rather than comparing propositions to some absolute, fixed world, though, pragmatists analyze them in practice in our current, lived experience. Of course, this analysis takes into account the realities in which we find ourselves, though philosophers would regard this as a form of weak realism.

Whereas analytic and purity truth theorists seek a truth that is independent of humans, including their processes of verification or whether the proposition matters for their lives, by emphasizing a correspondence with an objective world (strong realism) pragmatism emphasizes a dynamic relationship between what we believe, what we experience, and the process through which we test that belief in the world around us.[55] Finding such a believer-independent ideal nonsensical, Peirce proclaimed that since we have "no use for this meaning of the word 'truth,' we had better use the word in another sense."[56] He is not suggesting here that pragmatists simply give up on the epistemic notion of truth but, rather, is saying that our focus is better spent on practices that may get at truth, such as inquiry, and the knowledge those practices provide. Summarizing this Peircean take, Misak explains, "The focus is on the fact that those engaged in deliberation and investigation take themselves to be aiming at the truth—at getting things right, at avoiding mistakes, and at improving their beliefs and theories. Truth is not linked to the actual products of human inquiry, but rather, to the products of human inquiry, were they to be the best they could be, opening up some distance between what is justified now and what would really be justified."[57] Some summarize this view as "truth is the end of inquiry."[58]

Dewey and other pragmatists reject what Dewey calls "the spectator theory of knowledge." In that view, knowledge is that which accurately represents reality, apart from and unbiased by humans.[59] But Dewey and Peirce find that we cannot so clearly distinguish an objective world from our experience of it. Instead, they argue, our focus must be on how we act in the world, a world that we come to know through manipulating it in experimentation.[60] Lest the reader suspect that pragmatists doubt the reality of objects, let me interject James's words:

> Most of the pragmatist and anti-pragmatist warfare is over what the word "truth" shall be held to signify, and not over any of the facts embodied in truth-situations; for both pragmatists and anti-pragmatists believe in existent objects, just as they believe in our ideas of them. The difference is that when the pragmatists speak of truth, they mean exclusively something about the ideas, namely their workableness; whereas when anti-pragmatists speak of truth they seem most often to mean something about the objects. Since the pragmatist, if he agrees that an idea is

"really" true, also agrees to whatever it says about its object; and since most anti-pragmatists have already come round to agreeing that, if the object exists, the idea that it does so is workable.

Rather than seeing truth as that which "sets us free," pragmatists like James and contemporary pragmatist Colin Koopman recognize that truth is not "extrinsic to human action."[61] Truth results from our actions, our inquiry, and the reconstruction of our world to meet our needs and ensure our growth. Further describing the social process of knowing, Dewey adds that knowledge happens through "association and communication; it depends upon tradition, upon tools and methods socially transmitted, developed and sanctioned."[62] Whereas others have sought a disinterested truth, pragmatists see truth as necessarily interested, but it must not be narrowly self-interested, of the sort on display in our post-truth era. Intriguingly, pragmatists link truth to hope. Pragmatists uphold meliorism, the belief that, through effort, things can get better. Applying that hopeful lens to the process of truth as "what works" to enable us to flourish, Koopman rightly concludes: "Truth, understood melioristically, is an improvement resulting from our work."[63] Pragmatists pursue truth because they want to improve our lives.

Contemporary pragmatist Bianca Thoilliez adds, "If truth is something that happens to an idea, the most advisable approach from this position is to give the ideas as many opportunities (and points of view) as possible. . . . [W]e should promote habits of thinking and experimenting that are open to and appreciative of the plurality of specific facts and manifestations of the world."[64] In other words, we should enable many ways of seeing and experiencing the world to be brought forward, shared, and tested. This is a broader and more inclusive process for determining truth. It is aligned with a pragmatist commitment to pluralism. In a liberal democracy, pluralism allows for citizens to hold an array of worldviews, especially about the good life. Pragmatists take this commitment a bit further by placing it in the service of epistemic and civic life, where the views and experiences of others are valued, in part, because they extend our range of understanding of the world and our ability to adapt it to meet our needs. Being exposed to the views and experiences of others may broaden our own perspectives and help us to see aspects of reality that we did not previously detect, thereby providing more beliefs to test for truth and more fodder for analysis of the beliefs we bring to the table.

While pragmatist inquiry is most known for its empirical focus on understanding and reconstructing the natural world, it also uses a similar approach to questions of value and political life. In that context, moral claims are offered as hypotheses about which ways of understanding social and political concepts will prove to be most satisfactory. Moral claims entail hypotheses about which ways of living will prove to be most satisfactory. Those hypotheses are then tested through inquiry into our lived experiences to determine whether the moral claims hold, to what extent, and for whom.[65] Notably, the criteria used to evaluate moral claims are more than just utilitarian weighing of happiness. Rather, the pragmatist criteria of satisfaction and flourishing encompass many different types of goods, including freedom, justice, community, and more.[66]

Finally, an idea is no longer true when it no longer works for us—when it no longer helps us to make sense of or thrive in the world. As a result, pragmatists value fallibilism, acknowledging that anyone's beliefs might be mistaken and asserting that, in most cases, nothing is true for certain or always. Rather, truth depends on us. We must identify and be ready to let go of truths that no longer hold and be ready to acknowledge when we are mistaken. This fallibilism also serves to head off forms of extremist dogmatism and fanaticism because it changes the way that we hold our ideas, making them more tentative and revisable.

Describing truth in this way may make truth appear to slide too easily into the realm of mere opinion, as if we could proclaim, for example, that "masks are ineffective" simply because it doesn't "work" for us to wear them because they are uncomfortable or inconvenient for us personally. But that sets the bar for establishing truth too low as we ask "What should we do about COVID-19 or other communicable airborne diseases?" Pragmatism holds that such a declaration would have to be tested empirically, both in the realm of formal science and more casually in our day-to-day interactions with our neighbors, looking to see how their well-being is impacted by others wearing masks. Pragmatists do not stop just at our personal desires in the moment. They look at the impact on others and in the long run as they establish truth.

Recognizing the interconnectivity and interdependencies of living within a modern democracy, we have to take into account how to thrive alongside others as we determine what is true. In other words, even if a belief may seem to "work" for us individually, given our interconnectedness, the belief must also "work" for others in order to be true. It must facilitate their growth or ability to improve the world, not just our own. Additionally, the differences an idea will make are quite limited if relevant only to one person. Because of this, we must seek out the perspectives of and impact upon others in order to verify truth. Moreover, we must consider the well-being of others. Successfully leading through experiences almost always requires working and communicating together, so we must secure the welfare of others alongside our own.

What, then, are "facts" for a pragmatist? Facts don't exist as certain and permanent, apart from human interference, because all knowledge we hold is influenced by our social positioning and is falsifiable. But that is not to say that our external world is regarded with complete skepticism. Rather, what is awarded the label of "fact" are specific objects, propositions, and the referents of propositions that stand up to (typically repeated) empirical and community investigation. We determine facts through experimentation and dialogue. Facts result as maxims of such inquiry, as that which ongoing experimentation is trending toward and which can be asserted with rather strong assurances at this point in time. They are more justified than personal beliefs. Most facts, such as that the sun rises in the east, are reaffirmed in new contexts and with new people. Facts result from a process, even as they may point to seemingly objective aspects of our world and aim to capture them. Because of that source, pragmatist facts are always open to challenges and revisions due to new evidence, changes in the environment, novel perspectives in the dialogue, or shifts in the consensus. This basis in dialogue and community inquiry accentuates the need for honesty so that we can count on others when developing and assessing facts.

Unlike the accounts of epistemology and metaphysics of truth that undergird modern liberal democracy, pragmatism offers a very different perspective. Rather than aiming to be objective or trying to achieve a correspondence by neatly reflecting some objective real world, pragmatist truth is grounded in real people, their lived experiences, and inquiry into the world. Truth doesn't merely mirror some objective reality; pragmatist truth provides the tools for interpreting and improving the world to meet our needs. All the while, pragmatist truth does not get bogged down in debates about "truthiness" (the Merriam-Webster 2006 Word of the Year)[67] because it neither upholds some absolute reality as a reference point nor privileges the affective impact of what "feels" true as the definitive measure of truth. Part of such determination of truth entails considering the affective impact of beliefs and assessing whether they lead to fruitful outcomes. This might include determining whether a belief sparks anger that stalls and debilitates people, or whether the belief unites them and enables them to make productive change as a result. This shift of emphasis may be a helpful way to respond to our current situation, pushing us to look at how truth operates when asking "What should we do?" It reveals that what matters more about lying or deceit is not whether one is being morally irresponsible or whether one is out for personal gain but whether the consequences distort or derail civic reasoning.

The process of determining truth connects us with others and can present opportunities to share struggles and bear witness to the suffering and successes of others. This is a significant component of pragmatism given that, in today's society, the suffering of marginalized populations, in particular, is often hidden or ignored. Pragmatism pushes us to consider the well-being of others, urging us to shed light on their struggles and to attend to them in order to bring about greater flourishing for ourselves and others.

In today's polarized climate, where populism further encourages "choosing sides," facts are not a clear tool upon which everyone can agree and which can be used to easily change the minds of those who are mistaken. People double down on the facts proclaimed by their group because of their commitments to their tribe. What pragmatism does in response is to expand tribes and communities, showing how some views may not be facts because they do not hold up in other contexts or do not work for other people.

In sum, pragmatism offers a different outlook from common accounts of the epistemology or metaphysics of truth. Rather than dehumanized accounts of coherence or correspondence theories, pragmatist truth is grounded in real social living and inquiry, which convey the relevance and importance of truth. When pragmatist truth is defined as "what works" to enable growth and flourishing,[68] truth becomes more aligned with people and the civic relations between them than with objective mirroring of reality. This means that honesty, as sincere, accurate, and forthright seeking and telling the truth, becomes more contingent upon the context and needs of people as they determine what "works" for them.

Employing Pragmatist Inquiry

Focusing in on the relationship between inquiry and democracy, John Dewey pointed out that we tend to think of democracy as something that happens elsewhere and is carried out by other people, often elected officials in faraway capitals. Those leaders and their institutions may compose a part of the formal aspect of democracy. But, importantly, democracy is also a way of life that each of us carries out in our daily actions, especially as we solve problems with others.[69] Democracy is deeply social, dependent upon people who work together and are interconnected in significant ways as they traverse shared spaces.

Inquiry is a form of problem-solving central to democratic survival. Inquiry is the process through which we can sort out our beliefs, determine truth, and guide our actions, especially our collective actions aimed at solving shared problems. Inquiry is the way that we not only arrive at answers to "What should we do?" but also establish evidence that leads us to those answers. Dewey explains that we can best manage our life together when we "cultivate the habit of suspended judgement, of scepticism, of desire for evidence, of appeal to observation rather than sentiment, discussion rather than bias, inquiry rather than conventional idealizations."[70]

Inquiry proceeds by identifying problems, forming publics to address them, crafting solutions, testing those solutions, and evaluating them. Inquiry begins when we find ourselves in what Dewey calls "indeterminate situations." These are problematic situations where we struggle to make sense of the world around us and aren't sure how to proceed. They are genuine moments of puzzlement and uncertainty. The goal of inquiry is to get out of indeterminate situations by reconstructing the world around us to better fulfill our needs and restore coordinated action among members of a community.[71] So, inquiry is not something that just happens in our heads; rather, it changes the situation, which may include changing ourselves and our surroundings. Often indeterminate situations aren't just confined to individuals but, rather, relate to issues or problems that we share with those around us. When we move from identifying shared concerns toward beginning to articulate common interests, we become a public.

In the second phase of inquiry, we explore and pause to reflect so that we can better understand the problematic situation and how it impacts ourselves and others. We investigate the world around us so that we can better understand the problem. This entails seeking out empirical information. We think with information; it is an input to our thinking that may help us develop knowledge about the world.[72] We also seek out related opinions, experiences, and values about the problematic situation from an array of stakeholders through discussion. Dewey explains, "Discussion will bring out intellectual differences and opposed points of view and interpretations, so as to help define the true nature of the problem."[73] Celebrating the plurality of views and solutions that may come forward during discussion, Dewey adds, "The plurality of alternatives is the effective means of rendering inquiry more extensive (sufficient) and more flexible."[74]

Once investigation and discussion have clarified the problem, inquiry shifts to proposing and considering solutions. We use evidence and feedback to construct potential solutions. We then test those ideas to determine whether or not they are effective for alleviating our problem and helping us move forward smoothly, thereby helping us to grow as individuals and flourish as a society. It is during this phase that invoking pluralism and fallibilism is especially helpful, as they embody a spirit of intellectual humility and openness that may help us past epistemic blind spots and toward a fuller and more useful understanding of the world.

In the final stage of inquiry, solutions are implemented and continually assessed. Moral and political hypotheses, for example, are tested through lived experience to determine whether the moral claims hold, for whom, and to what extent.[75] They are always held open to revision and to the potential of being falsified as new evidence comes to light or changes occur in the environment.

Inquiry is a key part of a democratic way of life, both informally, in the way we interact with fellow citizens, and formally, through our democratic institutions and processes. The inquiry process translates into the method of democracy like this:

1. Identification of the problem (agenda setting): to this phase belong formal practices such as electoral consultations, informal practices such as opinion polling, meeting with citizens, public hearings, social surveys, forms of social protest, and NGO campaigns but also practices of whistleblowing that aim at raising awareness about critical aspects so far underestimated; 2. Formation of the public: to this dimension belong the activities of political parties and social movements, but also of all forms of civic non-political association (churches, recreational associations, solidarity movements, etc.) which aim more concretely at producing organized forms of response to collectively perceived problems; 3. Determination of solutions: to this dimension belong formal and informal political practices of political decision-making, including parliamentary debate, expert committees, practices of public deliberation, participatory practices, public hearings etc.; 4. Implementation of solutions: the realm of public policies, but also of actions carried out by administrations, public and private agencies; 5. Evaluation and feedback: to this dimension belong the formal political work of oppositions, voting, the work of journals and media, of NGOs and other formal and informal "watchdogs" and more generally the activities by which individuals manifest their agreement or disagreement with the results of a political action.[76]

Inquiry and democracy are social and political activities, where we determine for ourselves our desires and our means for achieving them, while providing mechanisms for citizens to identify problems with the status quo and to hold others accountable for harmful outcomes. Democracy helps us to coordinate our efforts with fellow citizens so that we can better realize an array of shared goods and flourishing.

In sum, expanding the sketch of honesty I offered in the first part of this chapter by situating it within a pragmatist account of truth and democracy: honesty entails a commitment to ongoing, evidence-supported, civic inquiry that one carries out through one's behaviors. To be honest is to be vigilant in seeking truth, but not in the sense of locating ready-made facts in an objective reality; rather, it is to continually engage in an inclusive process of determining truth. Honesty entails sincerely sharing the truth as what verifiably works to ensure personal and community well-being and to hold that truth open to being revised or falsified. But this definition is not yet sufficient. We must also consider how honesty operates. A pragmatist understanding of habits provides an important component.

Habits and Honesty

While habits are seemingly mundane, political philosopher Danielle Allen wisely proclaims, "The ordinary habits *are* the stuff of citizenship."[77] Most people conceive of habits as mere routines we repeat exactly and unthinkingly. Instead, pragmatists offer a unique account of habits that highlights their power, pervasiveness, and adaptability. Dewey sees them as dispositions, inclinations to act in certain ways. Dewey notes, "Any habit marks an *inclination*—an active preference and choice for the conditions involved in its exercise. A habit does not wait, Micawber-like, for a stimulus to turn up so that it may get busy; it actively seeks for occasions to pass into full operation."[78] Habits, then, strive to be put into intelligent action; they are not mere default patterns we thoughtlessly rely upon. They are active and energetic means that project themselves.[79]

Habits begin with natural urges, often in response to our environment.[80] As we grow and interact with the world around us, our impulses are crafted into habits. They are molded and shaped by contextual factors, including societal norms, experiences, and other people, including parents and teachers. People who have similar interactions with their environments tend to reinforce certain patterns of behavior and thereby develop similar habits. When those behaviors serve us well by meeting our needs, we tend to repeat them. We then largely perform these acts without conscious attention.

Habits sometimes cause us to desire particular outcomes or objects in order for our lives to flourish. Those desires align with our growth from one experience to the next. Those desires may unite our experiences or serve as ends-in-view to guide us. Importantly, habits also offer a way to pursue those desires, often through thought or bodily movement. For Dewey, habits "do all the perceiving, recognizing, imagining, recalling, judging, conceiving and reasoning that is done."[81] They organize our perceptions based on past experiences so that we can form ideas about the world that we test out in order to overcome indeterminate situations. As we encounter new stimuli, habits help us to filter and make sense of those encounters, enabling us to develop ideas about them. Habits then provide the know-how to act in the world because they entail our working capacities. Habits can take an array of forms, including how we tend to move our bodies (stand with erect posture, for example), communicate (listen carefully), and make judgments (reach hasty conclusions). Habits compose us, making us who we are. Finally, we reflect on our experiences and our inquiries to determine which habits bring about our growth by promoting smooth transactions with the world and with other people. For example, we may discover that our tendency to reach hasty conclusions leads us to rush through the evidence, perhaps overlooking or not thoroughly considering key pieces. Such a tendency may cause us to make faulty judgments that don't meet our needs. In this case, our reflection reveals that our habit of hasty conclusions making isn't serving us well.

Habits are formed through our exchanges with others and are stabilized by social institutions, yet they remain capable of being changed. And, because of the way that they transact with the surrounding world, habits can change other people and society. As a result, pragmatist habits offer epistemic benefits that grow out of their rich social context and can be harnessed to change the environment when it presents some of the very sort of problems we see today, such as confirmation bias. Habits that become stagnant and harmful, such as making hasty conclusions, can be prompted to change through processes of education and by changing conditions in the environment that cause friction or irritate the habit. This reflexive and adaptive aspect of habits situated in personal and social inquiry provides greater leverage for change than the moral, intrinsic motivation needed to propel one to demonstrate virtue.

Because habits can be shaped by intellectual reflection, they are elastic and capable of change. Good habits are flexible, enabling us to respond to our changing world by changing ourselves. Bad habits, however, are those that become fixed or disconnected from intelligence.[82] In the context of democracy, a bad habit is one that keeps democracy from functioning well. It may be one that is stagnant and doesn't keep up with the changing population or social needs, is exclusionary, blocks inquiry with others, or is unjust. To return to the example, reaching hasty conclusions may be a bad habit that prevents the sort of careful and deliberative decision-making required to sustain a healthy democracy. Unlike virtue theory, which bases judgments of the moral uprightness of one's traits or actions on some fixed foundation prior to or apart from our present human experience, such as the good, the quality of habits is determined relative to how they impact our lives and our environment. As contexts change, judgments about whether a habit is good or bad may change.

We cannot easily drop bad habits, but we can work through a process of changing and replacing them with better habits. Notably, habits can be cultivated and nurtured; they can be revised and improved through education, where teachers or other guides manipulate our circumstances to help us develop better ways of acting. While habits can sometimes be changed or new habits adopted through conscious reflection, on many occasions, a more effective route to changing them is to alter the physical, social, or affective environment. When we disrupt the workings of our habits, they are better positioned for revisioning. Many habits, including those tied to dishonesty, are deeply ingrained over time through the force of our environment, where lying or deceit may be widespread. Efforts to change them via simple direct instruction or moral imperatives fail to account for the lasting role of the environment and how it shapes our bodies. Carolyn Pedwell explains:

> Dewey is critical of modes of social reform that depend predominantly on thought (i.e., verbal instruction of particular moral imperatives) or on the production of certain feelings (i.e., the generation of empathy, compassion, or moral indignation). The problem with both strategies, he argues, is that they tend to remove thought from embodied action and the individual from the environment. They assume that new cognitive or affective knowledge is enough to instigate "ethical" or "progressive" change, without attending to the bodily and environmental factors that powerfully support and perpetuate existing patterns and behaviour.[83]

To change habits, then, we need to intervene in ways that bring about new environments that will positively affirm new patterns of behavior as useful and worthwhile. Rather than chiding people not to do bad things, we need to nurture their proclivity toward better behavior by showing them that it serves their needs well.

Ideally, because habits are "adjustments of the environment, not merely to it," adopting new habits through a careful process of environmental change and intellectual reflection may also change the very surrounding phenomena that produced the problematic old habit.[84] Changing our habits, then, may also change democracy, whether its formal institution or its cultural practices.

While honesty is widely described as a virtue, it might better be understood as pragmatist habits. I follow contemporary European pragmatist Roberto Frega in claiming "that habits have a marked superiority over virtues when it comes to conceptualizing their specific contribution to politics."[85] This is, in part, because virtues in political life occur in a narrower scope of individuals in service of the common good and engaged in specialized political practice, whereas pragmatist habits are demonstrated in much wider social interactions and everyday ways of life in a democracy. Some of our habits, such as the way we listen to others, we use across all spheres of our lives, rather than only in civic or political pursuits. Notice that I am not saying that honesty is not a virtue, a position that Miller cautions against, given that honesty is widely accepted as being one.[86] Rather, I am saying that focusing on honesty only as a virtue—an "excellence," as some philosophers would say—misses the point when it comes to democracy as a way of life. Our focus should be elsewhere. Understanding honesty as habits offers significant insight that a virtue view does not.

Pragmatists are concerned with a wider array of habits that contribute to democratic living, including those that shape epistemic and social endeavors, disposing citizens to be cooperative, inclusive, adaptive, and reflective. Moreover, pragmatists understand that what we see in democratic life is a reflection of widespread lived habits, rather than idealized moral or intellectual virtues. Seeing honesty in terms of habits rather than merely virtues would shift emphasis away from the moral motivations behind one's actions to the lived practice and implications of honesty in one's daily life, emphasizing civic motivations and, more importantly, civic outcomes. Relatedly, civic republicans and civic humanists, restricted to virtues invoked narrowly in the political domain, are left struggling to attend to recent social and psychological struggles impacting democratic life.[87] Pragmatist habits give us a way to make sense of how those struggles have developed as the result of bad habits shaped by changes in the environment, and they provide ways to ameliorate those struggles through the reworking of bad habits or cultivation of new ones. For example, people become trapped in filter bubbles via bad habits: a bubble initially serves their needs, but they fail to "pop" the bubble when it limits their access to or willingness to engage with alternative views that might better serve their needs in new or developing situations. Reflecting on how that filter bubble may restrict quality civic inquiry or lead to harmful results may provoke a reworking of that tendency, not because one desires to be good but, rather, because one's own personal and social needs aren't being fulfilled.

Dewey made a useful distinction that lends insight into a pragmatist notion of honesty as habit. He said, "The adverb 'truly' is more fundamental than either the adjective, true, or the noun, truth. An adverb expresses a way, a mode of acting."[88] Distinct from more general descriptions of people or descriptions of actions, a pragmatist definition of honesty emphasizes ways of acting. Honesty entails ongoing verification and falsifiability. Honest mistakes are more likely to be discovered within continuing pragmatist inquiry and righted over time.

We have now reached a definition of honesty as a pragmatist habit situated within civic reasoning. As a predisposition, honesty entails acting truly—confirming the consequences of beliefs in our lives and using them to reconstruct the world to improve it and ourselves. Recast within some of the more widely held criteria of honesty laid out by Miller and others, *honesty is a proclivity to not intentionally distort the facts as one sees them but, rather, to engage in ongoing thinking and behavior marked by forthrightness, sincerity, and accuracy regarding the establishment and sharing of truth. Unique to pragmatism, honesty is an urge to act in good faith to determine truth as "what works" to secure our flourishing in the world. It is a disposition to consider our relationships with fellow citizens and how the truth we assert may impact those around us as we navigate shared problems and figure out how to live together.* This definition allows for well-intended, "honest" mistakes, where one acts in good faith but the outcomes are faulty in some way.

Bringing Together Pragmatist and Populist Notions of Truth and Honesty

Presenting a viable account of truth and honesty for our world today requires wrestling with the promises and challenges to that account posed by growing populism. Moreover, constructing a case for how to teach honesty must grapple with the difficulties it will face in a populist context. To summarize key points of overlap so far, populist truth, like pragmatist truth, is partial, temporary, and constructed. Both pragmatists and populists care about truth, not because they merely desire objective knowledge about the world but because truth helps us fulfill our needs. Instead of looking to an objective, outside world to find truth, both look to humans and the impact truth has on their experiences in the world. Both take seriously the everyday experiences and firsthand knowledge of individuals. They also value the sort of common sense that arises from our experiences—from what we feel and do, rather than just from what we grasp rationally. To an extent, the pragmatist emphasis on personal experience also aligns with populist concerns for sincerity because what "rings true" to us is that which matches with our personal experience. While populism may rely on individual emotions to fuel a collective effervescence of fervor, that fervor is often directed through empty signifiers and chains of equivalence that anonymize individual experience and absorb the individual in populist discourse. So, while populism relies on the experiences of individuals, it also can prohibit the individual from staying individual. In this regard, pragmatism may be better able to welcome individual experience and preserve it in the long run.[89]

But, importantly, pragmatists do not just stop at the level of the personal. In order to check our experiences, help us make sense of them, and assist us in growing from one experience to the next, pragmatists also often turn to experts, scientists, academics, and others whom populists would likely label "elites" and therefore ignore or rebuke. From a pragmatist perspective, populist truth goes too far in embracing a simplistic celebration of the experiences and opinions of individuals without confirming them in evidence or checking to see whether the beliefs lead to productive consequences like growth or flourishing. Indeed, some populists appear to be emboldened by conflicting information, overconfidently asserting their stance in response. In other cases, those with real-world experience or specialized knowledge in some areas engage in "epistemic trespassing," where they assert their views in other domains, sometimes winning over uninformed listeners to misguided views, as has happened with some outspoken leaders within the anti-vaccination movement.[90]

Pragmatism offers an approach to truth where personal beliefs and direct experiences are foregrounded but are better balanced with scientific inquiry, expert knowledge, and assessments of their impact on oneself and others. Yes, pragmatism does attribute more epistemic authority to scientific approaches (more so than to scien*tists*), but it does so with a qualified view of science. It recognizes scientific inquiry as a deeply contextual and human endeavor, influenced by bias and errors, producing fallible outcomes, while also celebrating that, "though it 'grow[s] out of' commonsense inquiry . . . , [it] demands more, pushes further, and develops forms of inquiry more rapidly than other types of inquiry."[91] Whereas some populists seek to discredit and dethrone science, and whereas some scholars have resorted to championing science as the best way to know via the fourth lens described in the introduction of this book, I offer a more tempered middle ground, which may be better suited to aid civic reasoning.[92]

Populists emphasize the direct experience of the people as the source of common sense and the foundation of the will of the people.[93] This knowledge is immediate and does not necessarily rely upon the rational procedures of liberal democracy. This sort of everyday, everyman's knowledge is valued by populists and seen as authentic.[94] This sets common sense in opposition to the knowledge of experts, which is seen as too distant and "out of touch" with real life, thereby making it illegitimate. Remarking on the errors of "so-called experts" during the coronavirus pandemic that stood counter to the intuitions and desires of many people, DeSantis opined that their performance was "so dreadful that no sane person should ever 'trust the experts' ever again." He then recalled "President Dwight Eisenhower's admonition that public policy not be permitted to be taken captive by a scientific-technological elite."[95]

Aligned with aims of being objective or neutral, elite academics tend to speak without emotion and lack sincerity. Their tendency to go into great depth with their analyses frustrates populists who see a need for urgent action, especially when they are propelled by anger or resentment.[96] In academic spaces as well as government institutions, the experiences and opinions of everyday people are too frequently seen as having less worth because only those who are credentialed are entitled to have their voices heard in those spaces. And sometimes even credentialed scientists are policed as being outside the boundaries of science when they hold certain views or disagree with scientific consensus, as happened during the pandemic.[97] Expert knowledge can be rationalistic and exclusionary, while too often the experiences, emotional responses, and knowledge of the people are denigrated. To the frustration of populists, the institutions of liberal democracy are often run more like an expertocracy. Governor DeSantis voices concern with this expert leadership and how it jeopardizes political legitimacy reflected through the will of the people when he explains that elites "believe that society is best governed by 'experts' working in unaccountable government agencies, they advance major changes to American society, in matters ranging from energy to education, through bureaucratic fiat, not popular consent."[98]

Again, pragmatists' views have some similarities to these populists' views. Pragmatists assert that all people have epistemic value in that all can contribute to building and assessing knowledge through an array of contributions that go beyond formal reasoning or science. So, like populists, pragmatists celebrate the emotions, voices, and experiences of the people. But pragmatists value the epistemic contributions of nearly *all* people, including the elites that populists are quick to write off. Scholars and researchers have specialized knowledge that can help us understand and address problems in our world. Shutting down those experts can cause both epistemic and civic harm by prohibiting the building or validation of truths that might help us understand and navigate the world together.

Admittedly, "it often can be difficult for the average person to distinguish genuine experts from purported or self-styled experts. Moreover, in many domains (e.g., public health, economics, climate science, political science), even genuine experts disagree on substantive issues. If we often lack the ability to distinguish genuine from would-be experts, we are even less likely to know how to adjudicate these disputes."[99] As a result, citizens need to learn tools to identify the credentials of experts and how to detect their potential motives, looking for integrity and benevolence rather than a political agenda or a moneymaking angle. They also need to understand how disputes between experts are settled through disciplinary means, such as through empirical study, peer review, and replication, while other disputes go unsettled and yet experts must move forward making the most wisely informed decisions that they can.

For Dewey, experts should be guided, in part, by the needs of the public and should inform the public so that the members of the public can live their life better together. Getting at the sense in which the expert serves the public, Dewey famously uses the metaphor of the shoe that pinches: "The man who wears the shoe knows best that it pinches and where it pinches, even if the expert shoemaker is the best judge of how the trouble is to be remedied."[100] Here, the public sets the needs and agenda for inquiry. That is not to say, however, that all scientific inquiry should be only in the service of immediate human needs, though Dewey did express hesitation regarding the pursuit of "pure science."[101] Dewey was also concerned with how expertocracies alienate citizens from the political process. When we overrely on experts, we drive citizens away from actively participating in the inquiries of their communities— the very sort of practices that keep democracy vibrant. Moreover, Dewey had considerable faith in the intelligence and judgment of everyday folks, as long as they had the right conditions to support them, such as quality education. These concerns, again, align with populist frustrations.

The pragmatist approach also offers a more complex account that encapsulates more than populist commonsense sentiments, which are too often oversimplified. Such oversimplification is exacerbated by developments in the use of technology, where many people, not just populists, are increasingly satisfied with "Google-knowing," as they quickly scan for answers online rather than seeking deeper understanding or engaging with more cognitive complexity.[102] Significantly, the common sense of the people is also often tainted, for it is shaped and fed by social media campaigns and other targeted efforts by people with vested interests in ensuring that the people view or experience issues in specific ways. The fuller and more complex approach endorsed by pragmatists can help to reveal such influences and their effects, while also delivering a more sophisticated and nuanced understanding that brings together expert insight with common sense. That is not to say, however, that the resulting pragmatist truth is unbiased.

Additionally, whereas populists may more quickly throw in the towel on formal scientific inquiry, pragmatists uphold it. But for pragmatists, empirical inquiry is grounded in and paired with accessible, everyday investigation in which we encounter problems in our world, make hypotheses about how we might assuage them, develop potential solutions, deliberate among them, try them out, and then evaluate them. This sort of experimental thinking and social inquiry is the purview of all citizens, not just trained scientists. Dewey explains in *Logic: The Theory of Inquiry*:

(1) Scientific subject-matter and procedures grow out of the direct problems and methods of the common sense, of practical uses and enjoyments, and (2) react into the latter in a way that enormously refines, expands and liberates the contents and the agencies at the disposal of common sense. The separation and opposition of scientific subject-matter to that of common sense, when it is taken to be final, generates those controversial problems of epistemology and metaphysics that still dog the course of philosophy. When scientific subject-matter is seen to bear genetic and functional relation to the subject-matter of common sense, these problems disappear. Scientific subject-matter is intermediate, not final and complete in itself.[103]

Science, then, is not limited to highly trained experts employing sophisticated terminology and machinery in sterile laboratory spaces. Too often, contemporary understandings of science focus on rigorous methodology and supposed objectivity, failing to recognize that science grows out of real-life experiences that are value- and emotion-laden.[104] The results of inquiry are better because of the inclusive approach pragmatists champion. But within common practices and institutions today, scientific experts may fail to detect their own biases and may become overconfident in their views.[105]

Pragmatists would take issue with tendencies today to cordon off experts who generally speak only about and to each other, experts who are too often disconnected from the experiences of typical people and who too rarely encounter and must attend to criticism from those outside their ranks. Such criticism may rightfully come from the people who suffer the consequences of knowledge proclaimed by scientists and instituted within public policy. Some populists might argue, for example, that this tendency was particularly on display during the COVID-19 lockdowns, where the recommendations of elite scientists shaped public policy of closing businesses and schools with little uptake of the daily concerns of the people who were unable to work from home and who relied upon schools to house and teach their children while they worked. Notably, the frustrated responses of the people led scientists and policy elites to have to reshape their research to attend to the demands of the people, including determining new criteria and procedures for reopening businesses and schools. In this way, scientific study and results can be improved when the process is politicized and democratized.[106]

Pragmatists envision more inclusive communities of scientific inquiry, carving out space for the people within such endeavors. There, pragmatists believe, scientists and everyday citizens can learn *with* and *from* each other, while also correcting each other. They co-produce and verify truth together. Pragmatists argue that the people should inform experts in order to improve both what we know to be true, but also our democracy. In Dewey's words:

> No government by experts in which the masses do not have the chance to inform the experts as to their needs can be anything but an oligarchy managed in the interests of the few. . . . [But] the essential need . . . is the improvement of the methods and conditions of debate, discussion, and persuasion. That is the problem of the public. We have asserted that this improvement depends essentially upon freeing and perfecting the processes of inquiry and of dissemination of their conclusions. Inquiry, indeed, is a link that devolves upon experts. But their expertness is not in framing and executing policies, but in discovering and making known the facts upon which the former depend. They are technical experts in the sense that scientific investigators and artists manifest expertise.[107]

The people can be a check on the biases of scientists and academics, while also making sure that the values that guide intellectuals are aligned with the values held by wider swaths of the population. Now, because of their specialized knowledge or access to information, on some occasions elites may be justified in asserting their views over the people. Admittedly, deciphering these moments and determining the extent to which one group (either the people or the experts) should be able to question or limit the other is quite challenging. Determining the acceptable limits of this asymmetry can be very difficult. At the very least, we must develop better communication about such limits across group boundaries. Such conversations may require the invention of new methods for better enabling the people and the elite to talk to and check each other.

Additionally, these scientific communities of inquiry require some minimal degree of mutual respect and collaboration that may be difficult to achieve in our divided world today. It is possible that many populists may not be interested in working across tribal boundaries to determine truth with others. And many different parties may refuse to engage in conversations with each other, in large part because they do not trust each other. This is a significant problem for a functioning democracy because the division of epistemic labor in our contemporary world often requires that rather than verifying the truth of all claims ourselves, we must rely on others to verify some claims because there is simply too much to be known and some knowledge that is well beyond that which many people can grasp without advanced training. Our task then becomes assessing others' credibility to determine whether their claims are trustworthy.

We must figure out how to place such trust well. Bianca Thoilliez urges: "Thus, a more radical account is needed, one that sees post-truth as an issue of trust, of an expansive unwillingness to engage in conversations with others. We must think of answers to post-truth conditions that are educational rather than political."[108] That is the project I take up in this book, building a case in later chapters for a form of trust-building inquiry based on honesty that can work across boundaries to determine and share truth. Notably, trust is not an unquestioning attitude toward another person but, rather, a willingness to engage with them and the information they share in an open way, which may include questioning that information. One may be vulnerable by virtue of trusting others, enabling opportunities to be taken advantage of or deceived. But, in the spirit of shared fate and political friendship described later in this book, trust takes informed risks because the benefits to epistemic and civic life are significant.[109] Alternatively, one increases one's own trustworthiness by allowing one's own claims to be subject to inquiry.

But deeply entrenching dichotomous divisions, as populism does, only further prevents our ability to arrive at wise, informed decisions that meet our needs, while increasing our chances of being stalled in competing narratives. Moreover, pragmatists must sort out how and when to differentiate elites and the people, recognizing that neither group is homogeneous or static, as populists too often categorize them. Some voices may prove to be epistemically or morally suspect to such an extent that their views should not be equally weighted with others, while other voices within each group deserve to be prioritized. This is not an easy task.[110]

Whereas liberal and neoliberal forms of democracy often operate with elitist forms of intelligence, pragmatist democracy enables social intelligence, where increased and widened participation in inquiry improves the quality of the knowledge produced. In this context, citizens also develop what Tony DeCesare calls "democratic competence," where, to quote Dewey, one uses social knowledge intelligently "to judge the bearing of the knowledge supplied by others upon common concerns."[111] Moreover, like populism, the process of inquiry brings individuals and their personal experiences and opinions together around public problems that lead to political movements and action. David Ridley concludes that this "intelligent populism" is "an emergent, bottom-up and essentially democratic process of public self-education and mobilization."[112]

In sum, pragmatism aligns with the populist desire to value the experience and insight of the people, while providing middle ground between simplistic celebrations of common sense and an exclusionary adherence to expertocracy. In this regard, pragmatism may offer a better alternative to current problems in liberal democracy. At the same time, it opens pathways for achieving more informed collective intelligence and democratization that lead to action that can improve shared living. Pragmatism would see populism as useful for revealing indeterminate situations and sparking inquiry into them, and for generating publics that can determine and advocate for truth. Pragmatism shares some similarities with populist understandings of truth but provides an account of honesty that is more helpful for attending to struggles in our civic lives today. Importantly, however, pragmatist views on truth, social democracy, honesty, and ultimately civic education should not be understood as just a middle ground between liberal democracy and populism. They provide more radically inclusive ways to answer the question "What should we do?" that go beyond simply sorting out "the facts," listening to different "sides" of an issue, or engaging in struggles between competing tribes. Pragmatist approaches push us to figure out how to solve shared problems and figure out how to live together in ways that promote growth of individuals and flourishing of society. As such, they may help us ameliorate some of the problems we face in democracy today.

Using Pragmatism to Attend to Struggles in Democracy Today

I will not try here to fully diagnose the problems of democracy today, trace their history, or assess their severity. There is a mix of many contributing factors, including leaders and media that intentionally misrepresent facts in order to mislead the public for their purposes; psychological phenomena that drive individuals to like-minded peers and sources for information, sometimes causing them to double down on their views in the face of competing evidence; and growing distrust of the claims made by fellow citizens and democratic institutions.[113] In this section, I highlight some elements of these factors in order to demonstrate how pragmatist understandings of democracy, inquiry, truth, and honesty may provide helpful avenues for addressing or ameliorating aspects of these struggles.

To begin to make sense of some recent situations in democracies around the world, we must start with the "sobering evidence that our allegiance to truth tends to end where our self-interest begins."[114] The post-truth era is marked by the tendency to put our own opinions above facts. Often we are driven to do so because facts and experts don't align with our interests or don't help us get what we want personally. "Truth decay" describes the social phenomenon whereby members of a society increasingly struggle to draw clear and sharp distinctions between fact and opinion, where personal experience takes on amplified importance, and where traditionally respected institutions and sources of facts, such as newsrooms and scientific reports, are increasingly distrusted.[115]

Hyperpartisanship is shaping both the makeup of citizen groups and the inquiry that occurs in them. In self-serving ways, citizens increasingly seek like-minded peers whose views, shared on social media and in friendship networks, affirm their own. Online settings are especially ripe for these problems because social media friends tend to share like-minded ideas, leading to epistemic insularity. It can be done deliberately or inadvertently. It may create a filter bubble, where other voices have been left out, or an echo chamber, where some perspectives have been actively excluded or discredited, typically because they are not trusted.[116] Sometimes citizens may be prone to motivated reasoning, where they reject evidence or ignore alternative viewpoints that conflict with their values or worldviews. Directional motivation may lead them to justify views that align with their prior beliefs because it "feels right." Additionally, they may prioritize the stance of their social or political group over new information or counter-information. All of these can lead citizens to discount evidence that might jeopardize their opinion of their group or experience some sense of moral culpability for being a part of that group. And confirmation bias may lead citizens to seek only evidence that already aligns with their views. Echo chambers, filter bubbles, motivated reasoning, and confirmation bias are epistemic threats; they put our ability to make wise and informed decisions at risk. They sometimes lead groups to engage in groupthink, which blocks out alternative perspectives and information, thereby jeopardizing our ability to determine truth and achieve quality civic reasoning. They run counter to pluralism and fallibilism.

I want to suggest that a better way of understanding and doing democracy—one grounded in a wider understanding of social life and relationships—might head off the temptation to be dishonest for self-serving reasons. While there is considerable writing recently about the impact of lying among political leaders and distrust in institutional democracy,[117] I am focusing instead on how failing to be honest jeopardizes our relationships with each other as citizens and our ability to engage in civic reasoning together to fulfill shared goals.[118] My pragmatist emphasis is on the social nature of democracy. As a result, we must look at how honesty impacts relationships between citizens, especially across different social and hyperpartisan political groups where fear and anger are already high. And we must consider how honesty shapes the problem-solving inquiry they undertake together as they ask, "What should we do?"

From a Deweyan pragmatist perspective, democracy is the social arrangement where we work together to solve our problems in ways that are inclusive and cooperative. Our inquiries are improved when we draw upon a wide array of evidence, incorporating multiple constituencies into our investigations. Democracy celebrates these wide and diverse resources for epistemic decision-making, positively drawing conflicting views and dissenting perspectives to challenge the status quo and consider different alternatives. Even when deep in disagreement, democracy is, in Dewey's words, a "conjoint" and "cooperative" undertaking.[119]

A well-functioning democracy employs inclusion and cooperation to craft solutions. It provides the relational conditions that enable and encourage honesty via truth-seeking and truth-telling. Moreover, this social view of democracy brings matters of trust to the fore. Our ideas are more likely to be listened and attended to when we are trusted by others. The solutions we craft to shared problems are better-informed when their sources are reliable. Facing shared fates, individuals must learn whom to trust and how to trust. Engaging in inquiry with those different from ourselves, but who face mutually harmful or beneficial results, helps us identify justified rather than naive trust. Importantly, it also propels us to be trustworthy ourselves out of our personal *and* collective interests. As Tamar Frankel explains in *Trust and Honesty*, "Trust is based on belief in other people."[120] Honesty is a key component of trustworthiness because it demonstrates that we are forthright and sincere, that we are open and straightforward and do not seek to mislead others. Being honest helps other people to believe in us and in what we say.

Situating truth primarily within a social view of democracy, rather than merely a procedural or even a moral one, offers important insight. Whereas a moral conception of democracy explains the meaning of democracy with reference to values (equality, freedom) considered as ultimate ends,

> a social approach to democracy is based upon a sociological understanding of human interactions and of how social life should be organized in order to reconcile individual striving toward self-expression and societal constraints relating to social stability. The differences are to this extent major. While moral conceptions are usually introduced with the aim of subordinating politics to a normative ideal, such as that of respect (liberalism) or self-government (republicanism), a social conception integrates moral considerations into a broader picture which also takes conditions of social functioning into account.[121]

This social view enables us to better attend to changes related to how populists describe truth, employ fake news, and create echo chambers, seeing them as not just matters of immorality or mere problems of human psychology (cognitive bias, etc.) but also as changes in how people relate to each other (polarization, tribal epistemology).[122] For example, this perspective sheds light on how post-truth works to gain competitive advantages,[123] exposing matters of power and unjust relationships between citizens. It also offers insight into how post-truth claims work to signal like-minded audiences and do not merely manipulate those audiences but rely upon their collusion in order to flex power.[124]

In Dewey's discussion of the "problem of the public," we begin to see how his views on inquiry and truth relate to life in a democracy. There he explains that the public must figure out how to use inquiry, persuasive language, and even affect in order to arrive at truths that work. The "public" for Dewey should be understood as multiple small groups (publics). Dewey defines these publics as consisting "of all those who are affected by the indirect consequences of transactions to such an extent that it is deemed necessary to have those consequences systematically cared for."[125] They develop and shift over time as new problems and shared concerns arise. It is not an overarching, all-encompassing notion of a group, nor are groups predetermined and fixed, as in populism's "people versus elites."

Notably, the people who compose publics are often affectively connected to the problem or issue in some way, and this embodied, emotional response carries them into inquiry about it together. They are not bound by some sort of patriotic duty, nor are they motivated by mere rationalism. People group together initially around shared concerns for the impact of an issue and then become a public when they are able to express shared interests in the issue.[126] During inquiry, publics also work together to clarify their emotions, including the conceptual content they relate to, the identities they shape, and their impact on epistemic determinations of truth. Rather than the predetermined and dichotomous identities of populism, pragmatist inquiry enables publics to investigate together to better understand their world and shape their identity in it as a political group.[127]

These publics, like "the people" in populism, may put forward demands revealing problems in current ways of living, but they may take a wide array of forms and are not easily grouped into "people versus elites." Moreover, through the process of inquiry, pragmatists promote democratic involvement beyond making only demands. They goad hypothesizing and testing solutions to problems detected in the world, including problems with liberal democracy. At the same time, the spirit of democratic experimentalism of pragmatism suggests that the social institutions of democracy must adapt to the demands of the people and to changes in the environment. For pragmatists, inquiry and democracy are social activities where problems (including empirical, economic, moral, and more) are detected, investigated, and addressed. Democracy is what helps us to coordinate our inquiries with fellow citizens so that we can better realize an array of goods and flourishing.

More significantly, this social understanding of democracy and inquiry provides ways to respond to populist and other obstacles as well as the power dynamics that underlie them, while still celebrating disagreement as an epistemic resource for making better decisions through inquiry. Rather than common tendencies to assert, or gullibly follow, falsities in the post-truth era, pragmatism offers us a call not to assertion but to deliberation in an epistemic democracy where we engage in inquiry to arrive at justified conclusions and plans of action—even if only provisionally held or only partially instituted.

To summarize, pragmatism offers a better framework for honesty, truth, and democracy that can attend to populist challenges to liberal democracy today. Pragmatism is a call not to quickly assert truth but, rather, to inquire into it and to determine whether "it works," even if only briefly and always open to revision. And democracy is a social way of living where publics form to meet the needs of citizens in a changing world and where inquiry strives not just to determine what "works" but also to put forward alternatives to problems in liberal democracy.

Before I turn in the next chapter to laying out how to teach honesty from a pragmatist perspective, I must acknowledge a limitation to the pragmatist framework I have offered in this chapter. I recognize that the pragmatist vision I hold is quite different from what is typically held in society or reflected in school practices or curricula. I'm offering this framework as a way to imagine what it might look like to reorient our classrooms around that vision, acknowledging that it would be hard to achieve for an array of reasons. At the least, it can serve as a foil to help us identify shortcomings in our current approaches to teaching young citizens. At the most, it offers a melioristic approach that, with careful cultivation in our schools, might dramatically reshape and revive democracy and our practices of it.

Notes

1. Christian Miller, "The Virtue of Honesty Requires More than Just Telling the Truth," *Aeon*, December 13, 2021, https://psyche.co/ideas/more-than-just-truth-telling-honesty-is-a-virtue-to-cultivate.

2. Christian Miller, *Honesty: The Philosophy and Psychology of a Neglected Virtue* (New York: Oxford University Press, 2021), C4.P10.

3. Christian Miller, "Honesty," in *Moral Psychology 5: Virtue and Character*, ed. Walter Sinnott-Armstrong and Christian B. Miller (Cambridge, MA: MIT Press, 2017), 237–272.

4. Bernard Williams, *Truth and Truthfulness: An Essay in Genealogy* (Princeton, NJ: Princeton University Press, 2002).

5. Daniel Lapsley and Dominic Charloner, "Post-Truth and Science Identity: A Virtue-Based Approach to Science Education," *Educational Psychologist* 55, no. 3 (2020): 132–143.

6. Dewey describes this interconnectedness in "Democracy and Education," in *John Dewey: The Middle Works, 1899–1924*, ed. Jo Ann Boydston (Carbondale: Southern Illinois University Press, 2008), 9:282–283, 304; John Dewey, "Logic: The Theory of Inquiry," in *John Dewey: The Later Works, 1925–1953*, ed. Jo Ann Boydston (Carbondale: Southern Illinois University Press, 2008), 12:481.

7. "Word of the Year 2016," Oxford Languages, accessed August 23, 2022, https://langua ges.oup.com/word-of-the-year/2016/; "Cambridge Dictionary's Word of the Year 2017," Cambridge Dictionary, accessed August 23, 2022, https://dictionaryblog.cambridge.org/ 2017/11/29/cambridge-dictionarys-word-of-the-year-2017/.

8. I focus primarily on the U.S. educational context, but some of the claims I make extend elsewhere also. Much of my argument pertains to democracies around the globe even if particular aspects may not be a direct fit. Specific to the United States, for instance, the Common Core State Standards make no mention of truth or populism. "The Common Core State Standards: English Language Arts Standards—History/Social Studies," National Governors Association Center for Best Practices, Council of Chief State School Officers, 2010, http://www.corestandards.org/ELA-Literacy/RH/introduction/.

    Additionally, in one report by the Fordham Institute populism shows up in fewer than half of state standards for K–12 students and truth was mentioned fewer than ten times. Jeremy A. Stern et al., *State of State Standards for Civics and U.S. History in 2021* (Washington, DC: Thomas B. Fordham Institute, 2021), https://fordhaminstitute.org/natio nal/research/state-state-standards-civics-and-us-history-2021.

    Also, Educating for America puts forward recommendations to increase the teaching of truth and bias within their "contemporary debates and possibilities" theme for students in grades six through twelve, but even they shy away from an overt exploration of popu-lism. Educating for American Democracy, *Educating for American Democracy: Excellence in History and Civics for All Learners* (n.p.: iCivics, 2021), www.educatingforamericande mocracy.org.

9. Nicole Mirra and Antero Garcia, "Civic Participation Reimagined: Youth Interrogation and Innovation in the Multimodal Public Sphere," *Review of Research in Education* 41, no. 1 (2017): 136–158, https://doi.org/10.3102/0091732X17690121.

10. Mark Abadi, "One of Trump's Favorite Phrases Was Named the 2017 Word of the Year," *Business Insider*, January 8, 2018, https://www.businessinsider.com/word-of-the-year-2017-fake-news-2018-1.

11. Silvio Waisbord, "The Elective Affinity Between Post-Truth Communication and Populist Politics," *Communication Research and Practice* 4, no. 1 (2018): 19.

12. I follow Edda Sant in this approach. Edda Sant, *Political Education in Times of Populism: Towards a Radical Democratic Education* (London: Palgrave Macmillan, 2021).

13. Thomas Frank, *The People, No: A Brief History of Anti-Populism* (New York: Metropolitan Books, 2020). See also the work of Edda Sant, who chronicles this history as well as its critics, such as Richard Hofstadter.

14. Sant, *Political Education in Times of Populism*, 47–48.

15. Ernesto Laclau, *On Populist Reason* (New York: Verso, 2005), 8. Laclau warns against the tendency to ascribe particular social content to populism.

16. Cas Mudde and Cristobal Kaltwasser, *Populism: A Very Short Introduction* (Oxford: Oxford University Press, 2017), 17–18, 83; Sant, *Political Education in Times of Populism*.

17. For more on the problems of maximalist views of populism, see Sant, *Political Education in Times of Populism*, 48–52.

18. For more on the thin-centered ideology definition, see the work of Cas Mudde and Margaret Canovan.

19. Ron DeSantis, *The Courage to Be Free* (New York: Broadside Books, 2023), audiobook, n.p.

20. Marjorie Taylor-Green (@RepMTG), "I am being attacked by the godless left because I said I'm a proud Christian Nationalist . . . ," Twitter, July 25, 2022, https://twitter.com/RepMTG/status/1551705165983621120.

21. Brian Geurkink et al., "Populist Attitudes, Political Trust, and External Political Efficacy: Old Wine in New Bottles?," *Political Studies* 68, no. 1 (2019): 250.

22. "Donald Trump Speaks at Rally in Eugene, Part 2," YouTube, posted by The Oregonian, May 7, 2016, https://youtu.be/L48tAxU12u4.

23. William A. Galston, *Anti-Pluralism: The Populist Threat to Liberal Democracy* (New Haven, CT: Yale University Press, 2018).

24. DeSantis provides a list of exceptions, people of great wealth or high societal rank who he argues are not elites, such as Supreme Court justice Clarence Thomas (*The Courage to Be Free*, n.p.).

25. Michalinos Zembylas, *Affect and the Rise of Right-Wing Populism: Pedagogies for the Renewal of Democratic Education* (Cambridge: Cambridge University Press, 2021), 6.

26. Sant, *Political Education in Times of Populism*, 121.

27. DeSantis, *The Courage to Be Free*, n.p.

28. Here, I draw heavily on Mudde and Kaltwasser, *Populism*, 95.

29. Laclau, *On Populist Reason*; Sant, *Political Education in Times of Populism*; Geurkink, "Populist Attitudes, Political Trust, and External Political Efficacy," 250. Note that Guerkink makes an important distinction in the types of political trust.

30. President Donald Trump, Inaugural Address, January 20, 2017, https://www.govinfo.gov/content/pkg/CREC-2017-01-20/pdf/CREC-2017-01-20-pt1-PgS362-4.pdf.

31. These debates have occurred in many places, including among scholars like Randall Curren, who highlights the threats of populism, and leaders like the UNESCO director-general Irina Bokova, who says we need to protect students from populism. Randall Curren, "Populism and the Fate of Civic Friendship," in *Virtues in the Public Sphere*, ed. James Arthur (Milton Park, UK: Routledge, 2018), 92–107; political theorists like Mouffe, who celebrate the potential of certain types of populism; and philosophers of education like Sant, who invites pedagogies that curtail worrisome aspects of populism while remaining open to what populism might usher in as an improved form of democracy starting within our schools. Clearly, though, it's important to recognize that populism can lead down deeply problematic avenues to authoritarianism, oppression, and even genocide.

32. Mudde and Kaltwasser describe some of these problems in *Populism*, 83.

33. For more along these lines, see Kathleen Knight Abowitz, "Populism, legitimidad y escolarización estatal," *Teoría de la Educación: Revista Interuniversitaria* 35, no. 2 (2023): 37–55.

34. There are notable exceptions to this. For one, see Sharon D. Wright Austin, "Contemporary Black Populism and the Development of Multiracial Electoral Coalitions: The 2018 Stacey Abrams and Andrew Gillum Gubernatorial Campaigns," *Political Science Quarterly* 136, no. 3 (2021): 417–438.

35. Sant, *Political Education in Times of Populism*, 79.

36. *Oxford English Dictionary Online*, s.v. "post-truth, adj."

37. Waisbord, "The Elective Affinity Between Post-Truth Communication and Populist Politics," 19.

38. I am aware that "tribalism" invokes images of Indigenous peoples and Native Americans and can do so in ways that may be perceived as offensive or derogatory. I do not mean to invoke such understandings here. Instead, I am using "tribalism" in a sense common in literature in political science and social psychology to identify tendencies to privilege and protect those most like oneself, especially members of one's social or political group.

39. Waisbord, "The Elective Affinity between Post-Truth Communication and Populist Politics," 17.

40. DeSantis, *The Courage to Be Free*, n.p.

41. Rush Limbaugh as quoted in Jason Baehr, "Democracy, Information Technology, and Virtue Epistemology," in *Virtues, Democracy, and Online Media*, ed. Nancy Snow and Maria Silvia Vaccarezza (New York: Routledge, 2021), 13.

42. Thank you to Kathryn Purcell for drawing my attention to the adherence to a clear and shared truth among some religious populists.

43. Waisbord, "The Elective Affinity between Post-Truth Communication and Populist Politics," 25–26.

44. Bernard Arthur Owen Williams, *Truth and Truthfulness: An Essay in Genealogy* (Princeton, NJ: Princeton University Press, 2002).

45. Sant, *Political Education in Times of Populism*, 107.

46. While not wanting to go too far into a thick description, I'm making a distinction here between what is typical of Right populist views, as opposed to the views of recent Left populists, such as those supporting Bernie Sanders, who champion higher education and even want to go so far as making it free for all, and more historical Left movements related to civil rights that celebrated intellectualism.

47. I am grateful to Katheryn Purcell for pointing this out to me.

48. Liesbet van Zoonen, "I-Pistemology: Changing Truth Claims in Popular and Political Culture," *European Journal of Communication* 27, no. 1 (2012): 56–67.

49. After initially drafting this chapter, I discovered a similar argument made by Just Serrano-Zamora in "What Kind of Epistemology Is Required for Democratic Renewal?," Open Conference on the Future of Deliberation: Exploring Political, Social, and Epistemic Control, University of Iceland EDDA Research Center, June 3, 2023. He nicely grounds his argument in the work of Helen Longino on epistemic cooperativism. I am both writing alongside him and drawing upon his excellent work here.

50. I recognize that there are significant differences in the accounts of truth offered by pragmatists. I offer here broad and general views of pragmatist truth to provide a brief working definition. I am more indebted to Peirce and Dewey, who emphasize empirical

methods, than to James, who gives greater weight to how one feels about beliefs and propositions, an approach that may share some similarities to populist truth. I also recognize that while Dewey tended toward warranted assertability, Rorty sided with agreement within a community (solidarity). For more on these distinctions, see Cheryl Misak, "Pragmatism on Solidarity, Bullshit, and Other Deformities of Truth," *Midwest Studies in Philosophy* 32, no. 1 (2008): 111–121.

51. Richard Rorty, "Is Truth a Goal of Enquiry?," *Philosophical Quarterly* 45, no. 180 (1995): 281.

52. Daniel Dennett, "Postmodernism and Truth," in *Philosophy: The Quest for Truth*, 6th ed., ed. Louis Pojman (Oxford: Oxford University Press, 2006), 233; Williams, *Truth and Truthfulness*, 59.

53. William James, *The Meaning of Truth* (Mineola, NY: Dover, 2002), vi. Emphasis in original.

54. John Dewey, "Propositions, Warranted Assertibility, and Truth" (1941), in *The Essential Dewey*, ed. Larry Hickman and Thomas M. Alexander (Bloomington: Indiana University Press, 1998), 204:201–212.

55. Ira Allen describes the view of truth held by William James well in "The Hegelian Spirit of Jamesian Truth," in *New Perspectives on Realism*, ed. Luca Taddio (Sesto San Giovanni, Italy: Mimesis International, 2017), 31–58.

56. Charles Sanders Peirce, *Truth, 549–573*, ed. Arthur W. Burks (Cambridge: Harvard University Press, 1958), CP 5,553.

57. Misak, "Pragmatism on Solidarity," 114.

58. "Pragmatism," *Stanford Encyclopedia of Philosophy*, last revised April 6, 2021, https://plato.stanford.edu/entries/pragmatism/.

59. James, *The Meaning of Truth,* xi.

60. John Dewey, "The Quest for Certainty: A Study of the Relation of Knowledge to Action," in *John Dewey: The Later Works, 1925–1953*, ed. Jo Ann Boydston (Carbondale: Southern Illinois University Press, 2008), 4:19.

61. Colin Koopman, *Pragmatism as Transition: Historicity and Hope in James, Dewey, and Rorty* (New York: Columbia University Press, 2009), 21.

62. John Dewey, *The Public and Its Problems* (New York: Henry Holt, 1927), 102.

63. Koopman, *Pragmatism as Transition*, 22.

64. Bianca Thoilliez, "'Making Education Possible Again': Pragmatist Experiments for a Troubled and Down-to-Earth Pedagogy," *Educational Theory* 72, no. 4 (2022): 15.

65. John Dewey, "Theory of Valuation," in *John Dewey: The Later Works, 1925–1953*, ed. Jo Ann Boydston (Carbondale: Southern Illinois University Press, 2008), 4:1–68.

66. Notably, how we understand those goods, such as what freedom means, continues to shift based on our experiences. Michael Fuerstein, "Epistemic Democracy Without Truth: The Deweyan Approach," *Raisons Politiques* 81, no. 1 (2021): 81–96.

67. "'Truthiness': Can Something 'Seem,' Without Being True?," *Words at Play* (blog), Merriam-Webster, April 2020, https://www.merriam-webster.com/words-at-play/truthiness-meaning-word-origin#:~:text=In%202006%2C%20truthiness%20was%20chosen,Year%20by%20their%20dictionary%20users.

68. William James, "Lecture VI: Pragmatism's Conception of Truth," in *Pragmatism: A New Name for Some Old Ways of Thinking* (1907; n.p.: Project Gutenberg, 2013), ebook.

69. John Dewey, "Creative Democracy: The Task Before Us," in *John Dewey: The Later Works, 1925–1953*, ed. Jo Ann Boydston (Carbondale: Southern Illinois University Press, 2008), 14:224–230; John Dewey, "Democracy Is Radical," in *John Dewey: The Later Works,*

1925–1953, ed. Jo Ann Boydston (Carbondale: Southern Illinois University Press, 2008), 2:296–309.

70. John Dewey, "Education as Politics," in *John Dewey: The Middle Works, 1899–1924*, ed. Jo Ann Boydston (Carbondale: Southern Illinois University Press, 2008), 13:344.

71. I'm working here largely with a Deweyan understanding of the process of inquiry, though similar arguments could be made about the approaches of some other pragmatists, such as Peirce's doubt-belief arc. In Dewey's words, "Inquiry is the controlled or directed transformation of an indeterminate situation into one that is so determinate in its constituent distinctions and relations as to convert the elements of the original situation into a unified whole." Dewey, "Logic: The Theory of Inquiry," 12:108.

72. I'm grateful to Tony Laden for his insight on how we think *with* information.

73. John Dewey, "How We Think, Revised Edition," in *John Dewey: The Later Works, 1925–1953*, ed. Jo Ann Boydston (Carbondale: Southern Illinois University Press, 2008), 8:329–330.

74. Dewey, "Logic: The Theory of Inquiry," 12:500.

75. Dewey, "Logic: The Theory of Inquiry."

76. Roberto Frega, *Pragmatism and the Wide View of Democracy* (Cham, Switzerland: Palgrave Macmillan, 2019), 96.

77. Danielle S. Allen, *Talking to Strangers: Anxieties of Citizenship After* Brown v. Board of Education (Chicago: University of Chicago Press, 2004), 12.

78. John Dewey, "Democracy and Education," 9:53.

79. John Dewey, "Human Nature and Conduct," in *John Dewey: The Middle Works, 1899–1924*, ed. Jo Ann Boydston (Carbondale: Southern Illinois University Press, 2008), 14:67.

80. John Dewey, "Democracy and Education," 9:199–200.

81. Dewey, "Human Nature and Conduct," 124.

82. Dewey, "Democracy and Education," 9:54.

83. Carolyn Pedwell. *Revolutionary Routines: The Habits of Social Transformation* (Montreal: McGill-Queen's University Press, 2021), 42–43.

84. Dewey, "Human Nature and Conduct," 52.

85. Frega, *Pragmatism and the Wide View of Democracy*, 212.

86. Miller, *Honesty*, C1.P111.

87. For more along this line of critique, see Frega, *Pragmatism and the Wide View of Democracy*, 238.

88. John Dewey, *Reconstruction in Philosophy* (Boston: Beacon Press, 1948), 156.

89. I am indebted to Katie Sellers for pointing this out to me, and I borrow heavily on her phrasing here.

90. Baehr, "Democracy, Information Technology, and Virtue Epistemology," 2021.

91. Matthew J. Brown, "The Concept of 'Situation' in John Dewey's Logic and Philosophy of Science," presentation at the USCD History of Philosophy Roundtable, Winter 2017, https://www.matthewjbrown.net/professional/papers/situation-science.pdf.

92. Sarit Barzilai and Clark A. Chinn, "A Review of Educational Responses to the 'Post-Truth' Condition: Four Lenses on 'Post-Truth' Problems," *Educational Psychologist* 55, no. 3 (2020): 107–119. I also want to be clear here that I am not casting everyone who questions scientific consensus or offers competing scientific findings as a "science denier." Jacob Hale Russell, "Post-Truth and the Rhetoric of 'Following the Science,'" *Critical Review: A Journal of Politics and Society* 35, nos. 1–2 (2023): 122–147.

93. Mudde and Kaltwasser, *Populism*, 18.
94. Sant, *Political Education in Times of Populism*, 109, rightly points out that populists some-times overly romanticize authentic common sense.
95. DeSantis, *The Courage to Be Free*, n.p.
96. Margaret Petrie, Callum McGregor, and Jim Crowther, "Populism, Democracy and a Pedagogy of Renewal," *International Journal of Lifelong Education* 38, no. 5 (2019): 493. The authors describe "epistemological populism" as a disdain toward intellectuals.
97. Russell, "Post-Truth and the Rhetoric of 'Following the Science.'"
98. DeSantis, *The Courage to Be Free*, n.p.
99. Baehr, "Democracy, Information Technology, and Virtue Epistemology," 3.
100. Dewey, *The Public and Its Problems*, 207.
101. Laura M. Westoff, "The Popularization of Knowledge: John Dewey on Experts and American Democracy," *History of Education Quarterly* 35, no. 1 (1995): 34.
102. Michael Patrick Lynch, "Teaching in the Time of Google," *Chronicle of Higher Education*, April 24, 2016, http://chronicle.com/article/Teaching-in-the-Time-of-Google/236180/.
103. Dewey, "Logic: The Theory of Inquiry," 12:71–72.
104. Here I am referring to more generalist views of science than those found in philosophy of science literature.
105. For more along these lines, see Sophia Rosenfeld, *Democracy and Truth: A Short History* (Philadelphia: University of Pennsylvania Press, 2018), 86–90.
106. After drafting this, I discovered a similar case made about COVID-19 by Just Serrano-Zamora and Matteo Santarelli ("Experts and Citizens in the Times of COVID-19: A Deweyan Perspective," *Dewey Studies* 6, no. 1 [2022]: 378–415), which they built from the work on public movements shaping AIDS research done by James Bohman ("Democracy as Inquiry, Inquiry as Democratic: Pragmatism, Social Science, and the Cognitive Division of Labor," *American Journal of Political Science* [1999]: 590–607).
107. John Dewey, "The Problem of Method," in *John Dewey: The Later Works, 1925–1953*, ed. Jo Ann Boydston (Carbondale: Southern Illinois University Press, 2008), 2:365.
108. Thoilliez, "'Making Education Possible Again,'" 7.
109. I am grateful to Tony Laden for prompting me to describe the role of questioning within trusting relationships.
110. I am grateful to Veli-Mikko Kauppi for urging me to recognize the difficulties of distinguishing among those in each group (people and elite) and the challenges of facilitating inquiry between them.
111. Tony DeCesare, "The Lippmann-Dewey 'Debate' Revisited: The Problem of Knowledge and the Role of Experts in Modern Democratic Theory," *Philosophical Studies in Education* 43 (2012): 106–117; Dewey, *The Public and Its Problems*, 208.
112. David Ridley, *The Method of Democracy: John Dewey's Theory of Collective Intelligence* (Bern: Peter Lang, 2021).
113. Henry E. Brady and Thomas B. Kent, "Fifty Years of Declining Confidence and Increasing Polarization in Trust in American Institutions," *Daedalus* 151, no. 4 (2022): 43–66.
114. Philip E. Dow, "Developing Truth Seekers," in *Integrity, Honesty, and Truth Seeking*, ed. Christian B. Miller and Ryan West (New York: Oxford University Press, 2020), 275.
115. Erica Hodgin and Joseph Kahne, "Judging Credibility in Un-credible Times: Three Educational Approaches for the Digital Age," in *Unpacking Fake News: An Educator's*

Guide to Navigating the Media with Students, ed. Wayne Journell (New York: Teachers College Press, 2019), 93.

116. C. Thi Nguyen, "Escape the Echo Chamber," Aeon, April 9, 2018, https://aeon.co/essays/why-its-as-hard-to-escape-an-echo-chamber-as-it-is-to-flee-a-cult; Baehr, "Democracy, Information Technology, and Virtue Epistemology."

117. Glynis Gawn and Robert Innes, "Do Lies Erode Trust?," *International Economic Review* 59, no. 1 (2018): 137–161; Philipp Gerlach, Kinneret Teodorescu, and Ralph Hertwig, "The Truth About Lies: A Meta-Analysis of Dishonest Behavior," *Psychological Bulletin* 145, no. 1 (2019): 1–44; John Higley, "Elite Trust and the Populist Threat to Stable Democracy," *American Behavioral Scientist* 64, no. 9 (2020): 1211–1218; Hodgin and Kahne, "Judging Credibility in Un-Credible Times," 92–108; Kai Horsthemke, " '#FactsMustFall'?—Education in a Post-Truth, Post-Truthful World," *Ethics and Education* 12, no. 3 (2017): 273–288; Richard Scullion and Stuart Armon, "Democracy in a DeCivilizing Age: The Rise of Shameless Personal Truths." *International Journal of Media and Cultural Politics* 14, no. 3 (2018): 283–300.

118. I rely on some key ideas expressed in Anthony Simon Laden, *Reasoning: A Social Picture* (New York: Oxford University Press, 2012).

119. John Dewey, "Democracy and Education," 9:29.

120. Tamar Frankel, *Trust and Honesty* (New York: Oxford University Press, 2006).

121. Frega, *Pragmatism and the Wide View of Democracy,* 116.

122. Chris Heffer, *All Bullshit and Lies? Insincerity, Irresponsibility, and the Judgment of Untruthfulness* (New York: Oxford University Press, 2020).

123. Steve Fuller, *Post-Truth: Knowledge as a Power Game* (Cambridge: Cambridge University Press, 2018).

124. Ignas Kalpokas, *A Political Theory of Post-Truth* (Cham, Switzerland: Palgrave Macmillan, 2019).

125. Dewey, "How We Think," 8:246.

126. Dewey, "How We Think," 8:327.

127. For more along these lines of the role of emotions in Deweyan inquiry and their distinction from populism, see Matteo Santarelli and Justo Serrano Zamora, "The Affective Side of Political Identities: Pragmatism, Populism and European Social Theory," in *Pragmatism and Social Philosophy*, ed. Michael Festl (Milton Park: Routledge, 2020), 248–264.

3

Teaching Honesty

So far, I have described some contemporary struggles that reveal the heightened importance of honesty. I put forward a pragmatist account of truth, inquiry, and democracy to suggest a better framework for understanding and enacting honesty, all the while attending to some of the changes put forward by populism in particular. I begin this chapter by exposing the absence of quality teaching about and for honesty: in most schools, honesty is touched on only briefly as a part of character education, if at all. Filling that gap, I offer an initial sketch of how we might more thoroughly teach honesty and, thereby, improve democracy. In this chapter, I put forward a pragmatist account of habit formation to offer a better way to develop and encourage honesty. I then place citizenship education within the pragmatist democratic context in the final section of the chapter to present a way to provide an environment, via classroom inquiry, that promotes honesty. This environmental and intellectual process differs significantly from simple individual character education or moral blame. It develops more sustainable dispositions aligned with democratic, social living, where honesty is affirmed for the positive outcomes it provides to such living, while taking into account the social and political influences shaping it and which it may shape in turn.

Current Education and Its Shortcomings

While it is difficult to generalize across the country or even across school districts in one state, typically honesty receives little attention in public schooling, even in coursework that is overtly focused on developing citizens. That includes courses in social studies, civics, government, and more general approaches such as *Bildung* and liberal education. Coursework in civics and government, in particular, is often more concerned with civic content, such as history and law, than with civic behaviors or skills, where matters of honesty would more likely arise. When it does appear in classrooms, if at all, honesty is typically described in brief elementary lessons about good character—sometimes as a "trait of the week"—not appearing again until high

Teaching Honesty in a Populist Era. Sarah M. Stitzlein, Oxford University Press. © Oxford University Press 2024.
DOI: 10.1093/9780197775912.003.0003

school or college, where students may be required to pledge academic honesty with little discussion of what their vow means.[1] When honesty is taught, it tends to be as a form of personally responsible citizenship that lacks the sorts of "analysis of social, political and economic contests . . . [making it] inadequate for advancing democracy."[2] Even within democratic political theory, civic humanists, civic republicans, and republican liberals tend to emphasize teaching other civic practices, like tolerance, over honesty.

Largely missing from the formal school curriculum, teaching honesty is seemingly left up to parents or religious leaders. Often in those settings, honest behavior is what is said to make you a good person individually, with little discussion of the role of honesty in the problem-solving and public work of society. Rather than positively valuing honesty, there is a tendency to focus more on the opposite, seeing lying as what makes you a bad person (forbidden by the Ten Commandments, for example). When stories such as "The Boy Who Cried Wolf" are used to warn children of the dangers of not being honest, their social implications often fall to the side of selfish takeaways: if you lie, you might not get help when you need it.[3] Yet, we see that matters of honesty are increasingly significant in our current social and political struggles, suggesting that our schools may bear some responsibility for inculcating it so that students are better prepared for the larger struggles plaguing their democracy. In response, this chapter calls for a new emphasis on honesty within schools, with overt emphasis on its implications for shared social living.

Traditional education also rarely takes up matters of truth beyond simplistic assertions and messages within the hidden curriculum that accumulating knowledge of facts leads to a degree, which leads to a lucrative career, which ultimately facilitates the pursuit of happiness.[4] It tends to downplay the role of power in shaping not only relations among citizens but also the facts that they employ—the very sorts of power on display between the people and the elite. Some scholars concerned with students "not knowing how to know" (the first lens described in the introduction of this book) have suggested that to respond to growing populism or the post-truth era, we simply need to arm students with more facts or equip them with the ability to systematically determine facts from falsity through critical media literacy.[5] Aiming to head off the perceived ignorance of populism, neutralize the role of anger and resentment, and fight post-truth, this approach is far too simplistic.[6] Its rationalistic tactics fail to provide a sufficient response to populism, which is situated in a historical moment of political distrust and propelled by affect, revealing significant problems related to relationships, power, and emotion. Whereas populism operates under different epistemological assumptions and prioritizes conflict over consensus, a "more facts" approach to citizenship education may not even make sense in today's context, let alone deter populism, as advocates imagine.

Instead, I offer here some initial suggestions for how a pragmatist approach to citizenship education might better attend to struggles over power and between groups as truths are asserted, contested, and shared. Such teaching may make epistemic and civic aims more salient than other motivations toward dishonesty, including tribal loyalty and self-interests. This proposal grounds education for active and effective citizenship within the understanding of pragmatism articulated in the previous chapter, where schools would strive to cultivate pragmatist practices of truth determination and social understanding of democracy. I describe ways that we might better develop proclivities toward and practices of honesty. In particular, I will describe how to cultivate honesty as a habit, understood in the uniquely pragmatist sense.

Virtue-Based Education for Democracy

While honesty is not sufficiently emphasized in current classrooms, philosophers have provided frameworks for understanding and teaching honesty as a virtue. Philosophers tend to describe the promotion of honest behavior in terms of being virtuous, where our character has been shaped to act honestly in accordance with the good, rather than merely by consciously holding ourselves to rules about good living.[7] Employing the lens of virtue, some commentators on the struggles of post-truth, fake news, and other problems in our democracy today chalk those problems up to the vices of individuals, pointing fingers at key populist leaders who are said to be bad people for failing to fulfill the virtue of honesty. Instead, I take a different approach, one that moves beyond intrinsic moral motivations.

Unlike some virtue epistemologists, I do not believe that we must emphasize honesty as a good that one should be motivated to pursue intrinsically, simply because it is good.[8] Speaking of people who exhibit intellectual virtues, for example, philosopher Jason Baehr describes their "intrinsic motivation. At their best, intellectually virtuous people are motivated to think outside the box, take intellectual risks, ask thoughtful questions, and avoid intellectual errors because they care about things like knowledge, truth, and understanding at least partly for their own sake—not as mere means to other ends or goals."[9] When considered within the context of citizenship, I find that such a motivation to be good sets expectations too high for formal political participation and perfection, yet also does not go far enough in addressing some of the problematic trends we see in democracy today, including self-interestedness.[10] Instead, foregrounding a pragmatist account of truth and a social view of democracy, I turn to intellectual and, ultimately, civic reasons for being honest. According to Baehr, intellectual virtues are aimed at truth as an epistemic good and are conceived as having three components: a skill, motivation to employ the skill, and good judgment about when and how to deploy the skill.[11] Intellectual virtues aim for wisdom as deep, explanatory, reflective understanding and must be geared toward epistemically significant, rather than merely trivial, matters.[12]

While it is good to be honest, my account of civic reasoning and inquiry showcases *why* it's good to seek and tell the truth: because it helps us arrive at satisfactory solutions to our civic inquiries. Shedding light on recent U.S. struggles to protect our population in response to pandemics or brutality by police forces, for example, reveals a pressing need to engage in civic inquiry well so that conditions can be understood, solutions can be developed, and lives can be saved. The need to address those problems, especially when directly tied to the personal experiences of citizens, is more persuasive than just the drive to be good or to achieve wisdom. Honesty is concerned with finding and evaluating evidence as a part of civic reasoning. Moreover, given that such reasoning enables civic means and ends, including coordinated communication and living, it is valuable.[13]

Studies reveal that the desire to fulfill political agendas or align oneself with one's tribe can lead people to share less accurate information online. But, when provided financial incentives, citizens are better able to identify accurate information and restrict their sharing of inaccurate information.[14] This reveals that a central part of the problem is whether people are motivated to act honestly in the way they use information. In many cases, it's not really about being confused by sorting out the information. Perhaps, when civic motivations are supplied, honest actions may be increased. Honesty within civic inquiries may be propelled by a drive to ensure the well-being of one's community and oneself as a citizen within that community. The bar set for the motivation to be honest, then, is a more functional one, focused on what is needed for individuals and society to thrive, especially when engaging in civic inquiry. In other words, we are motivated to be honest for civic reasons, because it helps us successfully answer "What should we do?" as we navigate the world together. This motivation addresses some elements of self-interestedness insofar as civic inquiry may more directly or immediately benefit us than simply being good or pursuing truth may. Our well-being is often bound up with that of others.

Honesty is related to and supplements intellectual virtues celebrated by some theorists. Ethicist Etienne Brown rightly describes open-mindedness, intellectual caution, intellectual courage, and intellectual humility as virtues key to a functioning democracy.[15] That is largely because those virtues help us epistemically when solving problems—they help us find information and form decisions in wise ways. Scholars who advocate for intellectual virtues tend to uphold them as an educational solution to the lens of "not caring about truth (enough)." These virtues, compelled by a desire for wisdom, are believed to provide the motivation needed to "burst epistemic bubbles by encouraging a broader consideration of evidence and argument" and "work against the tendency to seek only confirmation of one's own perspective and to do justice to the other side of an argument or discussion."[16]

Intellectual humility has special relevance to matters of honesty and truth. Intellectual humility entails being aware of and responsible for gaps and mistakes in one's knowledge. It influences how we speak and contribute to civic discourse, and also how we listen. When we are listening, intellectual humility requires that we must be generous in how we interpret the speaker, keeping in mind that we may be incorrect ourselves or missing some important point being made. This may entail being curious and resisting quick judgments when listening.

Citizens today increasingly practice the opposite of intellectual humility, intellectual arrogance, asserting the superiority of their beliefs and seeking confirmation of them in echo chambers and through confirmation bias. Strong psychological and sociological trends make it increasingly challenging to engage in intellectual humility, yet we must push back against the pitfalls of intellectual arrogance. Epistemically, intellectual arrogance inhibits fallibilism. It makes us overly confident about the reliability of our beliefs and unwilling to revise our beliefs in light of new or contradictory evidence, especially if such evidence is presented by groups, leaders, or institutions that we distrust. Intellectual arrogance is often accompanied by a desire for power or to assert one's affiliation with particular like-minded groups by upholding certain beliefs as true.[17] This phenomenon is likely exacerbated by populism. And it is likely also increased by filter bubbles, which, having pushed out and discredited competing views, give the false impression of wide agreement, corroborating views with accounts from only the like-minded, thereby making the case appear certain.

One might be quick to suggest that perhaps, then, the best response is to educate citizens to be fully autonomous thinkers. But that would be foolish. It is quite clear that living in the world today requires us to depend on knowledge produced by others because we cannot know or verify all things. What we can do is change our orientation to the knowledge we receive and hold in light of our epistemic and civic aims. Intellectual humility offers one way to do that.

Intellectual humility has intellectual and civic justifications. Philosopher Michael Lynch explains, "To be intellectually humble is to see your worldview as open to improvement from new evidence and the experience of others."[18] Or, in Dewey's words, to uphold intellectual humility is to assert that "there is no belief so settled as not to be exposed to further inquiry."[19] Dewey might have connected intellectual humility to what he called "open-mindedness," a proclivity to engage in inquiry, public reason-giving, and reflection on how we come to believe something is true. To work against intellectual arrogance, individuals must shift their attitude toward truth and the reliability of their beliefs by changing what they value (away from power or tribalism). As with honesty, I base that value in civic life.[20] When situated within a focus on inquiry and in a deeply social account of democracy, one that affirms the need to work across political groups and care about other citizens, the value of acknowledging one's own cognitive limitations (prejudices, assumptions), holding one's views tentatively, and seeking out and being open to learning from others becomes clearer. Importantly, though, we must be careful not to misplace the civic virtue of tolerance when exercising intellectual humility. Tolerance is concerned with respecting fellow citizens and their right to uphold a diverse array of beliefs, including some that may be wrong or objectionable. When tolerance is misplaced and exercised in intellectual rather than civic matters, it can encroach on intellectual humility. This is because it endorses a sort of relativism when sorting out claims that can hinder our ability to determine truth because one is unwilling to pass judgment on the beliefs of another.[21]

The virtue of intellectual humility also enhances one's trustworthiness because it demonstrates to others a willingness to forgo one's own "rightness," to allow one's views to be subject to scrutiny, in order to pursue better outcomes of inquiry. Additionally, intellectual humility helps us navigate moments of disagreement because we recognize that we, like others, may be earnest and yet mistaken. And in many instances, all of us can learn from each other and revise our stances relative to each other. This is different from celebrating relativism; it is an acknowledgment that we must sometimes live with competing beliefs, and yet the process of determining truth continues and is aided by our willingness to acknowledge our own shortcomings and learn from others.

Finally, as a source of doubt, intellectual humility may lead the way to inquiry. Both Peirce and Dewey claim that doubt generates inquiry. Emphasizing intellectual humility, fallibilism, and honesty together may help students identify and appreciate doubt for how it opens us to new learning, provokes deliberation with others, and leads to better-informed outcomes, which are then held open to revision.

Within this pragmatist framework, the effects of honesty on democracy become clearer. Honesty has both content and relationship dimensions.[22] When grounded in civic reasoning, both are important. Our motivation to be honest in content (careful accounting as we seek and tell the truth) is tied to our motivation to flourish together (a relational dimension of interdependency). Finally, honesty and intellectual humility enable the justified trust—of institutions, of experts, of each other—necessary for democracy to thrive.[23]

Cultivating Honesty

Dewey argued that it was the responsibility of education to "cultivate deep-seated and effective habits of discriminating tested beliefs from mere assertions, guesses, and opinions; to develop a lively, sincere, and open-minded preference for conclusions that are properly grounded, and to ingrain into the individual's working habits methods of inquiry and reasoning appropriate to the various problems that present themselves."[24] How, then, does one cultivate pragmatist habits of honesty in young citizens? We identify and re-work bad habits, including those aligned with some of the problematic tendencies of populism and in democratic life today. We mold and shape new habits aligned with truth-seeking and truth-telling. We provide classroom environments and experiences that are conducive to employing honesty and witnessing its positive impact to affirm and further encourage habits of and related to honesty. In other words, we offer genuine opportunities to try out honesty, along with environments where honesty is a helpful disposition, and we reflect with students about those efforts and their outcomes so that we cultivate proclivities toward honesty in the future. Insofar as habits compose us and make us who we are, they become a part of our identity. Emphasizing habits of honesty within citizenship education may help our youngest citizens integrate honesty into their conception of good citizenship and come to identify themselves as honest. When habits become recognized as part of our identity, they can more firmly support us when we face conditions that might tempt us to lie or deceive.

Doing Democracy in Classrooms in a Populist Era

To begin, citizenship education must start where pragmatist inquiry is provoked: with the real, complex, and complicated struggles in our lives. It should be focused on the present and how democracy is currently playing out in these times of change and crisis, rather than emphasizing only its ideal forms. That is not to say that citizenship education should not entail learning the history of liberal democracy or key figures within it, but rather to suggest that we open the door to critiques of liberal democracy today alongside that history. It means recognizing the value of consensus, collaboration, and compromise in liberal democracy, and yet acknowledging that those aims may be suitably questioned and challenged by populists who rightly detect that those aims and practices have historically served some more than others. Populists today start in a space of conflict and see consensus as naive (because it is unlikely) and/or dangerous (because it risks the interests of the people); this suggests the need to help students learn how to navigate conflict. Students need to learn how to engage as adversaries rather than enemies and how to form political alliances as well as when to shed them.[25] Through learning about the history of liberal democracy and its shortcomings, students may come to value liberty and yet recognize that the ideal free, fully autonomous, rational, political subject is not feasible (and perhaps not even desirable) in a world of interdependency, relationships, and affect. Finally, classes should overtly discuss what it means to be a citizen, including formal rights and responsibilities, but also what it means to act as a citizen with others when engaged in coordinated living and civic reasoning. Explicit discussions like these help students to understand how honesty fits with the expectations of good citizenship and its practices in traditional liberal democracy and in emerging forms of democracy today.

Moreover, focusing on the present means recognizing that children are already political players, not just citizens in the making.[26] We must *do* democracy with them in the present in our schools, rather than holding off democracy as something that we just teach *for* later in adulthood. Citizenship education must employ democratic means to achieve democratic ends. Classroom pragmatist inquiry is one way to educate *through* democracy. Children are capable of civic thinking as they figure out how to answer the fundamental civic question "What should we do?" with their peers and adults. To see them as not yet rational enough, not sophisticated enough, is to operate with some of the blinders of the modern liberal democracy framework. It is to belittle what children have to contribute in some of the same condescending ways that populists chalk up to the elites. And it is to limit participation rather than expand it. Children bring valuable experiences, common sense, and emotions to the table. Children, often by nature of their position relative to parents, teachers, and other adults, have significant experience with and insight into dependencies, relationships, and learning from others. These can enrich inquiry.

Communities of Inquiry

While direct instruction about what honesty means and why it matters, as well as using content (stories, examples) that display honesty at work, is a helpful starting point for showcasing the value of honesty, emphasis should be on creating realistic problem-solving situations that provoke and develop habits so that they come more naturally when similar situations unfold in the future and a teacher is not present to give explicit guidance. The point is that experiencing honesty and its implications is a more sustainable way to develop proclivities to behave honestly in the future.

The means and ends of cultivating honesty should be deeply social. Such learning should be located within classroom communities of inquiry, where students, much like citizens in a democracy, work together to answer "What should we do?" as they develop understanding of the world and their agency in it. Inroads have already been made for such an approach within citizenship education, where inquiry-based and project-based learning, as well as action civics, are highlighted in major national initiatives and are on the rise in classrooms.[27]

Classroom communities of inquiry should take up real and pressing problems in our world—those that genuinely interest or impact students—so that they learn how to validate truth through determining the consequences of beliefs for themselves and others in meaningful contexts. They should be empowered to form publics, to propose solutions, and to actually implement them. Such endeavors invite the complexities and conflicts of democracy into our classrooms. Moreover, they enable children to *do* democracy while under the guidance of teachers, in spaces that support exploration, and in settings where relationships have been established that may help students learn how to work across differences without casting their classmates as enemies to be defeated. This more active orientation to citizenship education is one that can cultivate habits of democratic living.[28]

Topics of inquiry should be meaningful for students and their surrounding neighborhood in order for students to have a genuine interest in the inquiry and to recognize the stakes of their participation in it. Classrooms are especially ripe for shared indeterminate situations and resulting inquiry because students are typically surrounded by people from the same community and peer groups, resulting in similar moments of uncertainty when learning or facing shared problems. Classes of students can be small publics that form around common interests.

Inquiry begins by identifying and naming the problem, making it more meaningful for students and helping them to see not only what it's about but also how it is significant to them or their community. Understanding a problem often relies on gathering multiple different viewpoints on the issue—seeing how it impacts different people in various ways. Gathering those perspectives can help to pull stakeholders into the inquiry by showing them that they have been impacted and that their experience is valued. As students seek to better understand the problem, teachers can step in to remind students of the importance of pushing beyond those like them to see the problem in other ways. They may need to consult people outside of their class or even turn to historical or literature-based examples to introduce a wider array of perspectives and experiences with the problem at hand.

Next, students should seek answers to the problem, while the teacher both models and facilitates evidence-gathering and deliberation. As they do, they must work to validate the truth of relevant information empirically by weighing evidence and assessing the impact of beliefs on themselves and others to determine whether or not they "work." Of course, when students encounter evidence, they draw on their background experiences, directional motivation, and emotional reactions as they assess its quality and trustworthiness.[29] Teachers can guide students through analyzing those contributing factors, while also equipping them with scientific criteria for judging evidence in terms of validity and reliability. Simply giving students more information or loading them up with facts is an insufficient and wrongheaded approach to battling post-truth. Students must be engaged in practices of truth determination to develop a lasting inclination to act honestly. Foregrounding communal learning settings in schools can help reveal the epistemic and civic reasons for being honest as well as the positive consequences of honesty, for the knowledge and well-being of that group of students may improve as a result of inquiry guided by sincerity and fallibilism. Moreover, communities of inquiry become places to practice honesty, nurturing dispositions toward acting truly. Within these, students can be encouraged to be forthright, sincere, and accurate when dealing with claims. Teachers can call out instances of each to draw attention to their use and consequences.

Our contemporary world tends to operate with quickly located information and quickly stated opinions, yet it requires citizens to make careful decisions to navigate wicked problems.

Many issues that affect us as citizens are complex. Civic responsibility sometimes demands that we attempt to understand these issues, which in turn can demand a willingness and ability to think long and hard about them, weigh arguments and counterarguments, give fair and honest consideration to a wide range of perspectives, avoid drawing premature conclusions, and so on. An electorate with a low appetite or capacity for cognitive complexity will be ill-equipped to meet these demands.[30]

In the midst of inquiries, especially when a teacher detects a rush to conclusions or the operation of unchecked assumptions, teachers should interject with a call to doubt or to introduce nuance. The teacher might suggest an alternative view or point out some flaw with the current one dominating the discussion. Or the teacher might challenge evidence that appears to be overly simplified. This may push students to pause, bringing about slower and more careful inquiry. It may remind students of the importance of being inclusive of an array of perspectives. Teachers should goad students past mere "Google-knowing" to welcome deeper and more complex understanding, which may include having to hold or tease out competing views.[31] In an era when many students are content with the quick information provided through easy outlets, teachers must help students see how such accounts may be limited in ways that are not only epistemically harmful (because they are inaccurate, shortsighted, distorted) but also civically harmful (because they are exclusionary, biased, or oppressive). Teachers must nurture students' capacity for cognitive complexity and their desire for it, in part by demonstrating that it leads to better outcomes for the students and those they care about.

Such communities of inquiry should simultaneously work to cultivate complementary intellectual virtues, including imagination, criticality, curiosity, and intellectual humility. Like honesty, direct instruction about the meaning of these virtues is needed. In classroom settings, overtly identifying instances of veracity and mendacity is essential. Teachers should also provide feedback on how intellectual virtues are being used and how they might be improved.[32] Teachers can provide regular reminders about how honesty bears civic value, offering examples of its usefulness and impact. But direct instruction is not the most effective way to teach intellectual virtues or the habits of honesty. Modeling by the teacher provides helpful demonstrations. One way the teacher might do this is through thinking aloud for students, describing the ways in which he is engaging honesty, perhaps while conducting inquiry. Another approach is to analyze the past behavior of exemplars, examining how honesty has been invoked in real-life situations.[33] Moreover, setting up environments where students themselves practice is even better. While these ideally are authentic activities, they can also be constructed through vignettes, plays, and other role-playing activities.

Allow me to provide a few examples regarding the teaching of intellectual humility in particular. Teachers should begin by defining intellectual humility and its opposite, intellectual arrogance, explaining what each means and why they matter. Teachers might model their own humility by sharing moments where they realized they were wrong or changed their views in light of new evidence. Teachers should reward moments of intellectual humility they witness, giving praise to students who demonstrate openness to learning from others and acknowledge potential problems with their own views. Even reminding students of the need for openness has proven to facilitate better discussion.[34] To display general human fallibility, teachers can showcase historical texts—say, one describing a geocentric model of the universe—to show how even widely held views like these, which may have been supported by evidence at the time, were later debunked. Then, they can shift the attention to the potential for personal fallibility in each student. Citizenship education scholars Paula McAvoy, Diana Hess, and Kei Kawashima-Ginsberg encourage teachers to accustom their students to asking of themselves, "Could I be wrong?"[35] Such a question is helpful on multiple fronts. It introduces the sort of doubt that may prompt and propel inquiry. It keeps one open to the possibility of being wrong, thereby inviting a fallibilist stance. It offers a more open position to learn from others. Relatedly, teachers can engage Socratic questioning to lead students to a state of aporia, which may reveal shortcomings or false beliefs to students, and hopefully lead students to wonder about their world anew so that they will be motivated to seek the truth. Admittedly, achieving aporia in ways that are not disheartening can be challenging.[36]

Classroom communities of inquiry can push back against the sort of intellectual arrogance that leads citizens to put their own opinions above those of experts, science, and other traditionally trusted democratic institutions by demonstrating deep interconnections between classmates and fostering a sense of how their shared fate relies on making wisely informed decisions together.[37] Viewing citizenship as shared fate pushes us to foreground how we are linked together by location, history, and culture, with an eye toward how our answers to civic questions impact us as members of a shared community. It nurtures an inclination to care for others, in part because we recognize that our futures are bound up with each other politically, economically, and geographically. Sharing a fate is not the same as having a common fate because a shared fate takes a more active and cooperative role in shaping the mutual impacts of decision-making rather than just letting things play out. Practices of shared fate can build a sense of "us," but, notably, they cast a big tent, inclusively bringing in many people.[38]

These inclusive and trust-building communities provide a safer environment for sharing and affirming the opinions and experiences of class members as another potential source for evidence and solutions when engaging in inquiry together. This includes the sharing of counter-narratives, which may challenge more widely accepted views in the classroom. This process of developing social intelligence affirms recent trends of valuing personal experience and pushing back against some forms of elitism (but not expertise) that dominate political decision-making without sufficiently attending to the experiences of the poor or working class (including by heavy-handed philanthropists and wealthy corporate leaders). Simultaneously, teachers must carefully prevent each individual student's view from standing on its own.

Through dialogue and inquiry, students can come to see both their own cognitive limitations at work and how their beliefs can be improved through the experience and evidence offered by others.[39] Teachers can encourage what Dewey called "the habit of amicable cooperation," where students learn "to treat those who disagree . . . with us as those from whom we may learn."[40] While there are limits on what students should be expected to tolerate or engage in educational settings, learning how to listen to and then critique alternative views pulls those perspectives into consideration as potential epistemic sources, rather than excluding them or shutting down further discussion, which we witness in the worst forms of cancel culture today. In the midst of classroom inquiries, teachers should reaffirm inclusivity by creating space for all students to significantly contribute to classroom inquiries. And when groups with competing views or values form, teachers should guide students through how to work across those differences in ways that affirm their classmates as adversaries with a shared fate, from and with whom they can learn, rather than seeing them as enemies to defeat. In part, this sort of work entails pushing back against the tendency in populism to essentialize people in neatly ordered and opposing groups, often juxtaposed as good versus evil. Teachers must expose the faulty drawing of those lines, looking instead to reveal politically significant differences where students can disagree as adversaries, with a focus on the issues dividing them rather than on defeating each other as enemy combatants in a political war.[41] Those politically significant disagreements are of the sort that gets at truth.[42]

Successful classroom inquiries into real problems can affirm for students that truth and honesty serve their communities well, an experience that can be further highlighted with praise from teachers and through exercises that engage student reflections.[43] One example is "I used to think _____; now I think _____." Harvard's Project Zero uses this exercise to help students consolidate new learning. But it can be used as well to help students identify not just specific developments in their views over time but also how their views changed, including how they were influenced by new evidence and epistemic practices. Similarly, a technique called "What makes you say that?" engages that title question to push students to consider what leads them to believe what they do, thereby pushing them to reflect on how they think and prompting them to be open to reconsidering the beliefs they hold.[44] These metacognitive reflections, whether through journaling, verbal debriefing, or other techniques, can reveal for students the process of how truth was determined during their classroom inquiry and how honesty shaped that process and the sharing of its results, thereby helping students to see the valuable role of honesty. Within those metacognitive exercises, students come to better understand the content of their particular beliefs, and, importantly from a Deweyan perspective, *how* they think and believe. Students might also be encouraged to journal about instances where they have failed to be honest, reflecting on the impact on themselves and others, motivations for their actions, and ideas for how they might head off such action in similar situations in the future. This intellectual aspect of reflecting on honesty can further support its development and establishment as a lasting, yet adaptable, habit.

Engaging in real-life inquiry together does not stop with understanding the problem or gathering information about it. Students should be empowered to craft solutions to the civic question "What should we do?" Then they should try them out, testing and evaluating them in lived experience to see if they help students and/or communities thrive. This enables students to see positive implications of honesty affirmed in real life. Citizenship education scholar Meira Levinson explains that guided-action civics inquiry may form a feedback loop, wherein students' actions are affirmed and repeated.[45] Thereby, students nurture habits of honesty and larger skills of good civic reasoning.

Community inquiry allows students to build trust between participants.[46] These communities can strengthen relationships between students, not only enabling students to see how their actions impact each other but also encouraging them to attend to their mutual flourishing. These settings then provide the sense of relational safety and mutual care that can overcome, or at least work against, self-serving motivations to lie and the tendency to distrust.[47]

Teaching About Populism

Let me return, for a brief moment, to attend to matters of populism in particular. Students should overtly learn about what populism is and how it functions. While I have focused on a thin version of it in this book, students should also learn how populism may be related to problematic ideologies or practices, including xenophobia and authoritarianism, that threaten democracy. This overt instruction can call attention to the democratizing potential of populism, while also alerting students to worrisome possibilities. I certainly do not recommend that citizenship education turn itself over to an all-out celebration of populism. Instead, in the spirit of pragmatist experimentations with democracy, I recommend remaining open to new approaches to democratic living that may arise from populism.[48] When such approaches are taken up in school settings, teachers and students can lead inquiries to evaluate their effectiveness, thereby providing self-correcting educative measures to head off some potentially problematic or extreme forms of democratic living that might spring from populism.

Part of instruction about populism should focus on the ways in which populism relies on affect. "Critical affective civic literacy" is a technique whereby students examine why they feel the way they do, consider how their feelings may lead them toward or away from particular other people or evidence, recognize the legitimacy of other citizens, interrogate how emotions work in political life, and channel emotions toward better outcomes.[49] Building on the work of Sharon Stein, James Damico and Mark Baildon call for teaching affective literacy "to recognize and accept responsibility for the harmful impact of our desires, investments, and emotions while learning to manage challenging emotions without being overwhelmed or immobilized . . . this would mean staying engaged with each other despite our differences and the emotions they may elicit."[50] Such an approach should help students understand how affect is shaped and manipulated, and how it leads to the development of certain embodied proclivities that influence how we interact with other citizens, respond to populist leaders, and engage with truth claims.[51] This includes self-reflexivity regarding their own affect, including how their identities and experiences influence their emotional reactions as well as how they interpret a source more generally. Students might be encouraged to explain "why particular pieces of evidence might cause them alarm, concern, anger, or pleasure, and then to hypothesize by whom that same evidence might be experienced differently and why."[52] The intention here is to help students better understand how affect influences themselves and others, which might help them understand how others have equally strong but differing emotional responses, develop better perspective-taking, and open up new understandings. It should not be wielded as a weapon to trick or persuade others to one's "side." This educational approach is aimed not merely at showing *that* emotions matter but also at learning to question *how* emotions matter in the construction and determination of truth.[53]

These impacts are especially notable in social media. Students need to learn to interrogate how affect works in those settings, dividing groups into an "us" versus a "them" and provoking emotional responses according to one's tribe. This requires more sophisticated forms of critical media literacy that go beyond merely assessing the quality or trustworthiness of websites.[54] Students must learn not only how to make sense of the affect of others as they share and assign emojis to some materials and not others but also how to respond to it in critical and fruitful ways. In addition, they must be sensitive to how their own affect is impacted, which could help them identify key moments to slow or stop the spread of mis- or disinformation or pose a critical challenge to a viewpoint being advanced or attacked by others. Education about affect is suitable across multiple disciplines. Most obviously, the study of psychology can lend insight into affect as an aspect of human behavior, but other fields like economics and language arts can help students see how affect is shaped through financial motivations, rhetorical persuasion, and more.

Relatedly, citizenship education must help students interrogate not merely what is said by citizens and their leaders but also, and even more important, *why* it is said. Students should learn how to investigate political contexts and motivations that shape what is uttered and whether it is done so honestly. This would entail learning to detect and analyze audience, tone, and intention to see how they bolster or distort accuracy, sincerity, and forthrightness.[55] Students should learn how to closely read and analyze political speeches and advertisements not just for rhetorical understanding of persuasion and propaganda (as currently supported in many language arts teaching standards in the United States) but also to explicitly assess their employment of honesty.

I recommend nurturing pragmatist frameworks for truth, inquiry, and social democracy in schools as a way to value a constructed account of truth that is receptive to passionate claims and dissenting views but provides inclusive communities of inquiry that check nihilism and extremism. This pragmatist approach may help students form publics around their issues of concern and put forward new visions that do not fall prey to either the empty promises of liberal democracy or the fantasies of populism.[56] Finally, this approach can direct attention to the affective and embodied aspects of citizenship, working to cultivate Deweyan habits that better support the growth of individuals and the flourishing of communities, and direct attention away from misguided attempts to pile on more facts and redouble efforts to teach only rational deliberation.

Encountering Conspiracy Theories

Especially during times of political chaos or uncertainty, conspiracy theories bubble up. Classes should overtly discuss these instances, including how they foster conditions ripe for conspiracy theories. To begin with a definition,

students should learn that such theories "explain the ultimate causes of significant social and political events and circumstances with claims of secret
plots by two or more powerful actors." Those actors seek to "usurp political or
economic power, violate rights, infringe upon established agreements, with-
hold vital secrets, or alter bedrock institutions."[57] Notably, conspiracy theories
are connected to matters of both honesty and dissent. Conspiracy theories
question the veracity of those actors seen as out to gain in some way. In this
way, they may be seeking truth and exposing falsity; they may have epistemic,
civic, or even moral motivations. And conspiracy theories often entail a spirit
of dissent insofar as they question those in power or the status quo. But, too
often, conspiracy theories rush to hasty conclusions against those in power
and quickly spread unjustified views, often based on shaky evidence that does
not stand up to verification.

Overtly teaching about conspiracy theories can help students learn to appreciate skepticism toward official accounts, including how attributes of
doubt and criticality may undergird developing or adopting conspiracy theories. Particularly for populists who are dissatisfied with and distrustful of
elites, conspiracy theories are appealing "because they represent the antith-
esis of authoritative accounts."[58] Students need to understand how cynicism
and distrust, rather than principled dissent, may create "an epistemic vacuum
that is easily filled by misinformation" and thereby spur the adoption of conspiracy theories.[59] Students should learn how to determine when those theories are warranted and when they are not, lest we forget that some conspiracy
theories do, indeed, turn out to be true and that bringing them forward can be
a significant act of good citizenship. Some conspiracy theories even work to
preserve or improve democracy (such as the Watergate conspiracy theory).[60]
But far too many conspiracy theories lead to a radicalization of beliefs such
that those beliefs are no longer aligned with reality. Students must learn to
appreciate the spirit of truth-seeking and dissent that may propel conspiracy
theories, and also learn how to detect when they have been taken too far and
no longer stand up to scrutiny.

Widespread conspiracy theories, such as Holocaust denial, should be fodder
for classroom lessons.[61] Students should learn what beliefs those conspiracy
theories entail and why they are problematic, an approach that has been
shown to help inoculate students against adopting the beliefs themselves.[62]
They should also learn how and why the conspiracy theories are asserted
as true—again, so that students learn to detect them and prevent their own
adoption of future false conspiracy theories. Students need to wrestle with
why some fictions are upheld, including for self-serving reasons, for affirming
tribal affiliations, or even more existentially as a reaction to feeling powerless

and as a way of regaining some special agency through holding "insider" information during times of chaos or uncertainty. Students need to witness the tenacity with which some believers adhere to those theories in order to understand the force of emotional conviction, especially among the people toward the elite. That conviction may be exacerbated when the conspiracy theory is unfalsifiable, a trait teachers can expose by showing how believers respond to counter-evidence or how they operate heavily within echo chambers that affirm their views and undermine the trustworthiness of anyone who disagrees.

Students need to learn how to respond to their fellow citizens who endorse conspiracy theories in ways that nurture constructive dialogue and reassert the social and political stakes of misguided beliefs or dishonest practices. Given the recent rise of relativist accounts of truth endorsed by increasing numbers of conspiracy followers, where truth is just relative to each individual, teachers need to show how those views of truth differ from those of pragmatism.[63] When it is suitable to the knowledge level and subject matter of the classroom, teachers may even engage students in inquiries that debunk those theories as a way to further help students understand them and respond to them in informed ways. Such an approach may help ease concerns from critics who may see engaging conspiracy theories in classrooms as counter to the teaching of content and as problematically giving play to extremist views.

Additionally, students should be exposed to some significant cases and their impacts in order to affirm that honesty matters. One example might be learning about QAnon and its role in fomenting the bloody attack on the United States Capitol, resulting in the conviction of some believers, thereby demonstrating the high stakes for adherents. Another example might be Alex Jones, who claimed that the Sandy Hook school shooting did not really happen but rather was orchestrated by certain people to secure their political interests. Jones was found guilty for his false statements and was ordered to pay large sums for the damage he inflicted on mourning parents. This example can be used to foreground the role of honesty and how conspiracy theories can slide into slander, as false statements about a person.

Responding to Fake News

Fake news currently plays a worrisome role in the United States and elsewhere. "Fake news" no longer simply indicates that a report is false; it also refers to other problems. This includes news outlets sharing only limited information or prioritizing some stories over others, thereby offering a partial or distorted account that falls short of the forthrightness required for honesty.

It also includes circulating targeted disinformation to mislead citizens or back particular political positions. Sometimes a person, especially political leaders, may declare accurate news that runs counter to their political views to be "fake news." By analyzing examples of fake news, students can come to see how fake news sows confusion, thereby derailing civic reasoning. They can also see how allegations of fake news may shut down dissenting or alternative viewpoints that could be of civic or epistemic value. Finally, by investigating accusations of fake news waged against traditionally respected media sources, such as major newspapers (as President Trump frequently alleged of the *New York Times*), teachers may introduce and affirm the valuable role the media can play as a check on power within a healthy democracy and in the process of determining truth, while still acknowledging that news media may be biased, mistaken, or otherwise problematic.

Importantly, fake news is not just a matter of "alternative facts"; it is a matter of trust between citizens and trust in institutions that shape news. Fake news prevents citizens from drawing upon a shared set of information because they disagree about which sources are trustworthy. With that understanding, teachers should help students learn how to assess trustworthiness, not just of other citizens but also of authority figures, media, and institutions. Critical media literacy in the domain of fake news is important, and couching such literacy within a pragmatist framework can provide students with conceptual tools needed to question who benefits from fake news and whether such news really "works" in a way to warrant being called true. These sorts of exercises will invoke discussions of pragmatist truth and flourishing, showcasing how honesty facilitates good reasoning and beneficial outcomes.

Pulling It Together

In sum, this reflective, active, and community-based citizenship education works to develop and affirm the inclination to be honest. Through repeated exercise, students experience the benefits of honesty, nurturing a habitual bent toward such action when similar situations arise in the future. This form of citizenship education is more likely to have a lasting effect in shaping the practices and proclivities of young citizens than is memorization of civic content, learning about character traits, or simply being morally goaded to do what's right. Teaching honesty can be both done directly, through overt lessons, and achieved indirectly as a part of other classroom activities and content. I turn in the remaining chapters to consider two aspects of education that are especially ripe for closer analysis in light of recent challenges to liberal democracy: learning how to engage in political dissent and the teaching of controversial issues. Both reveal the importance of teaching honesty and how doing so may help alleviate some of our recent social and political struggles.

Notes

1. My son's elementary school took such an approach and used a packaged character education curriculum to highlight honesty one week, with no other overt discussion of it beyond that. And the university in our city requires students to pledge the "Bearcat Bond," which says "I will promote the highest levels of personal and academic honesty and aspire continuously to better myself, the Bearcat community, and the world" (https://www.uc.edu/cond uct/BearcatBond.html).
2. Joel Westheimer and Joseph Kahne, "What Kind of Citizen? The Politics of Educating for Democracy," *American Educational Research Journal* 41, no. 2 (2004): 248.
3. I thank Barrett Smith for this helpful example.
4. It seems important to acknowledge here my own role in advocating for some rather problematic forms of citizenship education, including authoring a major national report on citizenship education that falls under the sort of closed, strong, aspirational citizenship education debunked by Sant. In part, my goal here is to think through these shortcomings and to broaden my thinking in regard to the alternatives and opportunities presented by populism. Sarah Stitzlein, "Defining and Implementing Civic Reasoning and Discourse: Philosophical and Moral Foundations for Research and Practice," in *Educating for Civic Reasoning and Discourse*, ed. Carol D. Lee, Gregory White, and Dian Dong (Washington, DC: National Academy of Education, 2021), 23–52, https://naeducation. org/educating-for-civic-reasoning-and-discourse/.
5. Ellen Middaugh, "More than Just the Facts: Promoting Literacy in the Era of Outrage," *Peabody Journal of Education* 94, no. 1 (2019): 17–31.
6. Edda Sant, *Political Education in Times of Populism: Towards a Radical Democratic Education* (London: Palgrave Macmillan, 2021), 112–113.
7. Michael Sandel, *Justice: A Reader* (New York: Oxford University Press, 2007).
8. Etienne Brown, "Civic Education in the Post-Truth Era: Intellectual Virtues and the Epistemic Threats of Social Media," in *Philosophical Perspectives on Moral and Civic Education: Shaping Citizens and Their Schools*, ed. Colin Macleod and Christine Tappolet (New York: Routledge, 2019), 46.
9. Jason Baehr, *Deep in Thought: A Practical Guide to Teaching for Intellectual Virtues* (Cambridge, MA: Harvard Education Press, 2021), 31–32.
10. Frank Lovett, "Civic Virtue," in *The Encyclopedia of Political Thought*, ed. Mike Gibbons (New York: Wiley, 2014), 1–10.
11. Jason Baehr, "Democracy, Information Technology, and Virtue Epistemology," in *Virtues, Democracy, and Online Media*, ed. Nancy Snow and Maria Silvia Vaccarrezza (New York: Routledge, 2021), 27–46.
12. Jason Baehr, "Intellectual Virtues and Truth, Understanding, and Wisdom," unpublished draft, https://jasonbaehr.files.wordpress.com/2013/12/iv-and-tuw.pdf.

13. John Dewey, "The Public and Its Problems," in *John Dewey: The Later Works, 1925–1953*, ed. Jo Ann Boydston (Carbondale: Southern Illinois University Press, 2008), 2:235; Robert C. Roberts and Ryan West, "The Virtue of Honesty: A Conceptual Exploration," in *Integrity, Honesty, and Truth Seeking*, ed. Christian B. Miller and Ryan West (New York: Oxford University Press, 2020), 97–116.

14. Steve Rathje, Jon Roozenbeek, Jay J. Van Bavel, and Sander van der Linden, "Accuracy and Social Motivations Shape Judgements of (Mis)information," *Nature Human Behaviour* 7 (2023): 892–903, https://www.nature.com/articles/s41562-023-01540-w.

15. Brown, "Civic Education in the Post-Truth Era"; Julia Driver, "The Conflation of Moral and Epistemic Virtue," *Metaphilosophy* 34, no. 3 (2003): 367–383.

16. Daniel Lapsley and Dominic Charloner, "Post-Truth and Science Identity: A Virtue-Based Approach to Science Education," *Educational Psychologist* 55, no. 3 (2020): 133.

17. Michael Patrick Lynch, *Know-It-All Society: Truth and Arrogance in Political Culture* (New York: W. W. Norton, 2019).

18. Lynch, *Know-It-All Society*, 149.

19. John Dewey, "Logic: The Theory of Inquiry," in *John Dewey: The Later Works, 1925–1953*, ed. Jo Ann Boydston (Carbondale: Southern Illinois University Press, 2008), 12:12.

20. Dewey, "Logic: The Theory of Inquiry," 12:12.

21. I am drawing heavily here on Kirsten Welch, "Misplaced Tolerance and Educating for Intellectual Humility," *Educational Theory*, 71, no. 6 (2021): 681–702.

22. Janie Harden Fritz, "Honesty as Ethical Communicative Practice: A Framework for Analysis," in *Integrity, Honesty, and Truth Seeking*, ed. Christian B. Miller and Ryan West (New York: Oxford University Press, 2020), 127–181.

23. Gabriele Bellucci and Soyoung Q. Park, "Honesty Biases Trustworthiness Impressions," *Journal of Experimental Psychology: General* 149, no. 8 (2020): 1567.

24. John Dewey, "How We Think, Revised Edition," in *John Dewey: The Later Works, 1925–1953*, ed. Jo Ann Boydston (Carbondale: Southern Illinois University Press, 2008), 8:28.

25. Chantal Mouffe, *For a Left Populism* (New York: Verso, 2018), 91. Also see my earlier work on cultivating pragmatist habits of dissent in schools: Sarah Stitzlein, *Teaching for Dissent: Citizenship Education and Political Activism* (New York: Routledge, 2014).

26. See my response, "Children as Citizens," to Tony DeCeasare's paper "The Future Is Now: Rethinking the Role for Children in Democracy," *Philosophy of Education Society* 78, no. 3 (2022): 111. I'm taking up his challenge here.

27. The inquiry-based C3 framework promoted by the National Council for the Social Studies and the action civics approach of the Educating for American Democracy Roadmap are key examples. Kathy Swan et al., *College, Career, and Civic Life (C3) Social Studies State Standards* (Silver Spring, MD: National Council for the Social Studies, 2013), https://www.socialstudies.org/standards/c3; Educating for American Democracy, *Educating for American Democracy: Excellence in History and Civics for All Learners* (n.p.: iCivics, 2021), www.educatingforamericandemocracy.org.

28. I have described a habits-based approach to citizenship education throughout my work, including in all four of my books: *Breaking Bad Habits: Transforming Identity in Schools* (Lanham, MD: Rowman & Littlefield, 2008); *Teaching for Dissent: Citizenship Education and Political Activism* (Abingdon, UK: Routledge, 2014); *American Public Education and the Responsibility of Its Citizens* (New York: Oxford University Press, 2017); *Learning How to Hope: Reviving Democracy Through Our Schools and Civil Society* (New York: Oxford University Press, 2020).

29. Rebecca Jacobsen, Anne-Lise Halvorsen, Amanda Slaten Frasier, Adam Schmitt, Margaret Crocco, and Avner Segall, "Thinking Deeply, Thinking Emotionally: How High School Students Make Sense of Evidence," *Theory and Research in Social Education* 46, no. 2 (2018): 232–276.

30. Baehr, "Democracy, Information Technology, and Virtue Epistemology," 9.

31. Michael Patrick Lynch, "Teaching in the Time of Google," *Chronicle of Higher Education*, April 24, 2016, http://chronicle.com/article/Teaching-in-the-Time-of-Google/236180/.

32. Jason Baehr, "Education for Intellectual Virtues: From Theory to Practice," in *Education and the Growth of Knowledge: Perspectives from Social and Virtue Epistemology*, ed. Ben Kotzee (Malden, MA: Wiley, 2013), 106–123, https://intellectualvirtues.org/guiding-principles/core-practices/.

33. Linda Zagzebski, *Exemplarist Moral Theory* (New York: Oxford University Press, 2017); S. Algoe and Jonathan Haidt, "Witnessing Excellence in Action: The 'Other-Praising' Emotions of Elevation, Gratitude, and Admiration," *Journal of Positive Psychology* 4 (2009): 105–127.

34. Jiawen Zheng, "Motivated Open-Mindedness: Rectify Biased Perceptions in Preparation for Deliberation," *Communication and the Public* 1, no. 2 (2016): 193–210.

35. Paula McAvoy, Diana Hess, and Kei Kawashima-Ginsberg, "The Pedagogical Challenge of Teaching Politics in Like-Minded Schools," in *Crosscultural Case Studies of Teaching Controversial Issues: Pathways and Challenges to Democratic Citizenship Education*, ed. Thomas Misco and Jan De Groof (Oisterwijk, Netherlands: Wolf, 2014), 253.

36. I borrow the distinction between general human and personal fallibility from Nancy Snow and its uptake in the examples of historical writing and Socratic method from Welch, "Misplaced Tolerance and Educating for Intellectual Humility."

37. Michiko Kakutani, *The Death of Truth: Notes on Falsehood in the Age of Trump* (New York: Crown, 2018).

38. Sigal Ben-Porath, *Citizenship Under Fire: Democratic Education in Times of Conflict* (Princeton, NJ: Princeton University Press, 2006); Cong Lin and Liz Jackson, "From Shared Fate to Shared Fates: An Approach for Civic Education," *Studies in Philosophy and Education* 38 (2019): 537–547.

39. Lynch, *Know-It-All Society*.

40. John Dewey, "Creative Democracy: The Task Before Us," in *John Dewey: The Later Works, 1925–1953*, ed. Jo Ann Boydston (Carbondale: Southern Illinois University Press, 2008), 14:228.

41. Asgeir Tryggvason, "Democratic Education and Agonism: Exploring the Critique from Deliberative Theory," *Democracy and Education* 26, no. 1 (2018), 1–9.

42. Cheryl Misak, "Making Disagreement Matter: Pragmatism and Deliberative Democracy," *Journal of Speculative Philosophy* 18, no. 1 (2004): 9–22.

43. Baehr, "Education for Intellectual Virtues."

44. Rob Ritchart, Mark Church, et al., *The Power of Making Thinking Visible* (San Francisco: Jossey-Bass, 2020).

45. See Meira Levinson, *No Citizen Left Behind* (Cambridge, MA: Harvard University Press, 2012), 210–249.

46. Laura D'Olimpio, "Trust as a Virtue in Education," *Educational Philosophy and Theory* 50, no. 2 (2018): 193–202.

47. Steven L. Porter and Jason Baehr, "Becoming Honest: Why We Lie and What Can Be Done About It," in *Integrity, Honesty, and Truth Seeking*, ed. Christian B. Miller and Ryan West (New York: Oxford University Press, 2020), 182–206.

48. While I am not as thoroughgoing here in my openness as Edda Sant is, she does offer some helpful suggestions for what this might look like in the later chapters of her 2021 book, *Political Education in Times of Populism.*

49. Patrick Keegan, "Critical Affective Civic Literacy: A Framework for Attending to Political Emotion in the Social Studies Classroom," *Journal of Social Studies Research* 45 (2021): 15–24.

50. James S. Damico and Mark C. Baildon, *How to Confront Climate Denial: Literacy, Social Studies, and Climate Change* (New York: Teachers College Press, 2022), online version, n.p.

51. Michalinos Zembylas takes up matters of citizenship education and affect well in his article "Interrogating the Affective Politics of White Victimhood and Resentment in Times of Demagoguery: The Risks for Civics Education," *Studies in Philosophy and Education* 40, no. 6 (2021): 579–594. I follow him in his wider understanding of affect and its connection to pragmatist habits in "Dewey's Account of Habit Through the Lens of Affect Theory," *Educational Theory* 71, no. 6 (2021): 767–786.

52. H. James Garrett, Avner Segall, and Margaret S. Crocco, "Accommodating Emotion and Affect in Political Discussions in Classrooms," *The Social Studies* 111, no. 6 (2020): 320.

53. Michalinos Zembylas, "The Affective Grounding of Post-Truth: Pedagogical Risks and Transformative Possibilities in Countering Post-Truth Claims," *Pedagogy, Culture and Society* 28, no. 1 (2020): 81.

54. Zembylas, "The Affective Grounding of Post-Truth," 84.

55. Paul Adams briefly alludes to these important aspects of the impact of populism on democratic education in "Populism: A Possible Future for Democratic Education?," presentation at the conference International Network of Philosophers of Education, Copenhagen, Denmark, August 19, 2022.

56. Sant's *Political Education in Times of Populism* describes these fantasies well.

57. Karen M. Douglas, Joseph E. Uscinski, Robbie M. Sutton, Aleksandra Cichocka, Turkay Nefes, Chee Siang Ang, and Farzin Deravi, "Understanding Conspiracy Theories," *Political Psychology* 40, no. S1 (2019): 3, https://onlinelibrary-wiley-com.uc.idm.oclc.org/doi/full/10.1111/pops.12568.

58. Joseph M. Pierre, "Mistrust and Misinformation: A Two-Component, Socio-Epistemic Model of Belief in Conspiracy Theories," *Journal of Social and Political Psychology* 8, no. 2 (2020): 624.

59. Pierre, "Mistrust and Misinformation," 625.

60. Maria Martinez Castro, "How Did the Watergate Scandal Popularize Conspiracy Theories?," *Curiosity Gaps* (blog), UC Davis, last modified June 3, 2022, https://www.ucdavis.edu/blog/curiosity/how-did-watergate-scandal-popularize-conspiracy-theories.

61. Importantly, a topic like Holocaust denial must be handled very carefully so as not to legitimate or provide a platform for anti-Semitic views that might cause harm to students.

62. Damico and Baildon, *How to Confront Climate Denial.*

63. Emily Guerin, "Untangling Disinformation: She Was a Popular Yoga Guru. Then She Embraced QAnon Conspiracy Theories," NPR, last modified January 2, 2023, https://www.npr.org/2023/01/02/1146318331/yoga-guru-qanon-conspiracy-theories.

4

Teaching Honesty as a Part of Teaching Dissent

The aims of citizenship education and approaches we use to develop young citizens must adapt to changes in our social and political contexts. That is not to say that those changes should be automatically welcomed or immediately reflected in the curriculum, but they should be taken into consideration for the benefits and drawbacks that they pose to citizenship education. In this chapter, I first attend to recent developments in youth activism and growth in populist outcry to highlight opportunities for improving how we prepare students for the current political context, where students regularly witness protests online, in their schools, and/or in their communities. I define good political dissent and show how it relies upon honesty. I show how dissent is ineffective if it does not emphasize establishing and sharing truth with forthrightness, sincerity, and accuracy in order to bring about individual growth and flourishing of the community. I also show that dissent is crucial to the determination of truth because dissenting views showcase that a specific belief does not work for a particular person or population.

Effective political dissent has a long history of contributing to the establishment and improvement of democracies around the world. This includes the United States, where dissent against British rule led to the Declaration of Independence and set the course for a new country, one that values the role of dissent, though to varying degrees based on the shifting political climate. In recent years, U.S. streets, statehouses, and school board meetings have been filled with the sounds of protest as frustrated citizens point out problems and demand change. The ability to effectively dissent, however, is hampered when students are underprepared for their lives as citizens. To maintain and improve our democracy, we must better equip students for understanding, valuing, participating in, and responding to dissent, especially in light of recent developments in civic and political life that have made displays of public outcry more widespread. Teaching students how to dissent well requires helping them to be honest, for they must learn how to find and share the truth as they challenge previous beliefs, practices, and policies and put forward new ones.

Teaching Honesty in a Populist Era. Sarah M. Stitzlein, Oxford University Press. © Oxford University Press 2024.
DOI: 10.1093/9780197775912.003.0004

I began writing about the importance of teaching students how to engage in political dissent more than a decade ago.[1] Initially I argued that in order for the state to have legitimacy, it must have the consent of the governed. And in order to achieve that consent, dissent must be not only permitted but encouraged and supported, for dissent enables citizens to ensure that the laws guiding them are desired or just. Said differently, in order to fully give their consent, citizens must be able to dissent. Citizens, I claimed, then have the positive right to an education for dissent that enables them to enact this important duty of citizenship. I originally developed my views on dissent during the war on terror, where the United States faced significant pressures toward consensus and a climate of allegiance following the 9/11 attack. I feared that dissent might not be sufficiently present in the lives of students or celebrated in their classrooms. I also noted the potential of newly emerging protests and political resistance groups at the time, such as Occupy Wall Street and the Tea Party. Throughout my initial work on political dissent, I paid only limited attention to matters of truth or honesty, perhaps naively presuming citizens would value, pursue, and share truth as a part of their dissent.

The U.S. context today is considerably different, as political divisions have become more pronounced and public displays of citizen frustration are widespread, though not always emblematic of good dissent, such as the violent looting that followed the police slaying of unarmed Black citizens and the bloody January 6 attack on the Capitol. As noted in Chapter 2, growing populism, in particular, presents significant opportunities for democratization and yet also worrisome possibilities for derailing democracy. At the same time, we've also witnessed significant growth in youth activism, perhaps best demonstrated in the movements around gun control and climate change. Recognizing their rise, in 2017 the Cambridge Dictionaries selected "populism" as the word of the year[2] and the Oxford English Dictionary selected "youthquake"—defined as "a significant cultural, political, or social change arising from the actions or influence of young people."[3] Populism and youthquakes have continued to grow in the years since. All the while, the importance of truth and honesty has come to the fore as major movements and episodes of dissent have failed to sufficiently uphold them, including those seeking to overturn the 2020 election who perpetuated lies of election fraud and those fighting against vaccinations who offered faulty data about the supposed dangers of vaccines. Evidence shows that we cannot assume honesty among populist dissenters or movements, especially when the motivations to champion oneself or one's group over others are high.

I will use these recent developments to offer a revised understanding of dissent, one better suited for our needs and experiences today. I will draw on youth movements to see what can be learned from their recent successes and struggles in order to reveal what may be needed in contemporary citizenship education to help students more successfully traverse today's social and political context. Finally, I will highlight some of the key components of citizenship education that follow from foregrounding this updated notion of dissent as an educational goal. An enhanced citizenship education aimed at political participation and improvement may help shepherd the United States and other countries through populist and challenging times, as students learn how to attend to and participate in today's messy democracy rather than the idealized image traditionally presented in civics classes.

An Initial Definition of Dissent

While I will not rehash the case I made for dissent in my earlier work by tracing the ideas and practices of American Founders and the Progressive Era pragmatists who followed them, I will briefly highlight some of the key aspects of dissent as I defined it initially. I focus on describing good and effective dissent, acknowledging that there are efforts and examples that embody aspects of dissent without living up to high-quality dissent overall. Many aspects of this definition remain important today, but as I will show in my discussion of populism and youth activism, some aspects need to be revised.

Dissent begins when a citizen openly "disagrees with the consensus of a community or the dictates of those in power."[4] Dissenters aim to reveal problems with dominant beliefs, practices, or policies. Dissenters expose concerns, especially how those beliefs, practices, or policies may harm citizens or the world around them. Importantly, good dissenters do not stop there; rather, they go further by putting forward solutions or alternatives, sometimes assisting in their implementation. To understand the problems and put forward feasible solutions, dissenters must strive to understand complex situations and seek out an array of perspectives as they account for how various stakeholders are or will be impacted.

Effective dissenters employ means of struggle that are consistent with their desired ends, so that in many cases the very practice of dissent works to continually reveal the problem and reaffirm the desired improvements upon that problem. Often, dissent involves critique that is aimed toward seeking justice or truth. Because of this, "dissent is typically undertaken in the spirit of benefiting the community, which nearly always contributes to the wellbeing of others, but may or may not necessarily include oneself as a direct or immediate beneficiary."[5] In the case of lies and dishonesty, dissenters must first detect falsity or deceit and then show how they prevent flourishing. When revealing harm, dissenters must be careful to determine accurate causes before placing blame or demanding accountability. Pointing fingers at the wrong culprit may only further complicate the situation rather than delivering improved conditions. Guided by an aim of seeking truth, practices of dissent are more effective when done with honesty, emphasizing openness and forthrightness as dissenters seek and share information.

Sometimes dissent is risky, potentially bringing about threats, harm, or even violence against the dissenter. But dissenters greet such risk with a spirit of courage and hope. They develop a proclivity for such action, not limiting their dissent to one-off events or restricting it to only significant moments of revolution. They seek an array of outcomes, from deep and sustained change to small tweaks. While they may sometimes use negative critique, they work toward positive transformation, using imagination and engaging hope.

Dissent is important to a healthy democracy because it is a way of living that enables and invites change. It questions the status quo and keeps government accountable to its citizenry. Dissent works against stagnation, as it generates discussion of current practices and policies and brings forward new ideas. Dissent is integral to civic reasoning, as citizens solve shared problems. In sum, dissent provides avenues for keeping democracy adaptive and vibrant.

Populist Employment of Dissent

Populism presents opportunities for democratization that are related to good political dissent. Populists call for democracy to better reflect the will of the people and respond to their needs. Dissent is an important way to clarify that will and champion those needs. Dissatisfied with the outcomes of current democracy, especially when they feel that their personal well-being is harmed, populist individuals begin to raise questions and challenge norms. Populists goad change, especially during moments when the motivations of elected officials appear suspicious and when those leaders seem or are unresponsive to the demands of the people. Even though individuals or segments of the people may have different concerns, they become united in feeling they have been ignored or suppressed by the elite. They may form publics where they express their interests and exert pressure on those they see as standing in their way. Their demands tend to become aggregated into what Ernesto Laclau calls equivalential chains.[6] Robert Ivie explains how the dissent of the people develops:

Generally speaking, the articulation of a people develops through different levels of demands. At the lowest level, a demand is a request, which is a focused concern of a particular group (e.g. asking a local government to provide improved housing). A request can be transformed into a claim, or popular demand, when it goes unmet and is linked to other unmet demands perceived as rights (such as transportation, healthcare, security, education). The situation can escalate when a governing institution proves unresponsive or incapable of meeting demands so that what is "requested within institutions" becomes "claims addressed to institutions, and at some stage . . . claims against the institutional order." . . . When requests become claims, institutions are more likely to be subjected to critique than passively accepted. As unmet requests for relief escalate into a topologically linked ensemble of claims and a ruling order opens itself to increasing levels of critique, a "people" emerges in opposition to a regime. Their dissent promotes revision and reconstruction of an unresponsive political order.[7]

By calling attention to "common sense," populists aim to shift how citizens view the country and their place in it, thereby elevating their perspective. Common sense also plays an important role in political dissent. Ivie explains, "Dissent works toward the realignment of common sense, which is the modus operandi of democracy as a politics of contestation."[8] Populists, then, can use dissent to shape what is seen as normal or desirable, emphasizing the experiences of everyday folks rather than the elite leaders who oversee them. Populist dissent may entail assemblage of an alternative cast of "experts," rather than those currently in power, to put forward a competing view more reflective of common sense. And when paired with affect, citizens may be provoked to action aligned with those shared views. Moreover, narratives of populist dissent may be further enhanced and motivating when they juxtapose critique with exposure of corruptness among the elite.

In these ways, populism is capable of achieving some degree of democratization in that it draws attention to current problems in democracy and empowers the people to bring about political transformation.[9] It magnifies the voices of the people through encouraging more active forms of political participation to fulfill their demands, such as citizen referendums or protests, rather than relying on more passive participation as citizens who wait dutifully for the next election and may express their frustration in the interim through formal letters to their representative. Such political activism may mobilize previously passive citizens, energizing them and bringing them into the mix of those who create and legitimate knowledge (consider here the examples of citizen science on the Left or citizen responses to restrictive COVID-19 laws on the Right). These political actions can spur the political system to greater responsiveness and accountability. Once heard, those people may become better integrated in the political system, where their demands are addressed by the system, ushering in a period of greater political stability.[10]

Often, however, transformation is limited or insufficient, and calls for change continue. Some may tire of the seemingly unending frustrations expressed by populists, but those do play an important role in shaping the political context. Importantly, a climate where struggle and disagreement are present can help dissent to be more accepted and valued. This differs from the sort of post-9/11 environment I described earlier in this chapter where allegiance squeezes out dissent with a spirit of patriotic loyalty, and what dissent remains is typically disdained or collectively vilified, if acknowledged at all. "The challenge of democracy, then, is to legitimize dissent, not to put an end to polemics, disputation, controversy, and contestation."[11] The trick is achieving a form of dissent where competing groups are viewed as adversaries rather than enemies, so that the dissenting views put forward are treated with consideration, rather than quickly cast aside or shot down.[12] And this is one of populism's current shortcomings.

While there is considerable potential in populist dissenting groups to become democratic publics, most currently do not. Commenting on these shortcomings, Kathleen Knight Abowitz notes that while populists have the potential to form helpful publics, too many fail:

> Theirs is a problem-posing articulation; one that helps formulate a description of the problem that matches the lived and social experiences of those among their bounded association. . . . Their inquiry is thus far limited to the project of understanding and organizing the articulation of the demand. This is Mouffe's "political" arena of contestation and conflict. To enter the area of politics, of process and procedure among a pluralist, broader public, the inquiry must be opened up to broader reasoning and investigation, the condition of entering the democratic institutional arena.[13]

Too often populists become bogged down in perpetuating conflict with the elite rather than making, considering, or testing solutions. They lack the imagination, positive critique, and hope of good dissent; instead, they are too often mired by negativity and cynicism. They fall short of good inquiry to solve problems—that is, inquiry that is based in asking questions and widening circles to include more perspectives on problems and alternatives—instead focusing on just asserting demands. They fail to thoroughly consider or propose how things could be different.

Additionally, populism tends to emphasize political dichotomies to such an extent that as soon as a dissenter appears to veer out of the group, they risk being ostracized to the point that they lose all ability to participate in or shape the group anymore. One reason is that populists often devalue pluralism and seek homogeneity. And yet, valuing different views is a key part of both dissent and the democracy it protects, not only because democracies celebrate the freedom to pursue the good life as one sees fit but also because differing views about that good life can be a helpful source for shaping the quality of shared living.

Relatedly, some populist leaders write off dissenting views that disagree with their own—labeling them, in the case of President Trump, as "fake news." Even more alarming, many authoritarian populist leaders overtly suppress dissent in the name of keeping order, which may then lead such outcry to boil over into riots and violence. Some might argue that was the case in Portland, Oregon, where Trump called for increased militarization to stamp out those outraged by police brutality against people of color. Relatedly, populism has a tendency to fall prey to tribalism, where confirmation bias and other psychological phenomena predispose adherents to their own group and against another. This makes the need for in-group and between-group dissent more important than ever to prevent groupthink, narrow-mindedness, or reaffirmation of problematic conclusions through echo chambers and filter bubbles.

Indeed, while populism may be good at showing us that there is a significant problem with democracy, it isn't always, or even particularly, good at putting forward alternatives to that problem or engaging with the alternatives suggested by other citizens.[14] Frustrations, coupled with anger and a desire for quick resolution, breed an environment inhospitable to careful consideration of solutions. Moreover, populism has a tendency to disparage the sort of slow and careful inquiry that is often needed to fully understand complex issues and the correspondingly complicated solutions they require.[15] Relatedly, because populism devalues experts and their knowledge, it forecloses a potentially rich resource for informing and testing potential solutions. Specialized knowledge may be needed to reveal and explain problems and craft feasible solutions that are informed by history, science, or other data not readily circulating in common sense.

Populism provides avenues for integrating and activating citizens. Dissatisfaction with the elite and the shortcomings of current democracy leads populists to speak out in dissent. But their ability to see that dissent through to change and to respond to competing views is hindered by tendencies toward hasty action and vilification of those on the periphery of their group and, especially, those outside of it. Furthermore, "opening education up to the elements of populism could therefore be an opening for affects and demands that are not directed towards a democratic life."[16] For example, the demands articulated may trample the rights of minoritized groups traditionally protected in liberal democracies. In other words, populism may support dissent, but the dissent it puts forward may have both form and content that challenge long-standing aspects of democracy in potentially deeply harmful ways.

These shortcomings begin to expose the importance of truth and honesty in good dissent. Populists discarding expert knowledge show a lack of commitment to determining the truth. If populists are too quick to press for change without first carefully determining what works for not just themselves but also others, then they may end up backing untrue or even harmful ideas.[17] And if their motivations are more about rallying their tribe or placing blame on the elite, they may be persuaded to act dishonestly, perhaps by sharing false or incomplete information if it serves their narrow, self-interested goals.

Learning from Recent Protest

It is not just among populist adults that forms of protest have been on the rise. Increasingly, youth endorsing an array of political ideologies have become more active. Even as I ultimately call here for teaching students how to dissent and how to do so in ways that foreground honesty, I must acknowledge that many youth are increasingly already politically active and some are already fulfilling key aspects of good dissent.[18] In this section, I pause to consider what we might learn from recent youth political activism, especially in the age of populism. I do so, in part, to acknowledge that youth are not merely citizens in the making; rather, many are active participants in democracy in the present, though some may be struggling to fulfill their role as citizens well. Unlike the conditions in our schools that prompted me to initially write about the importance of learning how to dissent, where students too rarely engaged in political dissent, recent years have seen a proliferation of youth dissent movements, including March for Our Lives (arising from the Parkland, Florida, school shootings) and Fridays for Future (advocating environmental reform in response to climate change worldwide). A brief look at practices common in groups like these reveals important insights into how dissent needs to be understood and taught today, as well as the obstacles young citizens face and the ways in which current citizenship education may render them unequipped to do dissent well or honestly.

Let me begin by summarizing some themes in recent forms of student activism, many of which were catalogued and demonstrated in an issue of

Radical Teacher.[19] First, youth activists often use digital technology and the internet to reach a wider audience with more instantaneous impact than previous generations or approaches. The depth of injustice and the slow rates of change within traditional democratic avenues have driven some indignant youth to seek quicker alternative pathways online. Growth in online and social-media-based activism may indicate that youth experience more agency in those platforms than in more traditional formats like school newspapers. Moreover, digital platforms enable techniques that are less common in traditional spaces, such as employing satire through memes that critique the status quo, raising consciousness about problems through YouTube and TikTok videos, and using hashtags to organize.[20] Perhaps learning a lesson from a decade of the Occupy movement, students seem to grasp the importance of understanding how media works and how to use it to spread their message and develop a narrative.[21]

Digital platforms also offer more equitable access and provide lower barriers for entry.[22] Of course, COVID-19 necessitated a shift online, making such platforms not just a preference but a necessity. Digital natives took to this challenge more successfully than did many older citizens. Worryingly, digital formats also pose risks. For example, the algorithms of some social media may propel radicalization by bombarding viewers with one particular, extreme perspective.[23] Or online political groups may lure youth into extremist positions, pushing them into false conspiracy theories or violent views. These outcomes are more likely when adult supervision or educator guidance in helping them make sense of the content they find online is missing,[24] and especially when habits of acting truly are not valued or nurtured.

Recently, students detected that digital and social media spaces for expressing themselves may be in jeopardy in the United States in light of the Supreme Court case regarding a high school cheerleader sharing her frustration about her coach and team online.[25] Student school board members wrote in support of the cheerleader, not because they believed she was engaging in important political dissent (which she was certainly not) but because they feared that punishing her would chill student speech and hinder the practices of young citizens and their development. Notably, the students argued that there should be limited oversight of social media because the students saw it as an important space for them to learn how to collaborate and organize— key citizenship skills. At the same time, these students also advocated for a more formal organization for student school board members to pursue their political agenda, thereby simultaneously championing more traditional approaches alongside more recent digital techniques.[26]

Next, it's worthwhile to consider organization and interaction within youth political groups. In many cases, especially on the Left, students resist hierarchies.[27] They use horizontal participatory methods and open-source approaches. They respect and value differences among their members, including recognizing their varied identities with a welcoming spirit.[28] They foreground self-care and care for others. Again, seemingly learning from Occupy, youth today acknowledge that lack of clear leadership may hinder some aspects of advancing a cause, yet assert the importance of open membership by being careful not to limit messaging or exclude participants. They seek wider participation, but they also are more willing to empower smaller groups to break off or form distinctly.[29] That is not to say, however, that these groups are without identifiable members who have captured the spotlight. Greta Thunberg and Emma Gonzalez have become recognizable figures whose efforts have propelled their respective movements.

Recent youth groups aim to cultivate a "collective vision" while still valuing pluralism. They draw upon knowledge of past movements to learn how to fashion a common discourse and to tell stories that will unify participants, though often reaching those who already identify as activists or politically inclined than those who do not.[30] At the same time, they enable an array of goals. "Some do and some do not focus on movement building or imagine a revolution as their end goal."[31] Additionally, they may be product-focused (perhaps aiming at new legislation) or process-focused (where participation itself may be a goal).[32] Relatedly, they also vary in their approach to their goals, with some working inside the system and some outside it to bring about change. Such a variety of approaches and aims suggests that students may need to learn an array of different skills of dissent, for the knowledge required to write an effective formal letter to an elected official certainly differs from that needed to create a satirical meme.[33]

Finally, it's worthwhile to consider the types of problems and responses youth have faced. For example, when some youth express dissent online, their acts are discounted as mere "clicktivism" or "slacktivism";[34] they are not viewed as significant political action. Too often, as demonstrated in the studies of Judith Bessant and Analicia Mejia Mesinas of youth gun and environmental dissenters, "the dominant response from governments, political commentators, and many others in mainstream media, in both cases, was to try to denigrate and delegitimize the students and their actions. This time-honored strategy is used to restrict eligibility to the public sphere, and is designed to exclude students from engaging in free and open deliberation about issues in which they have a direct interest."[35] It is sometimes alleged that the students are mere puppets of other adults, that they have been indoctrinated, or that they are untrustworthy rabble-rousers. Rather than seeking to fully understand youth or the content of their political demands in thoroughgoing and honest ways, some adults misrecognize and misrepresent them, while political elites assert themselves as legitimate experts. Borrowing from the populist playbook of common sense, some youth have spoken back, reclaiming the value of their perspective and their role as citizens.

One example of students contesting derogatory representations of themselves was played out in an American national television interview between David Hogg and Cameron Kasky, two March for Our Lives leaders, and the host Bill Maher of HBO's "Real Time." Hogg and Kasky responded and challenged the popular misrecognition that being young meant they "lacked the expertise." In this instance, the two students did this by highlighting their expertise as eyewitnesses of the matter in question which gave them firsthand knowledge of what they spoke about. By implication, it was a form of knowledge and insight that Maher and many other "experts" did not and could not have. As Hogg and Kasky argued: "We've seen our friends text their parents goodbye. We are the experts." The students also identified themselves as the "grown-ups" and "the responsible ones" who have been left with the burden of a violent legacy brought about by their "irresponsible elders." As these students explained, we can and indeed will "rebuild the world that you fucked up."[36]

At the same time, student online participation may receive other problematic responses. Students face online harassment and trolling from adults, bots, and other youth who assault their ideas, or worse, the children themselves. Sometimes these attacks are identity-based, such as attacking the race of the young person rather than the cause they are advancing.[37] And when youth move from online to physical protests, they face threats of violence, such as drivers intentionally plowing their vehicles through protest marches. While lack of adult oversight online can pose its own problems, youth also face increased digital surveillance, especially by parents or educators who may be suspicious or fearful of their participation.

In sum, youth activism reveals a penchant for creative use of media to share and affirm dissenting views and their place as political agents. It also displays collective vision-building that remains open to a plurality of perspectives and welcomes an array of different types of people to participate. But it also suggests a tendency to rush, to preach to the choir, and to face potentially harmful kickback.

Learning from Populism, Youth Activism, Honesty, and a Divided Citizenry to Refine Dissent

In his recent critique of my work on dissent, Eric Luckey charges me with employing a dated definition of dissent that better reflects an era of patriotic consensus than the political fray of the United States and other polarized countries today.[38] As a result, he claims that the definition I employ is too broad, allowing most any type of disagreement to be viewed as dissent and not providing enough direction regarding the different types and skills of dissent that should be taught. He concludes:

> It is not enough, then, to merely refine the definition of dissent. For scholars of democratic education, the challenge is also to consider—and continually reconsider—the meaning and value of dissent within our changing political culture. At this moment, scholars would be wise to contemplate the meaning and practice of dissent—and how to teach it—in an age of polarization, negative partisanship, and misinformation.[39]

How, then, might populism and recent youth activism lead to a contextually informed and enhanced understanding of good dissent, which can shape and improve citizenship education and address the spread of mis- and disinformation, perhaps fulfilling Luckey's charge? First, they suggest that a duty to dissent may not be a sufficient motivator for youth today. Drawing on the words and authors of America's founding documents, I initially made the case that dissent is a duty, where citizens have an obligation to speak out when they witness injustice or when democracy is at risk. Such patriotic duty, however, likely will not win over Generation Z and Generation Alpha, especially in a populist context that emphasizes tribal political membership over national identity or pride. Instead, rather than seeing citizenship acts as patriotic duties, citizens today behave largely out of their own interests and experiences. Cho, Byrne, and Pelter found that "young people are less invested in 'dutiful' citizenship acts, favouring personalised engagement through digital networking, self-expression, protests and volunteerism."[40] They do so to protect their well-being and that of others, most often those they see as within their group, but love of country or democracy as a system of government has little role in that motivation.

This relates to my introduction to Chapter 2, where I described the problems with viewing honesty as a moral virtue one performs to be good. Instead of virtue or even duty obligations, we must emphasize how honesty as a set of habits serves to improve civic reasoning, thereby leading to improved life conditions for those who demonstrate it. We must nurture truth-seeking and truth-telling as a way of life that enables one to flourish, rather than only as an expectation of good citizenship. Also, while I initially cautioned against leading dissent with anger in my initial writings on dissent, recent youth movements and the affective impetus of populism reveal the igniting power of anger, especially as an apt response to injustice. So rather than avoiding anger in today's populist context, good dissent must effectively channel and wield it to spur and sustain action. Teachers must be aware of the risks posed by embracing anger, however. This includes how it may lead to closed-mindedness, as students "turn off" from other people and ideas.[41]

Second, populism and contemporary youth activism demonstrate that dissent defined initially as occurring "when a citizen openly disagrees with consensus of a community or the dictates of those in power" is far from sufficient.[42] That is not to say that I saw dissent as containing only that quality in my earlier writing. But what I now see is that this definition invites far too many forms of partisan polarization, or even just conflicting viewpoints, to be labeled dissent. As a result, the education for dissent that I recommend must be differentiated from activities such as teaching for political disagreement, as advocated best by Paula McAvoy and Diana Hess.[43] As I will describe later, educational gag orders are increasingly being passed, with the aim of stamping out controversial discussions in schools. In that context, I must not merely champion discussion for the sake of discussion. Instead, an education for dissent should develop the ability to detect lies and injustice inherent in controversial discussions and moments when those in power are stifling the views and lives of others or snuffing out pluralism. Such an education must help students identify those problems, name them and their sources, spread awareness of them, and work to craft and test alternatives. This may be especially important and challenging in light of Right populism, which itself tends away from pluralism and which has backed many of the restrictions as a way to limit the reach of the "woke" elite.[44] At the very least, though, students should be supported in learning how to determine truth about contentious matters and how to advocate for it in honest ways.

Third, populism and youth activism suggest a reworking of the aims of citizenship education and dissent in particular. In the past, including in a major report on civic reasoning commissioned by the National Academy of Education, I celebrated striking middle ground between competing views as a key goal of citizenship education.[45] As a result, I championed values of collaboration and compromise. Such aims, while still admirable in some situations, seem increasingly naive, failing to recognize the depth of divisions existing between political parties and groups today as well as the depth of disagreement about facts. More significantly, however, compromise may be actually be unjustified concession. Populists, for example, rightly detect that such aims have historically served some people—elites—more than others. Under the guise of middle ground, the tables have turned out to be tilted far more, and far more often, toward those with greater power.

Populists and an increasing number of other citizens today begin in a space of conflict and warn of consensus or compromise not only as unlikely but also as potentially dangerous, risking the interests of the people. As a result, dissenters today must learn how to navigate deep division and stay committed to the pursuit of truth in defiance of pressures to compromise. Some youth are already emphasizing that trait and bucking compromise, as evidenced by a recent National Public Radio showcase of Generation Z leaders who are running for office.[46] Moreover, in the United States, asserting that we have a divided country and seeking "middle ground" suggests that both "sides" need to move, but it's possible that one side is honest and truthful, while the other is not. In that case, seeking middle ground should not be a simplistic goal. The results of inquiry can help dissenters know when their position is civically justified and intellectually defensible, warranting that they stand their ground. Dissenters need to learn how to use truth claims and their process of justification as a basis for doing so.

Moreover, we must head off the problems that arise from pursuing compromise and consensus. Aiming to achieve smooth, peaceful compromise or consensus in today's divided political climate may set some students up for failure, thereby increasing their tendency toward cynicism or withdrawal from political life. Additionally, witnessing politics as merely a game to be won—one rigged and controlled by powerful elites—drives away some citizen participants. Still others may find that a goal of consensus leaves them without a drive to participate. Instead, we need a form of dissent that nurtures agency, imagination, inquiry, and problem-solving, helping to engage youth to feel heard and detect change in the midst of deep divisions or seemingly intractable problems, like climate change.[47] To summarize using the words of political theorist Deva Woodley:

> Social movements are a potential antidote to the politics of despair. They allow us to enact citizenship, not only through performing duties, but also by authoring new understandings, priorities, and even governing institutions. Unlike other forms of participation, which can also teach valuable civic skills, social movements show us how to make change. Even if we do not immediately change policy or restructure institutions, we change our ideas, we change our minds, we change our associations, we change public understandings, and we change the scope of political possibility.[48]

While she speaks of larger social movements, certainly the dissent that grounds and leads to them can have some similar impacts.

Finally, my initial discussion of dissent was largely confined to the realm of deliberative democracy, which I described largely in rational, proceduralist terms.[49] Key early criticisms by Iris Marion Young and others who have pointed out the valuable role of storytelling and emotions in deliberations highlight that populism reveals the importance of the narrative and affective dimensions of democratic discussion.[50] More recently, theories of deliberative systems have shifted to a wider view in which democratic participation and impact occur and are more inclusive of affective impact. Whereas historically only government and formal deliberations were seen as legitimate, the systems approach recognizes other public and private spaces as significant, including protests and digital platforms.[51] As a result, specific deliberative skills that dissenters need cannot be fully pinned down in advance, because they can vary widely and will continue to change based on shifting contexts. Moreover, "in a deliberative system, good deliberators should be understood not by their competencies but by the particular function of their activity in a broader system."[52] Our educational focus, then, should be less on specific deliberative competencies developed to be used in the future and the long run and more on how citizens can participate in and shape democracy now, including in a space of contestation between the people and the elite and in the process of determining truth.

Luckey suggests that dissent itself may bring forward new ways of communicating and thinking as our political culture changes.[53] Building on Ivie, Luckey even suggests that dissent may produce "a serious break in the political order"—a more radical departure than mere disagreement.[54] More disruptive forms of dissent may be necessary when traditional avenues within liberal democracy are limited or failing. Such disruptive dissent can change norms and shift power between the people and the elite, the youth and the aged.[55] As fewer young people see democracy positively or as a system of government "of, by, and for the people," disruptive dissent can bring forward improvements or revolutionary ways of doing things.[56]

To summarize, dissent must arise from citizens' needs and grow from their personal experiences. It should go beyond mere disagreement and be cautious about aims of consensus or compromise. It must help students know when to stand their ground and when to compromise in a culture that starts with conflict. It should empower students and encourage them to create and try out new ways of participating and new avenues for expressing themselves. All the while, dissent must build on inquiry aimed at determining truths that enable people to flourish. Sharing that truth through protest and developing new forms of democratic expression must be done honestly if it is to be effective at revealing problems and ameliorating them.

Improved Citizenship Education for Dissent

Increasingly, there is a mismatch between the idealistic version of democracy that is formally taught in school, with its normative visions of what counts as good citizenship (voting, patriotism, following the dominant social order), and what students experience in their own lives, both within and outside school walls. Students see protests in the streets, arguments in the news, and nasty comments about political parties on social media. Students witness or participate in populism and youth activism, both of which highlight significant dissatisfaction with democracy or the injustices it permits. Social studies educators Nicole Mirra and Antero Garcia raise similar concerns about this discrepancy. Like them, I argue that we need a citizenship education that goes beyond mere "civic participation and toward practices of civic interrogation and innovation."[57] We need citizenship education that teaches students how to recognize problems with democracy, to challenge the political world around them, and to work toward positive change.

Populism and recent youth movements expose ways in which current laws and practices are not aligned with the will of significant groups of citizens. This reveals that the political legitimacy of liberal democracy may be weak and in need of realignment or reform. Citizenship education that prioritizes dissent doesn't merely aim, as traditional citizenship education does, to develop the skills and knowledge that reproduce the current system. Instead, it seeks to ensure that the system is politically legitimate, and it brings about the changes needed to ensure that is the case. Of course, teaching for dissent doesn't merely celebrate change for the sake of change. This sort of citizenship education must also help students understand the justifications for democracy and the value of political agency so that they have normative guidelines to help them decipher when and how change is warranted.[58]

Students today have many reasons to engage in political dissent, yet most receive only limited knowledge, skills, and habits of dissent from their formal education, and some of those may not be effective in the messy context of partisan rancor today. This mismatch may not only render students unequipped to dissent in formal or informal contexts but also breed cynicism toward or disinterest in political life as students feel overwhelmed, frustrated, and ineffective. Dissenting is a way that students can overcome feelings of powerlessness to achieve agency and cultivate a disposition toward ongoing political

participation. And dissenting is a way that youth can *do* citizenship in the moment when many other avenues, such as voting and running for office, are not
yet open to them. Changes in political culture and students should influence
our goals for citizenship education and how we go about achieving them. In
response to those shifts, I offer a sketch of some revised and additional ways
in which we can teach for dissent. I recognize that incorporating all of these
may be quite difficult, especially when constrained by requirements to teach
more traditional civics education content about history, laws, government
processes, and patriotism.

To begin, in the same way as schools should teach honesty, classrooms
should take up real problems students encounter in the political world
today. Students can fulfill Generation Z's desire to go beyond mere lecture-
or textbook-based learning, or even community service, to work to understand and alleviate underlying problems through project- and inquiry-based
learning.[59] Authentic action civics lessons, for example, both bring the outside
world into the classroom and take students out of the classroom to immerse
them in their community context.[60] When injustice, lies, dishonesty, or other
problems are revealed through the course of inquiry, students can hone their
skills of dissent as they identify and develop avenues for expressing dissatisfaction, raising awareness, putting forward alternatives, and testing solutions.
Heading off youth tendencies toward hasty action, classroom investigations
must be grounded in careful inquiry, which entails analysis, often empirical, of
evidence. These approaches also help to ensure that the personal experiences
and opinions of youth reflect the real world and informed understanding of it.
These approaches nurture investigation and imagination. They build political
agency.

Digital platforms—a burgeoning space for democratic living—may be important spaces for such classroom inquiry and learning how to dissent. Many
schools have wisely begun integrating lessons about students' rights and
responsibilities online. Some schools, including recent initiatives in Illinois
and California, have begun critical media literacy lessons that help students
learn to detect mis- or disinformation online.[61] The landscape of media is
changing rapidly, making it challenging for critical media literacy techniques
to keep up. The emergence of "deep fakes" and the rapid expansion of artificial intelligence via ChatGPT and other tools are introducing new materials,
and their veracity can be harder to determine. A starting point for critical
media literacy today entails determining whether material has been human-
or computer-generated and whether that distinction matters for the issue at
hand. This is increasingly tricky. Setting aside examples of AI creation, when
the material is human-created, critical media literacy entails determining the

reliability of online sources by evaluating the experience and expertise of the author, the author's purpose, and the claims and evidence the author presents. It is helpful for teachers and students to agree on procedures for media literacy and evidence evaluation before undertaking an inquiry, so that all participants feel that the approach is fair and so that teachers can redirect students if they get off track and begin using less rigorous ways to evaluate sources and data. At multiple points during an inquiry, teachers should prod students to explain why they deem sources to be reliable and to justify those explanations, and provide them opportunities to reassess their initial findings in light of new evidence presented.[62] And critical media literacy must be couched within citizenship education that helps students understand the social, political, and economic contexts of digital media. For example, social trends in communication emphasizing affective responses lead digital algorithms to privilege information that gets attention and is shared and reshared quickly, even though it may be biased or false. Similarly, economic incentives behind social media sometimes encourage sharing information that is distorted or untrue because it sparks spending or shapes economic behavior.[63]

Teachers should build out from their classroom settings to nurture the disposition to be honest and practice dissent in national and global settings. Transitioning between local and larger arenas, critical media skills become especially important in online spaces where civic reasoning increasingly occurs. Given that online sources are often used to find information, students need to learn how to scrutinize and verify that information. Students should develop strategies to ask useful questions, investigate sources, and verify claims.[64] As they do, teachers should help students see the influence of power, emotions, intellectual arrogance, and more not just on information but also on how students perceive and respond to it, including manipulations of their feelings and cognitive biases.[65] Whereas websites and social media sometimes spread false narratives, critical media literacy can help students detect lies, confronting them before they fester and grow, and asserting instead the value of truth and honesty.[66] Teachers can guide students in learning how to "call out" their peers and strangers online for spreading mis- or disinformation in ways that value pluralism and openness to an array of beliefs and experiences. And teachers can encourage students to "call in" their classmates when they are dishonest to enable a peer-to-peer learning experience where the implications of dishonesty are discussed and trust is reaffirmed between classmates.[67]

Critical media literacy also should help students learn how to detect legitimate dissent and differentiate it from unfounded conspiracy theories and mis- or disinformation.[68] These approaches fall under what Damico and Baildon call "excavation practices," which are concerned with carefully inspecting a text. They also call for "elevation practices," which consider the larger context in which the text or website is being shared. Going beyond excavation practices, students should be taught elevation in terms of political psychology, where a key aspect of context is the affect and affinities that the text or website provokes.[69] Students should learn how to identify the ways in which their affect and beliefs are shaped and manipulated by what they encounter online. At the same time, they should be equipped with knowledge of how psychological and sociological phenomena operate so that they are on the lookout for related shortcomings. For example, echo chambers are perpetuated, in part, because we have a tendency to weigh most heavily the first evidence we encounter, and that evidence tends to come from like-minded sources, often shared on social media.[70] During a well-facilitated inquiry, teachers might remind students of that tendency and push them past initial evidence and perhaps even remind them of the unique insight sometimes gleaned when minority reports are considered, including counter-narratives. Similarly, research shows that people often fail to even consider the accuracy of a social media post before sharing it, and yet simply nudging them to rate the accuracy of that post or others can lead them to redirect their attention to matters of accuracy and then more careful and accurate dissemination.[71] Moreover,

> experimental studies have found that providing social rewards for sharing high-quality content and punishments for sharing low-quality content improves the quality of news people report intending to share. Additionally, making people publicly endorse that the news that they share is accurate, or showing people that fellow in-group members believe content is misleading, also improves people's sharing intentions.[72]

Teachers can provide these sorts of rewards while also affirming social norms around the importance of sharing accurate information. Finally, research shows that media literacy can help students foreground accuracy over directional motivations. When such teaching is accompanied by an effort to instill "critical loyalty," students are enabled to strongly and emotionally hold their own views while adopting a critical stance toward information online, even if it may appear to support their views.[73] These approaches attend to the second lens of "fallible ways of knowing," introduced at the outset of this book, and respond by helping students identify ways in which political influences and cognitive limitations distort our civic reasoning.

Importantly, though, online spaces also offer opportunities for students to construct new media, where they put forward better-informed narratives.

Students must learn that the internet doesn't just reflect reality but also creates it, thereby heightening the need for skepticism toward it, but also appreciation for its significance as a democratic medium. A component of that appreciation is learning about the role of news media as a check on power, where reporters ideally uncover corruption and shed light on falsity, thereby helping to keep democracy healthy. As a part of honesty is sharing truth, students can learn how to develop websites, blogs, news reports, videos, and other media with honesty as not just a descriptor of their content but a more overt goal, shaping their work and the relationships it fosters with other citizens.

Students should learn how to create and share digital media to express and affirm political dissent. Effective dissenters build on their knowledge of a group, including its worldview, to craft their messages and demands. Students need to learn how to create and adapt media that exposes problems in society or government. They need to learn how to use that media to both push back and move forward. This might include learning how to creatively play with or alter mainstream images and words through memes, short videos, and other formats that travel widely and quickly through social media.[74] Students should learn how to elevate the common sense of the people by sharing their experiences and bringing forward voices that are often unheard, especially when they conflict with dictates of the elite. Part of that task entails clarifying the demands of the people. Students should learn how to use digital media to craft a narrative that persuades other citizens to join movements or take action.

Teachers should alert students to instances where the narratives they create deepen problematic aspects of us-versus-them thinking, such as when one group is painted in a positive moral light and the other is denigrated as immoral or dehumanized. These narratives should unify and expand groups in ways that don't just preach to and activate more of the choir. Part of such lessons should focus on the power of political framing and how to use key phrases to be provocative and to capture attention, as Occupy did with "the 1 percent." Citizenship education should also entail learning how to share counter-narratives that expose problems or imagine alternative ways of living. These critical media literacy lessons might also teach students how to head off potential problems from digital surveillance or trolling.[75] And they might work against allegations of mere clicktivism by showcasing successful digital impact, demonstrating how and why youth dissent matters.[76]

Citizenship education can also improve the way that students work with other citizens in both online and face-to-face contexts. These lessons might begin by laying groundwork for understanding the complex identities of fellow participants and how identities might lead them to experience political issues in varied ways. Such efforts must move past mere essentialism or stereotyping and toward a "politics of difference," a more situated knowledge of particular individuals as well as the groups to which they belong.[77] They might build on recent youth movements emphasizing horizontal participatory methods to help students consider how to develop the care for others and mutual responsibility that sustains groups using such approaches. Such within-group care may help motivate actions to lessen or dissuade the impact of those who aim to harm dissenters.

Within and across groups, students need to learn how to build and sustain political friendships and agonism rather than enemies and antagonism.[78] Allen argues that such friends recognize their shared life (rather than a common one) and try to be trustworthy to each other because their shared flourishing depends on it.[79] Here, friendship is a relationship based on equal recognition and sharing power, not to be confused with merely being kind to or getting along with others. Allen describes how we begin by "talking to strangers" and move toward seeing each other as political equals. Listening demonstrates that one acknowledges the interlocutor as a political equal whose perspective and concerns are worthwhile and should be given fair consideration. It helps to build trust, which is deepened when political friends demonstrate for each other that they are open to being moved by each other and changing their views in light of the reasons and stories provided. Political friendship is what calls citizens back into conversation again if trust is damaged or the results of inquiry prove to be inequitably burdensome or harmful to one party over another. This spirit is reflected in the pragmatist emphasis on both individual growth and mutual flourishing as the criteria for determining whether or not an indeterminate situation has been successfully resolved through inquiry. Such practices can help to build and restore trust during times of great suspicion toward those from differing backgrounds or political parties.

Robert Talisse, a scholar of pragmatist political philosophy, describes "fellow feeling" between citizens and how they might best regard each other:

> Democratic citizenship also requires capacities of a different sort. In order to sustain democracy in the face of political losses, citizens must be able to regard each other with a certain kind of empathy or fellow feeling. That is, they must be able to recognize each other as persons who, like themselves, aspire to deploy democratic politics for the sake of their sincerely held values. And they must be able to sustain that sympathy even when they staunchly object to the values that drive their fellow citizens' political views. That is, democratic citizens must have the capacity to recognize that harboring incorrect or even distasteful views about justice

and other great political values does not necessarily disqualify a person for proper democratic citizenship; they must be able to judge that their political opponents are mistaken or misguided without regarding them as therefore unfit for citizenship. We can call this overall capacity democratic sympathy.[80]

This sort of mutual regard can help to work against the problems of polarization and the tendency to see others as political enemies to be defeated.

This is a very hard task in an era of "us versus them," but one that is key to heading off populism's tendencies to vilify those outside of their group or, worse, to threaten the protections for minorities in a liberal democracy. Nurturing care and trust within groups and learning how to extend that care and trust out to others is a starting point. But it must be informed by the depths of conflict in our divisive context, for some youth and many adults do indeed seek to dominate their enemies, like at political rallies.[81] And it should not be motivated by a wrongheaded goal to end all political disagreements, which are key to pluralism, democracy, pursuit of truth, and improved living. Rather than focusing on trying to debunk or disprove truth claims, students should spend some time trying to understand how those claims originate, which may be facilitated by engaging in empathy to better understand the experiences and beliefs of others, including their experiences of suffering and exclusion. That is not to say that one must come to agree with the claims of others or to strike middle ground. Empathy, or the "fellow feeling" Talisse describes, may activate affective responses to one another that cultivate trust and move students past seeing others as simply morally good or bad. As a result, students may be better positioned to see complexity and humanity in each other, paving the way for political friendship and political agonism.[82] They may be better poised to work to improve the conditions in each other's lives to eliminate future suffering.

One helpful starting point is to look at effective civic reasoning, especially within the context of shared fate. When citizens must solve a problem in their lives, their efforts are often enhanced or more successful when supported by or engaged alongside those of other people. When they recognize the limitations of their own agency, they may be ushered into conditions that urge or require them to trust others. Those situations are more likely to achieve a successful outcome if truth is sought and shared honestly. Teachers can help students to see interdependence and how civic reasoning is more successful when we not only work with others but also offer them honesty and trust. These moments can build political friendships.

To prevent naive trust, where individuals may be taken advantage of by others, teachers can engage classmates in open discussion of their motivations, risks, and benefits. They may also expose how dishonesty has justified mistrust in the past or is perpetuating it in the present. It has been well documented that when individuals work on local issues with someone different from themselves—tasks of the very sort taken up by classroom communities of inquiry I described in the last chapter—they become more trustful of not only that person but also others of similar demographic background. This suggests the possibility of opening up networks of burgeoning trust by starting with local inquiries. The starting point for such work relies heavily on teachers establishing a trusting relationship with each student individually and creating a culture where students can further build trust with each other.

Working against problematic tendencies of populism to protect only the interests of those in one's own group, teachers can help students to see how the well-being of those outside of their group may be at stake, thereby expanding the realm of who is served by their dissent. This part of instruction will explicitly raise concerns about how truth as "what works" is determined and assessed relative to the interdependencies citizens experience in modern life. Identifying shared fate and building relations of care around it may be useful. Students need to see that while others outside of their group may not have an experience identical to their own, they do have what Allen calls "a *shared life . . .* one with common events, climates, built-environment, fixations of the imagination, and social structures."[83] Relational ties and political friendships that enable agonism start there. Developing citizenship as shared fate based on a shared life nurtures the relational aspects of citizenship. It builds the inclination to care for others across that community because we recognize the many ways in which our futures are bound together politically, geographically, economically, and culturally, and that they can be improved by cooperating together.

Within and between groups, students should learn how to practice intellectual humility and fallibility. In a context of confirmation bias, backfire effect, and other tendencies to affirm like-minded viewpoints and discount others, good dissenters must learn how to seek out fuller, richer, and more accurate accounts of truth. They must work against a climate of certainty and self/group assurance, which entails not just questioning the other group, but also one's own. Psychologist Todd Kashdan found that

in the absence of dissent, homogeneous groups fell prey to strong confirmation biases, primarily seeking information that justified their premature conclusions while ignoring highly useful information that conflicted with group momentum. Although the homogeneous, dissent-free groups sought only half of the available information to make decisions, they felt an alarmingly high level of confidence compared to the broader thinking, questioning attitude of groups with dissenters.[84]

Students should study examples of the phenomenon described by Kashdan, and when they display such behavior themselves, teachers should pause to expose it. Moreover, students need to see examples of groups that arrive at better decisions and outcomes when they detect errors in their views, admit mistakes, seek counterevidence, are open to alternative views, and more. Students can learn about these instances through personal narrative accounts of them (journals, podcasts) or outside reports about them (newspaper articles, academic studies). Or key figures within the group may be invited into the classroom to talk about those instances with students so that students more directly appreciate the significance.

Lessons should demonstrate how being critical and skeptical may help young citizens from being lured into extremist positions or false conspiracy theories. In part, they need to learn about how affect *works* in both helpful and harmful ways to propel citizens to quickly adopt a view without carefully considering its truthfulness or to build allegiances between like-minded people by sharing information dishonestly.[85] Increasingly often, anger is the guiding emotion. Students need to see its power, including how it shapes action and may even manipulate responses. Citizenship educators might consider how to foreground not just negative emotions like indignation, which can produce an affective response impelling people to action, but also positive emotions like joy, which can give young citizens reasons to carry on with dissent even when it is challenging, risky, or exhausting.

Given that many people seek instant gratification today, teachers must help students see the advantages of slow, careful, and informed inquiry, the sort of inquiry that enables citizens to determine truth as "what works" to enable us to thrive. Students need to see that the results of inquiry, honesty, and dissent may take considerable time and ongoing effort. And teachers should give students pause when the dissenting views or approaches they put forward substantially challenge or risk long-standing democratic values or practices, urging students to carefully consider their ramifications. This may especially be the case with some forms of Right populism that endorse nationalism, which, while potentially aligned with patriotism, may slide into blind loyalty or virulent exclusion. Such types of populism may also be coupled with xenophobia or calls for authoritarian leaders who can protect and assert the dominance of the nation rather than democratically govern it alongside other countries.

Finally, citizenship education should not just emphasize the value of dissent or the making of dissenters; it must also teach students how to see, hear, and learn from the dissent of others. While traditional citizenship education emphasizes civility as polite and respectful engagement with others,[86] such an approach often perpetuates the status quo of power among adults and the elite and squelches the justified anger of marginalized populations because it is viewed as inappropriate for civil conversation. Instead, teachers might emphasize civility as a commitment to ongoing dialogue, a spirit of responsiveness to others best articulated by philosopher Anthony Laden.[87] Practices of civility enable groups to uphold pluralism and provide the space within deliberations for differing and contrary views to bring forward new and improved ideas. And in cases where some ideas proposed may be morally abhorrent or otherwise deeply problematic, civility enables us to remain open to the person, even if we are justifiably closed off to a particular idea they may endorse. Civility is a difficult aim in an era of populism where the outcry of those outside of one's immediate group may be quickly written off and where, despite significant examples, the protests of youth are often downplayed or ignored by older adults.

We must nurture student curiosity and the desire to seek out new ideas and be open to hearing counter-narratives that may differ from or challenge mainstream views. Counter-storytelling not only provides a fuller account of the situation but also works against the constraints of traditional conceptions of civility by privileging voices that are not typically centered, emphasizing collective solidarity rather than just individual viewpoints, often challenging the status quo, and putting forward visions of how life could be better.[88] Students must learn not just to celebrate free speech but also to practice reciprocal listening to what others say, even when they say those things in ways that demonstrate anger and outrage. Students must learn how to listen generously to others to better understand the perspectives and experiences of others. Students must learn how to be responsive to what they hear so that they can discern and incorporate good ideas into their own efforts at enacting and improving democracy, especially as they seek to determine truth and share it.[89]

In sum, citizenship education that foregrounds a revised understanding of dissent alongside honesty includes engaging in inquiry about wicked real-world political problems, nurturing a proclivity to determine truth and fight to share it honestly, using digital media to craft narratives that persuade other citizens to join movements or take action, developing relationships of care among dissenters, practicing intellectual humility, employing affect to enhance dissent, and responding to the dissent of others in receptive and open-minded ways.[90]

Notes

1. Sarah Stitzlein, *Teaching for Dissent: Citizenship Education and Political Activism* (New York: Routledge, 2014).
2. "Cambridge Dictionary's Word of the Year 2017," Cambridge Dictionary, accessed August 23, 2022, https://dictionaryblog.cambridge.org/2017/11/29/cambridge-dictionarys-word-of-the-year-2017/.
3. BBC News, "'Youthquake' Declared Word of the Year by Oxford Dictionaries," BBC, last modified December 15, 2017, https://www.bbc.com/news/uk-42361859.
4. Sarah Stitzlein, "Democratic Education in an Era of Town Hall Protests," *Theory and Research in Education* 9, no. 4 (2011): 74.
5. Stitzlein, *Teaching for Dissent*, 54.
6. Ernesto Laclau, *On Populist Reason* (New York: Verso, 2005).
7. Robert Ivie, "A Democratic People's Dissent from War," *Javnost: The Public* 24, no. 3 (2017): 203.
8. Robert Ivie, "Enabling Democratic Dissent," *Quarterly Journal* 101, no. 1 (2015): 51.
9. Petrie is one example of a scholar who highlights the democratic potential of populism—notably, one where traditional liberal democracy and its shortcomings are transcended.
10. For more on the democratic potential of populism, see Cas Mudde and Cristobal Kaltwasser, *Populism: A Very Short Introduction* (Oxford: Oxford University Press, 2017), 17–18, 83.
11. Robert Ivie, "Democratic Dissent and the Trick of Rhetorical Critique," *Critical Methodologies* 5, no. 3 (2005): 276.
12. Ivie, "Democratic Dissent and the Trick of Rhetorical Critique"; Chantel Mouffe, *On the Political* (New York: Routledge, 2005); Claudia W. Ruitenberg, "Educating Political Adversaries: Chantal Mouffe and Radical Democratic Citizenship Education," *Studies in Philosophy and Education* 28, no. 3 (2009): 269–281.
13. Kathleen Knight Abowitz, "Populism, legitimidad y escolarización estatal," *Teoría de la Educación: Revista Interuniversitaria* 35, no. 2 (2023): 37–55.
14. There are notable exceptions to this. For one, see Sharon D. Wright Austin, "Contemporary Black Populism and the Development of Multiracial Electoral Coalitions: The 2018 Stacey Abrams and Andrew Gillum Gubernatorial Campaigns," *Political Science Quarterly* 136, no. 3 (2021): 417–438.
15. I'm responding here to a provocative question posed to me by Jane Lo, who asked whether populism results from impatience.
16. Andreas Mårdh and Ásgeir Tryggvason, "Democratic Education in the Mode of Populism," *Studies in Philosophy and Education* 36, no. 6 (2017): 610.
17. Clearly, there may be times when dissenting action may be warranted before a thorough inquiry has been completed. In such cases, good dissenters are committed to continuing that inquiry and openly revising the demands or proposals that arise from it if they prove to no longer be accurate or helpful.

18. Center for Information and Research on Civic Learning and Engagement, Tufts University, "So Much for 'Slacktivism': Youth Translate Online Engagement to Offline Political Action," October 15, 2018, https://circle.tufts.edu/latest-research/so-much-slacktivism-youth-translate-online-engagement-offline-political-action.

19. Fall 2020 issue.

20. Nicole Mirra and Antero Garcia, "Civic Participation Reimagined: Youth Interrogation and Innovation in the Multimodal Public Sphere," *Review of Research in Education* 41, no. 1 (2017): 136–158, https://doi.org/10.3102/0091732X17690121; Alexander Cho, Jasmine Byrne, and Zoe Pelter, "Digital Civic Engagement by Young People," UNICEF Office of Global Insight and Policy, February 2020; Janay Kingsberry, "Gen Z Is Influencing the Abortion Debate—from TikTok," *Washington Post,* last modified June 28, 2022, https://www.washingtonpost.com/nation/interactive/2022/gen-z-tiktok-abortion-debate/.

21. James A. Anderson, "Some Say Occupy Wall Street Did Nothing. It Changed Us More than We Think," *Time,* last modified November 15, 2021, https://time.com/6117696/occupy-wall-street-10-years-later/.

22. Zoë Pelter, "Pandemic Participation: Youth Activism Online in the COVID-19 Crisis," UNICEF Office of Global Insight and Policy, last modified April 14, 2020, https://www.unicef.org/globalinsight/stories/pandemic-participation-youth-activism-online-covid-19-crisis.

23. Annie Y. Chen, Brendan Nyhan, Jason Reifler, Ronald E. Robertson, and Christo Wilson, "Exposure to Alternative and Extremist Content on YouTube," Anti-Defamation League, last modified May 3, 2022, https://www.adl.org/resources/report/exposure-alternative-extremist-content-youtube; Brandy Zadrozny, "'Carol's Journey': What Facebook Knew About How It Radicalized Users," NBC News, last modified October 26, 2021, https://www.nbcnews.com/tech/tech-news/facebook-knew-radicalized-users-rcna3581; Olivia Little and Abbie Richards, "TikTok's Algorithm Leads Users from Transphobic Videos to Far-Right Rabbit Holes," Media Matters, last modified October 5, 2021, https://www.mediamatters.org/tiktok/tiktoks-algorithm-leads-users-transphobic-videos-far-right-rabbit-holes#paragraph--section-heading--3421981.

24. Tom Dreisbach, "UCLA Student Charged in Capitol Riot Took Inspiration from Online Extremist, NPR, last modified March 15, 2021, https://www.npr.org/2021/03/15/971931742/ucla-student-charged-in-capitol-riot-took-inspiration-from-online-extremist; Dina Temple-Raston, "A Tale of 2 Radicalizations," NPR, last modified March 15, 2021, https://www.npr.org/2021/03/15/972498203/a-tale-of-2-radicalizations.

25. *Mahoney Area School District v. B.L.,* 594 US _ (2021).

26. Stephen Sawchuk, "Student School Board Members Flex Their Civic Muscle in Supreme Court Free-Speech Case," *Education Week,* last modified April 7, 2021, https://www.edweek.org/policy-politics/student-school-board-members-flex-their-civic-muscle-in-supreme-court-free-speech-case/2021/04.

27. Jacqueline Brady, "Introduction: Visions of New Student Activism," *Radical Teacher* 118 (2020): 1–7, https://doi.org/10.5195/rt.2020.868.

28. Brady, "Introduction."

29. Anderson, "Some Say Occupy Wall Street Did Nothing."

30. Brady, "Introduction."

31. Brady, "Introduction," 4.

32. Cho, Byrne, and Pelter, "Digital Civic Engagement by Young People."

33. Eric Luckey, "Refining Dissent: Response to Sarah M. Stitzlein's 'Democratic Education in an Era of Town Hall Protests,'" *Theory and Research in Education* 20, no. 1 (2022): 119–124.

34. Center for Information and Research on Civic Learning and Engagement, "So Much for 'Slacktivism.'"

35. Judith Bessant and Analicia Mejia Mesinas, eds., *When Students Protest* (Lanham, MD: Rowman & Littlefield, 2021), 38.

36. Bessant and Mejia Mesinas, *When Students Protest*, 48–49.

37. Seo Yoon Yang, "I Arranged a Protest at My High School. The Reactionary Racist Attacks Changed Me," Daily Kos, last modified August 17, 2020, https://www.dailykos.com/stories/2020/8/17/1969290/-I-arranged-a-protest-at-my-high-school-The-reactionary-racist-attacks-changed-me.

38. Luckey, "Refining Dissent.'"

39. Luckey, "Refining Dissent," 122.

40. Cho, Byrne, and Pelter, "Digital Civic Engagement by Young People," 3.

41. Douglas Yacek, "Should Anger Be Encouraged in the Classroom? Political Education, Closed-Mindedness, and Civic Epiphany," *Educational Theory* 69, no. 4 (2019): 421–437.

42. Stitzlein, "Democratic Education in an Era of Town Hall Protests," 74.

43. Paula McAvoy and Diana Hess, "Classroom Deliberation in an Era of Political Polarization," *Curriculum Inquiry* 53, no. 1 (2013): 14–47.

44. Stuart Sim, *A Call to Dissent: Defending Democracy Against Extremism and Populism* (Edinburgh: Edinburgh University Press, 2022).

45. Sarah M. Stitzlein, "Defining and Implementing Civic Reasoning and Discourse: Philosophical and Moral Foundations for Research and Practice," in *Educating for Civic Reasoning and Discourse*, ed. Carol D. Lee, Gregory White, and Dian Dong (Washington, DC: National Academy of Education, 2021), 23–52.

46. Elena Moore, "The First Gen Z Candidates Are Running for Congress—and Running Against Compromise," NPR, last modified July 6, 2022, https://www.npr.org/2022/07/06/1109193929/the-first-gen-z-candidates-are-running-for-congress-and-running-against-compromi.

47. Deva Woodley traces this repoliticization of recent activists well in her book *Reckoning: Black Lives Matter and the Democratic Necessity of Social Movements* (Oxford: Oxford University Press, 2022).

48. Woodley, *Reckoning*, 16.

49. Stitzlein, *Teaching for Dissent*.

50. Iris Marion Young, "Activist Challenges to Deliberative Democracy," *Political Theory* 29, no. 5 (2001): 670–690.

51. Nicole Curato, John S. Dryzek, Selen A. Ercan, Carolyn M. Hendriks, and Simon Niemeyer, "Twelve Key Findings in Deliberative Democracy Research," *Daedalus* 146, no. 3 (2017): 28–38; Kei Nishiyama, "Democratic Education in the Fourth Generation of Deliberative Democracy," *Theory and Research in Education* 19, no. 2 (2021): 109–126.

52. Nishiyama, "Democratic Education in the Fourth Generation of Deliberative Democracy," 120.

53. Luckey, "Refining Dissent."

54. Luckey, "Refining Dissent," 121.

55. Karen O'Brien, Elin Selboe, and Bronwyn M. Hayward, "Exploring Youth Activism on Climate Change," *Ecology and Society* 23, no. 3 (2018): 42–55.

56. "Language Perceptions Project," Philanthropy for Active Civic Engagement, April 19, 2019, 14, http://www.pacefunders.org/wp-content/uploads/2019/05/PACE-Language-Percept ion-Project_May-16.pdf.

57. Mirra and Garcia, "Civic Participation Reimagined," 138–139.

58. Julian Culp, "Democratic Citizenship Education in Digitized Societies: A Habermasian Approach," *Educational Theory*, 73, no. 2 (2023): 178–203.

59. Corey Seemiller and Meghan Grace, *Generation Z: A Century in the Making* (New York: Routledge, 2018).

60. Generation Citizen offers an action civics curriculum based on systemic impact (getting at the root of the problem), action, and open-mindedness, as well as resources for digital storytelling. See "Democracy Doesn't Pause," Generation Citizen, https://generationcitizen. org/democracy-doesnt-pause/, accessed February 8, 2023; "Our Curriculum," Generation Citizen, https://generationcitizen.org/our-programs/our-curriculum/, accessed February 8, 2023. Other excellent educational resources are available from Youth in Front, which grew out of the Parkland shooting; see "Understanding and Supporting Student-Led Activism," Youth in Front, https://www.youthinfront.org/student/collection/744064-understanding- and-supporting-student-led-activism, accessed February 8, 2023.

61. Isabelle Hanson, "Illinois High School Students Will Learn Media Literacy Skills Next School Year," KFVS, last modified October 25, 2021, https://www.kfvs12.com/2021/10/ 25/illinois-high-school-students-will-learn-media-literacy-skills-next-school-year/; Erin McNeill, *U.S. Media Literacy Policy Update 2021* (Watertown, MA: Media Literacy Now, January 2022); Carolyn Jones, "Media Literacy Would Be Required for California K–12 Students Under New Bill," EdSource, June 5, 2023, https://edsource.org/2023/media-liter acy-would-be-required-for-all-california-students-under-new-bill/691667?amp=1.

62. James S. Damico and Mark C. Baildon, *How to Confront Climate Denial: Literacy, Social Studies, and Climate Change* (New York: Teachers College Press, 2022).

63. Culp, "Democratic Citizenship Education in Digitized Societies."

64. Sarah McGrew, Teresa Ortega, Joel Breakstone, and Sam Wineburg, "The Challenge That's Bigger than Fake News: Civic Reasoning in a Social Media Environment," *American Educator* 41, no. 3 (2017): 4–9. The Digital Inquiry Group of Stanford University offers ex- cellent guidance in this area.

65. National Council for the Social Studies, "Position Statement: Powerful and Purposeful Teaching and Learning in Elementary School Social Studies," *Social Education* 73, no. 5 (2009): 252–254.

66. Wayne Journell, ed., *Unpacking Fake News: An Educator's Guide to Navigating the Media with Students* (New York: Teachers College Press, 2019); Joseph Kahne, Jacqueline Ullman, and Ellen Middaugh, "Digital Opportunities for Civic Education," in *Making Civics Count*, ed. David E. Campbell, Meira Levinson, and Frederick Hess (Cambridge, MA: Harvard Education Press, 2012), 207–228; Peter Levine, "Media Literacy for the 21st Century: A Response to the Need for Media Education in Democratic Education," *Democracy and Education* 23, no. 1 (2015); McGrew et al., "The Challenge That's Bigger than Fake News"; Lee McIntyre, *Post-Truth* (Cambridge, MA: MIT Press, 2018); Joseph Kahne and Benjamin Bowyer, "Educating for Democracy in a Partisan Age: Confronting the Challenges of Motivated Reasoning and Misinformation," *American Educational Research Journal* 54, no. 1 (2016): 3–34.

67. Thanks to Danny Foster for suggesting the "call in" follow-up exercise to "calling out."

68. Sarah McGrew and Virginia Byrne, "Who Is Behind This? Preparing High School Students to Evaluate Online Content," *Journal of Research on Technology in Education* 53, no. 4 (2020): 457–475.

69. Wayne Journell and Christopher H. Clark, "Political Memes and the Limits of Media Literacy," in *Unpacking Fake News: An Educator's Guide to Navigating the Media with Students,* ed. Wayne Journell (New York: Teachers College Press, 2019), 109–125.

70. C. Thi Nguyen, "Escape the Echo Chamber," Aeon, April 9, 2018, https://aeon.co/essays/why-its-as-hard-to-escape-an-echo-chamber-as-it-is-to-flee-a-cult..

71. Gordon Pennycook, Ziv Epstein, Moshen Mosleh, Antonio A. Arechar, Dean Eckles, and David G. Rand, "Shifting Attention to Accuracy Can Reduce Misinformation Online," *Nature* 592 (2021): 590–595.

72. Steve Rathje, Jon Roozenbeek, Jay J. Van Bavel, and Sander van der Linden, "Accuracy and Social Motivations Shape Judgements of (Mis)information," *Nature Human Behaviour* 7 (2023): 892–903.

73. Joseph Kahne and Benjamin Bowyer, "Educating for Democracy in a Partisan Age: Confronting the Challenges of Motivated Reasoning and Misinformation," *American Educational Research Journal* 54, no. 1 (2017): 3–34.

74. The YaYa Network provides lessons on how to make Educational Comms (videos that teach other people about political issues) and AgitProp (enables one to spoof well-known figures with memes in order to share a political idea).

75. One example of youth using storytelling to empower change is featured in the writing of Alan McCullough, Felton Morrell Jr., Bernard Thomas, Vicente Waugh, Nicholas Shubert, and Amy Donofrio, "The EVAC Movement Story: Why Youth Storytelling Is Powerful . . . and Why It's Dangerous," *Harvard Educational Review* 90, no. 2 (2020): 195–228. An organization that is helping youth to craft effective stories using a populist approach is Dēmos. An example of a political leader and her organization working to navigate both building knowledge from crowds and heading off problems with them is Danielle Allen and the Democratic Knowledge Project.

76. "Digital Civics Toolkit," Project Zero, 2018, https://pz.harvard.edu/resources/digital-civics-toolkit, offers a helpful digital civics toolkit that demonstrates how detractors may write off online action as "slacktivism," yet showcases how "flash activism" can generate the steam necessary to bring an issue to the fore and create impetus for change.

77. Iris M. Young, *Justice and the Politics of Difference* (Princeton, NJ: Princeton University Press, 1991).

78. Danielle S. Allen, *Talking to Strangers: Anxieties of Citizenship After* Brown v. Board of Education (Chicago: University of Chicago Press, 2004); Mouffe, *On the Political*; Chantal Mouffe, *For a Left Populism* (New York: Verso, 2018).

79. Allen, *Talking to Strangers.*

80. Robert Talisse, *Overdoing Democracy* (New York: Oxford University Press, 2021), 147.

81. Adam Harris, "Conservative High Schoolers Want to 'Own the Libs,'" *The Atlantic*, last modified July 26, 2018, https://www.theatlantic.com/education/archive/2018/07/conservative-high-schoolers-are-ready-to-own-the-libs/566177/.

82. Michalinos Zembylas, *Affect and the Rise of Right-Wing Populism: Pedagogies for the Renewal of Democratic Education* (Cambridge: Cambridge University Press, 2021).

83. Allen, *Talking to Strangers*, xxi.

84. Todd Kashdan, *The Art of Insubordination: How to Dissent and Defy Effectively* (New York: Avery, 2022), 47.

85. Megan Boler and Elizabeth Davis, "The Affective Politics of the 'Post-Truth' Era: Feeling Rules and Networked Subjectivity," *Emotion, Space and Society* 27 (2018): 75–85.

86. Stitzlein, "Defining and Implementing Civic Reasoning and Discourse."

87. Anthony Laden, "Two Concepts of Civility," in *A Crisis of Civility? Political Discourse and Its Discontents*, ed. Robert G. Boatright, Timothy J. Shaffer, Sarah Sobieraj, and Dannagal Goldthwaite Young (New York: Routledge, 2019), 2–6.

88. Melissa Gibson, "From Deliberation to Counter-Narration: Toward a Critical Pedagogy for Democratic Citizenship," *Theory and Research in Social Education* 48, no. 3 (2020): 431–454.

89. Bryan Warnick, Douglas Yacek, and Shannon Robinson, "Learning to Be Moved: The Modes of Democratic Responsiveness," *Philosophical Inquiry in Education* 25, no. 1 (2018): 31–46.

90. Of course, such citizenship education will require substantial emphasis and development within teacher education programs also, where some evidence suggests that activism is too rarely discussed now. Jim Carlson, "In-School Discussion About Activism Not Consistent, Research Shows," last modified June 21, 2021, https://www.psu.edu/news/research/story/school-discussion-about-activism-not-consistent-research-shows-0/.

5
The Role of Honesty in Teaching About Controversial Issues

In this chapter, I consider recent efforts to curb the teaching of controversial issues in schools, especially those concepts or matters perceived to be divisive because they entail contentious aspects of race, gender, and sexuality, as well as injustices that may relate to each. I describe how honesty is essential in both *what* we teach and *how* we teach. Honesty enables students to better understand, navigate, and solve problems related to potentially divisive issues. This case and the one presented in the last chapter grow out of recent struggles in our democracy and both demonstrate the need to better teach honesty.

On Constitution Day, September 17, 2020, President Donald Trump told participants in a conference on American history at the National Archives, "Our mission is to defend the legacy of America's founding, the virtue of America's heroes, and the nobility of the American character." He went on, "We must clear away the twisted web of lies in our schools and classrooms and teach our children the magnificent truth about our country."[1] In the same month, President Trump issued an executive order that forbade federal workplace trainings about "divisive concepts." That order became a template for legislation that popped up across the country aiming to prohibit teaching of such concepts in schools also.

This situation draws our attention to not just the difficulties of teaching controversial issues, especially those labeled "divisive," but also to whether and how we do so when the histories and information that undergird those discussions are themselves contentious matters of truth and partisanship. Trump saw a particular version of American history, one that celebrates its exceptionalism and progress, as true, while others, presumably the teachers he implies in his statement, put forward a different account, one he saw as "lies." Indeed, a central part of the problem has become not just whether divisive concepts should be discussed but whether agreement can even be reached about the truthfulness of histories and ideas related to those concepts, especially in "purple" communities with stark division between Right "red" citizens and Left "blue" ones. For example, in a poll conducted of school

Teaching Honesty in a Populist Era. Sarah M. Stitzlein, Oxford University Press. © Oxford University Press 2024.
DOI: 10.1093/9780197775912.003.0005

principals, nearly two-thirds reported "that parents or community members pushed back against information used in classrooms. And this tug-of-war over facts 'grew almost three-fold in purple communities between 2018 and 2022.'"[2] In part, growing polarization does not just divide people by what they agree upon; it may also be challenging how schools have traditionally determined which matters are worthy of classroom study and which are not.

In the years since Trump's declaration, many states have introduced or approved legislation that bans teaching about divisive concepts, including aspects of racism, sexism, and equity in public K–12 classrooms and sometimes in university courses too.[3] Problematically categorized as concepts, they might be better understood as political, moral, and sociological beliefs about aspects of race, gender, sexual identity, as well as injustices related to those aspects of identity. While "concepts" is not the best term, for the sake of alignment with the language of the bills I will stick with the term.[4] In some cases specific concepts have been listed; in others they have been left quite vague. For example, recent legislation introduced in my home state catalogues some key divisive concepts but then goes on to include "any other concept that the state board of education defines as divisive."[5]

Many of these laws were created in reaction to critical race theory, which emphasizes the enduring and ongoing role of systemic racism, and the 1619 Project, which centers Black Americans in the historical narrative of the United States, including their contributions and their experiences of racism.[6] In response to the legislation, some teachers and scholars of education have been quick to defend the importance of teaching about the concepts banned in the bills, such as systemic racism and privilege, with some of them calling for classroom discussion about these concepts.[7]

While I certainly believe there is value in students learning about many of the identified concepts and the beliefs or phenomena they describe, I want to offer an alternative focus in this chapter. Here, to the extent one ethically can, I largely set aside the content of the particular concepts and their relationship, if any, to critical race theory, the 1619 Project, or their uptake in schools.[8] Instead, I contend that we should be deeply concerned with banning learning about things that divide us because it prevents us from solving problems in our democracy, perhaps deepening our divisions in ways that impair our ability to take up an array of better ways of living together. Answering the fundamental civic question "What should we do?" is an aim held across political parties and one aided by inquiry. Rather than excluding divisive concepts or the divisions they may provoke from our classrooms, in order to figure out how to live together we need educative spaces where we inquire into what divides us, why we are divided, and how we might respond to such division.

Within that inquiry, we can better attend to our divisions while also taking up the specific concepts prohibited in recent legislation. This may involve "forensic work," where students engage in historical and genealogical work to trace how particular concepts or positions have evolved into divisive issues and battlegrounds in the school "culture wars," including how such concepts may serve the power and interests of some populations more than others.[9] Moreover, through inquiry we can bring competing or contested beliefs and histories into consideration to sort through determining their truth as "what works" and in accordance with empirical evidence. Within such endeavors, classrooms can yet again affirm the value of acting truly, and foster habits of honesty among students in ways that may resolve political tensions or prevent future divisions.

In this chapter, I begin by describing recent divisive concepts legislation, speculating briefly on the motivations behind it and the implications resulting from it. I will then describe how discussing divisive concepts in classrooms may be a helpful way for students to better understand the particular concepts and for students to take a stand on them. While I will briefly argue for the importance of classroom discussion of divisive concepts, my central claim will be that we must do more than merely discuss these concepts. Instead, we should engage in classroom inquiry about them. It is through this inquiry that a commitment to truth and honesty becomes apparent and through teaching such inquiry that we can further nurture habits of honesty in students.

While there are many different forms of classroom discussion, the dominant or typical approach entails exposing students to opposing perspectives on an issue and sometimes then requiring students to take a stand and provide reasons for their preferred perspective. Classroom discussion, though a valuable tool, is too often quickly championed as a solution to dealing with controversial issues. Inquiry, which often includes discussion, avoids some of the shortfalls of only doing discussion and goes further in helping students not just learn about divisive issues but also engage them in more richly democratic ways. At the same time, an inquiry approach may head off some of the very concerns used to justify divisive concepts legislation, such as Trump's allegations of lying teachers.[10] Inquiry is more effective than banning divisive concepts or pushing them to the background, insofar as inquiry can reveal the root causes of political, ideological, and sociological division and their implications in our lived experience, while also putting forward solutions that can move us forward.

Finally, teachers should guide students through lessons in distinguishing fact from opinion of the sort needed to combat truth decay and offer an informed response. Such distinction can be difficult. Controversial issues offer opportunities to help students confront ambiguity and negotiate new meaning together as they honestly seek and share truth. It prepares them to tackle other social and civic problems where histories are unknown, unclear, or contested. Moreover, inquiry positions students to not be silent regarding divisive concepts. Inquiry positions students to not just talk about divisive concepts but also solve social problems related to them in our world today. In other words, inquiry enables us to *do* something about divisive concepts, rather than just learning *about* them, as some educators currently advocate in calls for classroom discussion. That doing, as a form of civic reasoning and action, is improved when truth and honesty are prioritized.

Recent Legislation

Divisive concept bills and laws label certain understandings of or beliefs about race, gender, and sexuality as too divisive or inappropriate for classroom curriculum and instruction, or even for the professional development of teachers. Florida, in an approach that drew widespread attention and served as a model for legislation in other states, forbade schools to use instructional materials that discuss sexual orientation or gender identity to students before grade four. More recently, Florida carried out its divisive concept ban by prohibiting the teaching of a newly developed Advanced Placement course on African American history for being uncompliant with the law and for allegedly teaching historically inaccurate information, thereby also raising matters of honesty.[11] In this case, Governor DeSantis specifically made his decision a matter of truth when he justified his ban by saying, "Education is about the pursuit of truth, not the imposition of ideology or the advancement of a political agenda."[12]

Bills and laws in other states have forbidden teaching the concepts of "white privilege" and "systemic racism." Rhode Island took a broader approach, prohibiting ascribing "character traits, values, moral and ethical codes, privileges, status, or beliefs to a race or sex or to an individual because of their race or sex."[13] Still, other states, like Iowa and Oklahoma, have prohibited teaching concepts that cause students to "feel discomfort, guilt, anguish, or any other form of psychological distress" about their own race/gender.[14] In proposed legislation in my home state of Ohio, divisive concepts include teaching that the "United States is fundamentally racist" or "assigning fault, blame, or bias to a nationality, color, ethnicity, race, or sex."[15] In Indiana, the state representative sponsoring their bill listed more than three pages of concepts to ban, including some race-related concepts like "intersectionality," "white supremacy," and "racial prejudice," gender-related concepts like "patriarchy," more general concepts like "critical self-reflection" and "educational justice," and concepts that may appear to be tangentially related, like "social-emotional learning" and "land acknowledgments."[16]

Some bills, including one in my state, call for more than just a ban on specific concepts; they actually prohibit assignments, like position papers, or class activities, such as debates, that require students "to advocate for or against a specific topic or point of view."[17] This ban applies to all topics, not just those that are controversial or divisive. Finally, lumped in with divisive concepts legislation, some states prohibit "action civics," where students engage in projects that seek some sort of change in their school or community. In my state, this includes forbidding "any practicum, action project, or similar activity that involves social or public policy advocacy."[18] Such bans, then, may also limit the sort of education for dissent that I described in the previous chapter because those may lead to policy advocacy.

Aims of Legislation

Divisive concept legislation originated from conservative policymakers. Their motivations can be read in more and less generous ways. These policymakers and their supporters can be understood as trying to improve harmony across America's demographic groups and among America's increasingly politically polarized citizenry. They aim to do so by stamping out teachings that emphasize differences or hierarchy between racial and gender groups and fending off the emotions that such teachings may raise, including anger and resentment toward other identity groups or guilt toward one's own group. Additionally, they seek to assert the importance of seeing each citizen as an individual, rather than primarily as a member of various identity groups. Providing a formal statement for such concerns, the National Association of Scholars expressed that curricula should not engage in identity politics that pits groups against each other and should not teach hostility toward America or its heritage.[19] Calls to focus on individuals, rather than groups, are common among legislation proponents, and some are especially concerned with portraying particular groups as "oppressors" and others as "oppressed," with these terms also banned in some bills. For example, Ohio HB 327 sponsor Representative Diane Grendell said in her testimony:

> Teaching our children that they are either victims or victimizers does not inspire change or love, but rather is divisive and creates a conundrum in their minds. America, since its inception, has stood firm on the grounds of individual excellence. In our bill, we promote respect for all.

Later she adds that her bill is "an affirmation, that no matter the color of your skin, the ethnicity your ancestral family calls home, your gender, you are an individual."[20]

Another shared motivation behind these bills is a concern for indoctrination in classrooms, where content is taught in ways that lead to an unshakeable commitment even if that content is inaccurate or politically biased.[21] Indeed, citizens from across the political perspective should be alarmed if teachers are indoctrinating students into false, deceitful, or otherwise incorrect interpretations. The proponent testimony of Ohio H.B. 322 sponsor Representative Don Jones is illustrative:

> The purpose of school is to educate students. Classrooms are not indoctrination centers, nor should they be. . . . Whether these points of indoctrination are referred to as divisive concepts, critical race theory, or whatever else may be out there, at the end of the day the name doesn't matter. Indoctrination is indoctrination. The goal of that indoctrination is to alter how our children view the United States. The goal is to train children to believe the United States is fundamentally racist, and by association our children are somehow inherently racist.

He concludes:

> Too often teachers are telling students what to think, and not teaching them how to think. HB 322 is about protecting the integrity of our education system and ensuring our students are learning real facts, and not being told to feel or think a certain way.[22]

Here Jones distinguishes fact from political opinion and affect, perhaps detecting the role of each in our current times and trying to foreground truthfulness as objectively distinct from opinion and affect. He also argues against action civics, largely because it is seen as putting indoctrinated views into action:

> Our children absolutely need to learn our government processes, but not because they are pushing an agenda from a teacher or school, or even potentially being dinged by a teacher for advocating for the "wrong position." Coursework should be about learning, not advocating and lobbying.[23]

A more generous take on these laws, then, emphasizes the long-standing significance of individualism in America, the desire for citizens to get along, the value of truthful accounts of history and the experiences of citizens, and the goal of schooling free from political indoctrination.

A more nefarious interpretation of these policies suggests that conservative officials are trying to restrict how concepts of race, gender, sexuality, justice, and equity are defined and taught in schools, prohibiting alternative, often more complex historical accounts that portray systemic injustice. Some critics feel that these leaders fail to seek or provide an honest account of history, one that is full, forthright, and accurate. Notably, one such group of largely progressive critics in my home state calls itself Honesty for Ohio Education. These restrictions silence the voices and experiences of minorities, who may view matters of race, gender, and sexuality in ways that differ from the views held by proponents of divisive concepts legislation, the majority of whom hold a majority position as straight white men. Prohibiting talking about these issues may also prevent discussions of responsibility for past and ongoing harm as well as (arguably justified) feelings of guilt or shame that may arise from them, especially among students who are white. From that perspective, guilt or shame may not breed divisiveness, as conservative leaders warn, but rather provoke action to stop or prevent harm.

Additionally, under this less generous interpretation, the harmony and consensus sought seem to be more aligned with assimilationist goals of *e pluribus unum*, where we aim for a citizenry united as one. While being "one" may sound like an admirable goal, especially during times of populism and polarization, the drive toward oneness may expunge differing opinions and ignore or deny the experiences of minorities. It actually runs counter to the values of liberty and pluralism central to democracy, and may assert the dominant views of political leaders over the everyday experiences and wishes of common people.

Finally, it should be noted that while I focus more on legislative action on the Right, some on the Left have made more informal suggestions or called for school policies that also chill classroom environments and limit the ability to teach divisive concepts well. These include some calls for rather extreme forms of safety, where it is argued that students should be protected from topics or words that might upset them. It also includes silencing or "canceling" people who make some contentious claims, rather than working through the conflict they cause or dialoguing about or inquiring into the substance of their claims.

Implications of Legislation

While these proposed and approved laws are quite new and their impacts are not yet fully known, some practical and theoretical implications are already becoming clear. First, more practically, divisive concept legislation not only outlines what should not be taught in schools but also has given rise to mechanisms where citizens can report teachers for perceived infringements of the law. Punishment then may follow, from loss of school funding to firing teachers to suspending teaching licenses.[24] This has led some commentators to describe these as "teacher gag laws."[25] Teachers, fearing repercussions, may resort to teaching to the lowest common denominator, teaching only material or views that are unlikely to be seen as objectionable to anyone. As a result, teachers will likely avoid taking up real matters of equity and identity that students and families are struggling with both in and outside of schools. They may also feel restricted from seeking or sharing the truth about divisive issues and thereby allow faulty views to not only go unchallenged but also be passed on unquestioningly to students.

Second, in a matter of both practice and theory, divisive concept legislation precludes classrooms from taking up what Diana Hess describes as "open" issues. These are issues where multiple reasonable positions can be taken.[26] These may be issues where the truth of the matter has yet to be determined or is currently being reconsidered. Open issues offer learning opportunities where students engage with an array of differing perspectives and analyze the merits of competing positions. They can come to better understand how others view an issue and may reach a stance themselves. While it can be hard to distinguish which issues should be seen as open, and therefore worthy of classroom consideration, one criterion for doing so asks whether the issue is politically authentic. One way to determine this is by looking to see if the issue is being openly debated in public legislation. Obviously, this is the case with the concepts leading to the bills themselves, but it is also evidenced in other public policy debates around related matters like transgender athletes in schools and school racial integration programs.[27] Interestingly, the effect of the bill seems to contradict the call of some proponents, such as Indiana representative Chuck Wichgers, who argues in his proponent testimony:

The problem is that critical race theory and its related ideas form a closed system. It is a perspective that leaves no space for anyone, no matter how well-intentioned, to see the world differently. When presented as the singular valid worldview, it is not a productive way to engage with students, groups, or with one another.[28]

Unfortunately, banning discussion of these concepts further prevents multiple interpretations of them from being considered in schools and prevents challenges being raised that might work against a singular and entrenched view. These laws, then, bar discussion of concepts that should be seen as open issues worthy of engagement. They block key opportunities to seek truth and to determine how upholding divisive concepts as true might impact stakeholders.[29]

Finally, I offer a more theoretical implication. Exploring disagreements about important social and political matters is a source for making better decisions about how we live together in a democracy. Yet, divisive concept legislation forecloses not just opportunities to do so in classrooms but also the ability of young citizens to see and value disagreement as a benefit to democracy. Proponents of this legislation seem to fear antagonism in their quest for harmony and oneness.[30] As a result, they miss out on antagonism as a source for different ways of thinking about, and potential solutions to, our shared problems. In their effort to stamp out the wars of antagonism between citizen enemies, proponents of divisive concepts legislation may also stamp out opportunities to productively engage with adversaries. Instead, we might pursue a more democratically justified form of harmony by promoting wholeness, best described by Allen. Wholeness seeks a cohesive community that is tied together by political friendship and shared fate, where we are bound together by our shared problems and experiences of having to figure out how to live together. It does not homogenize or erase differing views as oneness or bans on divisive concepts do.

Discussing Divisive Concepts

Some people, including many social studies teachers and higher education scholars who prepare social studies teachers, are quick to suggest that controversial issues should be discussed in classrooms.[31] Typically, that's well justified. Discussion and related approaches like deliberation and debate are important avenues for enacting democratic life, as we make sense of and respond to contentious issues. Students should practice them. The benefits of classroom discussion are well supported in the literature. Some benefits, such as producing respect for those with differing opinions and increasing the perspective-taking abilities of students, have also been affirmed in empirical studies, though some findings are mixed.[32] The "Civic Mission of Schools" report was the first to strongly push two related classroom practices: discussing current events and debating current events and controversies. These have since been shown to have positive effects, including on National Assessment of Educational Progress (NAEP) civics scores.[33] The call to discussion has grown since the report's release, but it is one that we should heed carefully in light of some potential complications.

Importantly, when discussing open political issues—those with multiple reasonable positions—the discussion should be taught "non-directively," where the teacher doesn't try to impart a particular belief or position. This differs from teaching about settled issues, where there is only one reasonable position and that position should be taught directively.[34] Even the best teachers, however, sometimes struggle to teach about the first type of issues in genuinely open ways, without bias or unintentionally favoring some positions over others. Their shortcomings may be perceived as indoctrination—though, I believe, wrongly so in many instances. Nonetheless, such potential is aligned with the concerns raised by policymakers authoring divisive concept bills.

Not all aspects of divisive issues should be taught in thoroughly open ways, however. Take, for example, the perpetually thorny issue of racism in the United States. It is not possible to honestly and fully teach the history of the United States (or even the historical context of many works of American literature) without encountering horrific instances of historical or contemporary racism. While some textbooks try to sanitize or obscure this history,[35] any sober look at the historical record is clear. In most cases, teachers ought to present these histories as settled and reserve discussion and deliberation for related issues that remain open. For example, how to grapple with the historical legacies of discrimination is still very much an open question, worthy of discussion in our schools. It is not appropriate, however, to frame discussion in ways that students are invited to argue for historical atrocities (such as the Tulsa race massacre) or the limitations of others' rights on the basis of protected categories such as race. While there is room for tension, deliberation, and constructive dissent around open issues, fostering it around settled questions is likely to misrepresent historical evidence and harm classroom relationships.[36]

Discussion emphasizes stating one's opinion and giving reasons for it. Again, this helps instill important citizenship skills, especially in more deliberative accounts of democracy that rely upon rational argument exchange. However, emphasizing reason-giving and one's personal stance may not focus enough on learning how to gather evidence to better initially understand the issue and to support the reasons one gives for one's developing stance on it. Teachers and students may also fall short of the more rational, non-emotional discussion that is described in the literature on deliberative democracy, in part because it requires skills students have not yet developed in school or may not be appropriately expected of students at their age. Discussions can become heated.[37] And, when they do, they may reify divisions between students. Relatedly, studies show how debate, for example, may further entrench people in their positions, reduce diversity of views within a group, and exacerbate polarized views.[38]

Sweeping calls to discuss controversial issues, then, may not be well-justified in matters of divisive concepts and may foreclose other useful approaches. As Kauppi and Drerup argue:

> As soon as it is established that an issue should be taught as controversial, it is usually regarded as rather uncontroversial that discussion of some type is the natural way to proceed. Thus, despite the significant variation in what counts as a controversial issue and what makes an issue controversial, in educational discourse, a uniform solution to approaching these issues has been presented.[39]

Indeed, we have been inundated with calls to discuss controversial issues in recent years. It is an approach that is reflected in studies of best practice in social studies education, and an approach that I generally endorse and have even called for in a recent national citizenship education report.[40] However, what I want to suggest here is that pragmatist inquiry may be a better way to approach controversial issues like divisive concepts, especially when viewed through a lens that values the role of truth and honesty in democracy. Inquiry may achieve the benefits of discussion while avoiding some of the shortcomings. It may offer other educative experiences and outcomes, including the ability to determine truth and nurture habits of honesty. So, rather than responding to bans on teaching divisive concepts with a call to discussion, I respond with a call to inquiry.

Inquiry in the Classroom

So, what would a call to inquiry, as opposed to discussion, look like when it comes to divisive concepts? I will present just a brief sketch here—an overview that matches the process of inquiry described in Chapter 3 regarding matters of truth and honesty. The process is similar because engaging in civic reasoning and dialogue about controversial issues and divisive concepts is a matter of determining the truth about those phenomena and then treating them honestly. We need accurate, sincere, and forthright accounts in order to make sense of and respond to those phenomena.

Inquiry is a conjoint undertaking and is based in a community setting where students work together, drawing upon their shared experiences and relationships. To foster high-quality inquiry, teachers must first work to establish a sense of community connectedness and personal relationships between students in the class. This sort of environment can help sustain conversation when it faces moments of tension or conflict. And it can help humanize political divides by enabling students to see that their classmates may be on "the other side" and yet still be kind, pleasant, smart, and funny people. Relationships and care for each other may also be needed to head off the potential for inquiry to be experienced as an attack when it comes to matters of personal identity, where classmates recognize the potential for hurt and work to support each other. Establishing such a climate of care goes beyond the scope of this book but is an essential starting point for the approach outlined here.

Inquiry starts with real problems and uncertainties that students face. These might be moments of prejudice they encounter in their school, moments of doubt about their gender identity as they mature, moments of questioning Indigenous mascots representing their local team, or moments of confusion as students witness protests over police brutality against people of color. Typically, these are not problems that need to be artificially introduced in the classroom; rather, they arise on their own. On some occasions, students may fail to detect problems related to divisive concepts or to experience them as problems, especially if the situation serves them well. In these cases, teachers may need to help some students understand why a given problem is indeed a problem for themselves and/or others, and help them to see how students different from themselves may experience it as such. These problems should then be taken up carefully as matters worthy of reflection that prompt the gathering of related evidence and the seeking out of relevant experiences among a host of stakeholders. Students might share personal narratives about their own experiences with identity and discrimination or their desires for harmony and unity. They might search for the stories of their classmates or peers in other communities to determine differences and similarities in their experiences. Evidence can take multiple forms (scientific, political, artistic) and should be identified using multiple sources.

This phase of inquiry necessarily entails unearthing and including a diverse range of opinions on an issue and even possibly conflicting beliefs about it. This should be a slow, deliberate, and outward-oriented process, rather than a rush to assert one's own stance, as is too often the tendency in discussions about controversial issues. It entails discussion, which, Dewey says, "will bring out intellectual differences and opposed points of view and interpretations, so as to help define the true nature of the problem."[41] It is aimed at getting a rich and thorough understanding of the situation and the stakeholders.

Rather than inflaming identity politics or pitting identity groups against each other, as some legislators posit, Deweyan inquiry proposes a way to solve problems that begins with those experiencing them most directly as individuals. This sets up more of what Iris Marion Young would call "a politics of difference" that moves past the essentialism that the legislators abhor and moves toward the situated knowledge of particular individuals as well as the groups to which they may belong.

Inquiry is content-rich; it is not merely a skill. Historical and political knowledge is often required to make sense of indeterminate situations and propose solutions to move forward. Knowledge of what has been tried and accomplished in the past and historical consciousness can help students make wiser judgments for the future.[42] Skills of historical interpretation may be needed to distinguish facts from stories or myths and to reach conclusions based on evidence from multiple sources and the contextualization of texts.[43] These include identifying legitimate sources, attributing the source to an author contextualized historically, understanding that author's perspective, and corroborating the source to assess its reliability.[44] Again, key aspects of learning honesty and the process of truth determination play out in inquiry about divisive concepts.

During the next stage of inquiry in a classroom community, students might put forward potential ways to understand, confront, or eliminate identity-based struggles or injustices they encounter in their schools or lives. This could include developing language or locating terms that best describe their findings, including determining whether some of the banned concepts are a useful fit. Finally, they should test and assess those proposals to see if they bring about better ways of living together and as individuals. This evaluation phase foregrounds the shared fate of participants as they face together the benefits and risks of their hypotheses. Students thus arrive at truths that can be held tentatively, remaining open to falsifiability or new evidence. However, inquiry does not always produce new insight or lead to epistemic improvement.

Classroom inquiry about controversial issues engages honesty as a pragmatist habit insofar as it cultivates a proclivity to be forthright, sincere, and accurate regarding the truth. It urges students to consider the impact of divisive concepts on themselves and their fellow citizens, while seeking mutual well-being. In this way, recent uproar over the teaching of controversial issues in schools reveals the importance of being honest not only in how one approaches controversy but also in how one teaches students to understand and respond to it.

Benefits of Inquiry

Discussion is certainly a part of inquiry, especially when reflecting on the significance of a situation, one's personal experience of it, and potential approaches to improving it. But inquiry goes well beyond discussion, offering some additional perks and heading off some of the shortcomings of discussion. In a post-truth context, inquiry helps us to foreground the value of honesty as truth-seeking and truth-telling. Good inquiry demonstrates that honesty helps us get a fuller and more accurate account of problematic issues. If we foreground the pursuit of truth, inquiry is an apt process for determining what is true. It pushes us to investigate our world, empirical evidence, and the consequences of our beliefs more thoroughly than mere discussion does.

Whereas dominant forms of discussion often urge students to remain calm and rational, pragmatist inquiry attends to affect. It sees affect as a valuable source of information. Moreover, affect can prime some psychological conditions that lead to better engagement and learning. This includes feelings of frustration and moments of doubt, which help students appreciate why an issue is genuinely controversial as they sense its heft in their embodied responses to it.

Importantly, inquiry is a collaborative process—one that brings students together around a problem in a spirit of shared fate. In this regard, even as divisive concepts may give rise to contention between individual students or identity groups in the classroom, the process is undertaken as seeking to achieve and preserve wholeness. Inquiry doesn't pit one interpretation of a concept against another as merely right or wrong, good or bad, as a classroom discussion might or a classroom debate most certainly would. Neither does inquiry simply juxtapose the views of dueling political parties and their takes on divisive concepts. Rather, inquiry engages collective effort to sort out the issues.

Typical discussions frame controversial issues as either/or matters, presenting just two or some other small number of stances on an issue. This setup limits ways of thinking and ways of solving problems. Inquiry, though, invites alternative perspectives to be introduced, expanding options and encouraging more complex takes on the issue at hand. When issues are not raised directly as fodder for discussion but rather come about through indeterminate experiences that need to be resolved, the drive to make more informed and careful decisions pushes students past choosing among preformulated options and simplified perspectives. Unlike the rush to assert one's opinion in a classroom discussion, inquiry encourages students to remain open to new evidence as they construct and revise their position, including moments where they may be moved by others. Moreover, inquiry, unlike discussion, exposes the potential harms of choosing too quickly and of being intellectually arrogant.

Inquiry, with its close pragmatist connection to the empirical method and scientific fallibilism, assumes (and sometimes even reveals) that any of us can be wrong about our opening stance on an issue. It urges us to remain open to competing views and to the evidence gathered before reaching a conclusion about it. In this way, inquiry encourages intellectual humility and works against further entrenching polarized positions, as classroom debate tends to do.[45] When facilitated well, teachers can help students identify that it's okay to change one's mind, especially when the evidence indicates shortcomings in our views. Such a spirit of humility and self-criticality seems especially valuable right now given that our citizenry appears to have a range of ways of defining and experiencing divisive concepts. That is not to say that inquiry champions relativism about them, however, for decisions must be made. Hypotheses must be tested and assessed to determine their truth through how well they work to help us move forward and flourish. It is, however, a call to slow, informed, and careful exploration and judgment-making.

The best forms of classroom inquiry, much like the best forms of classroom discussion, encourage students to be open-minded and to listen to each other well. Inquiry entails learning not just to speak out when one disagrees with others but also how to listen to and respond to the disagreeing views uttered by classmates. But unlike discussion, inquiry intentionally opens spaces for minority views because they offer insight into problems and possible solutions. Inquiry foregrounds the democratic commitment to pluralism. Facilitated inquiry can also help students learn how to be responsive to and be moved by others, a conjoint experience of encountering and responding to a shared problem that may change the student in terms of their identity, the reasons they give regarding the problem, their position on the problem, or how they view other people impacted by the problem.[46] Inquiry can even lead to "civic epiphanies," where students can be surprised by each other and come to see the world, our shared problems, and the divisive concepts related to them in new ways.[47] For example, social studies scholars Nicole Mirra and Antero Garcia describe how they brought together students from different parts of the United States to share their experiences with guns. Perhaps some from rural areas used guns for hunting, some from suburban areas rarely even saw guns, and some from large cities witnessed gun violence regularly. Each may have stereotypes about and limited understandings of the others' experiences and beliefs. "As students heard about these different realities it helped shift students' own understandings of the issue and the legitimacy they accorded to political and policy perspectives that diverged from their own."[48] Students, then, can come to better understand "the other side" and to shape middle ground or more inclusive alternatives as a result. In inquiry, more so than discussion, students don't just learn how to live with disagreement but also figure out how to use it to arrive at better-informed solutions.

Relatedly, while discussion may reach moments of useful consensus or compromise, too often it doesn't offer an avenue for assessing or revising that agreement once the discussion ends. Inquiry builds in assessment and revision as key steps, recognizing that the process is always ongoing. Finally, participating in inquiry can help students see how knowledge is arrived at. This metacognitive aspect of inquiry is valuable because it helps students understand *how* they think and believe, not just *what* they think and believe.

These skills can help budding citizens better learn how to work across lines of division in society today. Inquiry offers opportunities to learn how to be political adversaries and disagree, yet reach better understandings and to guide their shared fate together. While not necessarily a goal held by all citizens or political groups today, inquiry builds relationships, and by doing so may help us work across our points of difference because those relationships help us to better understand others and perhaps even care about them, their needs, and their struggles. During classroom inquiries, teachers can encourage and support civility as a way of forming and sustaining relationships and communication across political and other divides. This foregrounding of relationships emphasizes that while new divisions and new divisive concepts may arise, we must continually come together in a spirit of wholeness to continue communicating about them. This relational civility is fostered in an environment that protects what Eamonn Callan calls "dignity safety," where students can participate without fear of being attacked or demeaned as people. Notice that this differs from "intellectual safety," which would shield ideas. Instead, dignity safety still allows for key ideas to be questioned or challenged. It focuses instead on the humanity and participation of all students.[49] Teachers can set norms that affirm this approach by emphasizing "challenging ideas, not people."

Whereas many proponents of divisive concept laws are concerned about potential indoctrination from teachers, inquiry is the best pedagogical rebuttal.[50] Indoctrination positions students passively, receiving dogma without question; inquiry is an active process that should largely be student-generated and student-led. While teachers facilitate inquiry and may help students by posing key questions, providing resources, and more, students are at the helm. This heads off the potential for substantial intentional and unintentional bias, deceit, or distortion on the part of teachers. Moreover, when inquiry is conducted with a critical, democratic spirit, it necessarily investigates bias, ideology, and other factors influencing problems and our understanding of them. Rather than foreclosing open issues or indoctrinating predetermined answers to them, inquiry explores questions and keeps the door open for returning to them for future revisions and keeps discourse open. It empowers students to take on this questioning role, even in their exchanges with teachers. As guides rather than experts on matters of divisive concepts, teachers can model ongoing learning and open-mindedness for students.

While the sort of inquiry I promote here is not activism, it may lead to action. As such, it may fall under the category of "action civics" when explicitly paired with citizenship education that encourages using the formal democratic system or informal processes like coalition-building to bring about change. Activism of the sort that concerns legislators and has led to bans on action civics is primarily charged with being politically partisan, emphasizing protest, and encouraging students to lobby for matters that arise from or serve the interests of teachers. Stanley Kurtz, in a piece that has influenced some conservatives, warns, "Action Civics, to the contrary, skips a step, moving uncritically to turn grievance and anger into protest and lobbying. Too often this has the effect of forestalling self-examination and dampening tolerance of alternative perspectives. Critical self-examination and thoughtful debate are easily avoided in the heat of collective political action."[51] While pragmatist inquiry may grow out of emotional turmoil and may lead to political action, the process I have outlined and advocate is slower, more careful, and more reflective than the picture of rash action Kurtz paints.

Instead, inquiry raises hypotheses about how to understand and act upon divisive concepts in ways that alleviate confusion and provide useful pathways forward for students and their communities. Pragmatist inquiry is less concerned with taking sides on a controversial issue or even amassing information about it than with figuring out how to live together, perhaps in spite of the divisive issue and perhaps in ways that bring an end to it. This may mean making small changes to the ways they live together with peers in the classroom or larger proposals for changing policies in their schools or neighborhoods. Importantly, the particular action is not defined in advance; rather, it arises from the solutions generated by the students in response to particular indeterminate situations. Additionally, the solutions posed by students may take on any political slant, regardless of the personal views of the teacher. Protest may be one tool for raising awareness about the issue and potential solutions to it, but it is not the only or preferred approach. In these ways, while it can be aligned with action civics, inquiry actually prevents many of the problems lawmakers fear.

Finally, while inquiry into divisive concepts may be pertinent to an array of subject areas, it is most relevant to social studies classes, which are most overtly tasked with helping students understand society and engage in practices of citizenship. Notably in the U.S. context, the College, Career, and Civic Life (C3) Framework for Social Studies State Standards is an inquiry-based approach. Pragmatist inquiry is different, but it has many similarities to the four dimensions of inquiry outlined in the C3 Framework: "1 Developing questions and planning inquiries; 2 Applying disciplinary [civic, economic, geographical, or historical] concepts and tools; 3 Evaluating sources and using evidence; and 4 Communicating conclusions and taking informed action."[52] This suggests that there may be an opening in social studies classrooms for a more Deweyan take on inquiry, as it encompasses and goes beyond these four dimensions.

More recently, in 2021, the Educating for American Democracy Roadmap, developed by a large team of scholars and K–12 teachers, has reaffirmed the value of an inquiry-based approach to social studies in general, though it largely reasserts the call by the report "The Civic Mission of Schools" for discussion, debate, and deliberation about controversial issues in particular.[53] The Roadmap also asserts goals of civil disagreement and political friendship that are fostered within the inquiry approach outlined in this book. Co-authored by Allen, the Roadmap draws upon her earlier work on political friendship. Perhaps most interesting, the Roadmap proposes that, through "design challenges," classrooms take up many of the sorts of questions that underlie lawmakers' motivations for recent legislation, including concerns with alternative histories that emphasize the role of racism and a "more plural and therefore more accurate story of our history."[54] The Roadmap argues:

> Rather than thinking that it is possible to solve up front all the challenges of how to deliver effective history and civic education, we argue that the nation's community of educators—and indeed our students—should be brought into the work of experimentation and discussion necessary to build solutions.[55]

Thus, I follow suit in arguing that in a country torn over what divisive concepts mean, how they relate to the history of America, and how to teach about them, if at all, the proposed approach should be one that invites students and citizens to the table for inquiry and experimentation, rather than an outright ban.

Limitations to Inquiry

Throughout this book, I have described pragmatist inquiry at its best, yet there are certainly many classroom efforts at inquiry that fall far short of the depiction I've offered. Before closing, I want to touch on just some of the potential limitations of inquiry. Most notably, schools in the United States are increasingly segregated along lines of race, class, and even political ideology relative to the communities where they are located. This situation makes it increasingly hard for a genuine plurality of opinions and experiences on social and political issues to arise on their own. Teachers must be careful that their classrooms do not become a filter bubble or echo chamber for like-minded views to become compounded or even further polarized. McAvoy, Hess, and Kawashima-Ginsberg warn that teachers should "not reify the worst tendencies of the polarization within the walls of their classrooms by simply providing airtime to what will likely be to homogenous views. Quite the opposite, they should purposely and explicitly create a curriculum and use pedagogies that expose their students to cross-cutting views."[56]

Teachers may have to introduce additional perspectives. They might begin by tasking the students themselves with doing so through an activity called "True for Who?" from Harvard's Project Zero. This activity entails brainstorming multiple different points of view that one might hold about a claim, then imagining the stance a person from that viewpoint might take. This can be a challenging technique because sometimes students fall prey to stereotyping or using faulty or limited information to imagine other perspectives, but there is value in helping students develop the proclivity to imagine and consider other perspectives. A teacher might complement or replace such an activity by providing narrative accounts, polling data, and interviews so that students have a fuller and more accurate picture of the issue. When doing so, teachers must also uphold honesty by being cautious not to provide limited or biased accounts that might distort the investigation or bias the findings of students. Notably, while filter bubbles can more easily be burst by exposure to counter-evidence, echo chambers are harder to break down because they work to render all of those who hold differing views as untrustworthy. Simply exposing those within an echo chamber to competing views may not be enough to overcome their distrust. One approach, which is admittedly difficult to deliver in classrooms, is to engage students in building relationships, and thereby trust, with someone who has a very different identity or experiences. A particularly noteworthy example is Derek Black, a former neo-Nazi, who broke out of his echo chamber, in part, by befriending a Jewish man in college.

Inquiry also does not escape the forms of dominance that are seen in classroom discussions, where some members dominate, especially those who tend to speak from or use the rational and linguistic approaches of educated white masculinity.[57] Teachers must work to detect and right these imbalances, in part by foregrounding relationships, civility as a call to ongoing communication, and political friendship. Balances of power and perspective are also exacerbated by increasing polarization, with the political views of some cit-izens moving farther toward the extremes. This can create challenging class-room dynamics where extremist positions may increasingly be endorsed. Often, good inquiry will reveal these perspectives for what they are, but teachers may have to play a more active role in helping students identify them as such.

Teachers must also be prepared to attend to media influences and an array of emotional and psychological phenomena that distort inquiry, such as motivated reasoning, filter bubbles, echo chambers, confirmation bias, and backfire effect—influences that limit exposure to alternative accounts and encourage doubling down on one's original stance or that of one's polit-ical tribe.[58] Developing skills of critical media literacy, especially regarding the finding and evaluation of evidence, will be key, yet far too few teachers have received training in these aspects of psychology and media.[59] Moreover, carving out space for inquiry within the school day will be challenging when social studies is rarely tested and has increasingly been cut from school time and budgets, largely in order to focus on math and literacy.[60] STEM initiatives do offer some helpful tools for discerning truth through learning about the scientific method, the design process, measurement, and the like. But we must avoid the trap of thinking that STEM is politically "safer" and offers clear right or wrong answers. Relatedly, more classroom time must be saved for human-ities and social science learning that is deeply nuanced and narrative in struc-ture. Such learning can help students better navigate gray spaces where right and wrong are not clear, whether that be in science, politics, or more.[61]

Inquiry offers wonderful opportunities for deep dives into particular con-tent and situations, often drawing upon interdisciplinary approaches to un-derstanding and addressing them. It also models how to engage in similar investigations and experimentations in the future, thereby showing students how to continue to learn and engage when novel situations arise in the future. It does not, however, move quickly, enabling teachers to cover a breadth of material or long lists of standards. Inquiry takes considerable time and focus, a privilege available in too few classrooms today, even if it proves to have a lasting impact on the habits of graduates to be honest and engage in civic rea-soning well.

Inquiry requires time, money, and clarity as a pedagogical approach. Preparing teachers to guide inquiry would require substantial training to un-derstand what pragmatist inquiry is and how it is invoked as a pedagogical practice that goes beyond the sketch I have offered here. Teachers must learn how to overcome tendencies to be teacher-focused, shifting their role to-ward facilitation and empowering students to lead. They must be aware of the age-appropriate expectations of what students can handle, while being willing to scaffold and challenge students to take up the difficult tasks of citizenship.

Similarly, classroom inquiry into divisive concepts must be undertaken with careful teacher oversight, drawing upon knowledge of the proclivities, strengths, and weaknesses of the students. While inquiry can be undertaken with students of any age, taking up divisive concepts in thorough ways may best be reserved for older students (those in high school or college) who have more sophisticated moral and reasoning skills as well as broader real-world knowledge to help them traverse this contentious terrain.

Inquiry, Honesty, and Controversial Issues in Schools

Inquiry is a way of *doing* democracy. Matters of diversity and equity are already present in students' lives both in and outside schools. Engaging in inquiry into them enables students to take up and shape pressing issues in their communities. In this way, learning to engage in inquiry is more effective at preparing and presently engaging citizens than merely talking about democracy or future citizenship in a traditional civics course or even discussing controversial issues. Inquiry enables students to actually interact with and impact the world around them in more tangible and significant ways than mere discussion provides.

Inquiry better prepares citizens for the messy world of democracy outside school walls—one where citizens are increasingly divided. Engaging in inquiry can help students learn how to work across those divisions, arriving at better understandings of contentious issues, developing better-justified stances based on evidence and multiple perspectives, and crafting stronger solutions to shared problems, including how we understand and define terms related to identity and justice. Democracy thrives when citizens, even those young enough to still be in school, wrestle with open controversies and solve public problems about them, including how to understand race and gender, and how to alleviate racism and sexism. Rather than banning divisive concepts from our schools, let's encourage classrooms to inquire into them honestly.

Conclusion

Throughout this book, I have described some current problems in democracies that relate to matters of honesty. I have clarified how honesty is connected to truth and contributes to a vibrant democracy. I have defined honesty as a habit, a proclivity to be forthright, sincere, and accurate in seeking and telling the truth, where truth is understood as "what works" to enable growth and flourishing. Those who think and behave honestly work in good faith to sort out truth and thereby secure well-being for themselves and their fellow citizens. I have recommended inquiry-based approaches to cultivate habits of honesty. I have couched these recommendations for improved citizenship education within a pragmatist account of truth and social democracy. I offer this new pragmatist framework in order to suggest potential pathways for improved citizenship education that go beyond the content focus of traditional civics and fill gaps in more recent national and international proposals that presume honest and trustworthy behavior.[62]

Populism, as a response to liberal democracy and its shortcomings, pushes us to reconsider the way truth is understood and taught in traditional citizenship education. Populists employ truth not as an objective or common good but as a tool for aligning the people against the elite. Truth is constructed from the real-life experiences of the people, which populists believe have been undervalued by elite academics and institutions of democracy. Sensing that liberal democracy has not fulfilled some of its promises, populists push for democracy to better reflect the will and needs of the people. While I have not endorsed populism here, I have taken up aspects of the spirit of populism to provide a different way to address populist concerns, one that may renew democratic living. In particular, I have expanded upon the spirit of political dissent underlying populism and provided a more sophisticated account of how good dissent works. I turned to recent examples of dissent to showcase how good dissent requires learning to be honest and to value truth.

By turning to pragmatist accounts of truth, inquiry, and social democracy, I have offered a better way to widen participation and keep democracy accountable to the experiences and values of the people, while also heading off problematic populist tendencies that divide citizens, ignore insights from experts, and diminish the role of verifying truth. As a result, students today need to learn about populism, including how to understand it as a vague and thin ideology that works performatively and through discourse. But more importantly, they need to learn how to engage with it by taking up some of the real challenges it poses in their communities today.

Citizenship education that overtly talks about how truth operates and demonstrates how inquiry can be used to determine "what works" better prepares students for the flawed democracy we see at play today and provides pathways for improving it in the future. Our ability to answer the key civic question "What should we do?" relies upon our ability to engage in civic reasoning, gather information, deliberate among courses of action, and test out potential solutions. The likelihood with which we will arrive at answers that support the growth and flourishing of our citizenry depends on our disposition to honestly determine and share the truth.

Notes

1. "Trump Gives Remarks at White House History Conference at National Archives Museum in DC," *PBS NewsHour*, September 17, 2020, https://www.youtube.com/watch?v=Pd9j Q2KY4fs.
2. Corey Turner, "School Principals Say Culture Wars Made Last Year 'Rough as Hell,'" NPR, last modified December 1, 2022, https://www.npr.org/2022/12/01/1139685828/schools-democracy-misinformation-purple-state.
3. Sarah Schwartz, "Map: Where Critical Race Theory Is Under Attack," *Education Week*, last modified February 3, 2023, https://www.edweek.org/policy-politics/map-where-criti cal-race-theory-is-under-attack/2021/06; Adrian Florido, "Teachers Say Laws Banning Critical Race Theory Are Putting a Chill on Their Lessons," NPR, last modified May 28, 2021, https://www.npr.org/2021/05/28/1000537206/teachers-laws-banning-critical-race-theory-are-leading-to-self-censorship; Brooke LePage, "These Are the States That Passed Laws Restricting the Teaching of Racial History," The 74, last modified September 3, 2021, https://www.the74million.org/article/these-are-the-states-that-passed-laws-restricting-the-teaching-of-racial-history/.
4. In some cases, the banned concepts are topics and in other cases they are issues. Wayne Journell distinguishes these and their educational implications well. "This distinction natters because topics and issues are often conflated. Take, for example, the issue of police violence against African Americans. . . . At the heart of this issue is race, specifically how Americans of a certain race are perceived and treated unfairly by police in the United States. Race, however, is not an issue unto itself; race is a topic. It is impossible to separate the topic of race from the issue of whether police are disproportionately using violence against a certain demographic of the population based on the color of their skin. It is important, however, for teachers to be able to distinguish between topics and issues for the purposes of leading discussions. Without the distinction, students may choose to focus on the topic and not the issue, which ultimately is not productive. One cannot rationally deliberate a topic; therefore, the focus should be on the issue with related topics used as a context for better understanding nuances of that issue." *Teaching Social Studies in an Era of Divisiveness: The Challenges of Discussing Social Issues in a Non-Partisan Way* (Lanham, MD: Rowman & Littlefield, 2016), 3.
5. "Regards Promotion, Teaching—Divisive, Inherently Racist Concepts," Ohio HB 616, 134th General Assembly (2021).
6. Richard Delgado and Jean Stefancic, *Critical Race Theory: An Introduction* (New York: New York University Press, 2012); Nicole Hannah-Jones, "The 1619 Project," *New York Times*, last modified September 4, 2019, https://www.nytimes.com/interactive/2019/08/14/magazine/1619-america-slavery.html.
7. "Discussing Controversial Topics in the Classroom," New Jersey Education Association, last modified February 28, 2021, https://www.njea.org/discussing-controversial-topics-in-the-classroom/#:~:text=Whenever%20a%20controversial%20topic%20is,appropriat

ely%20while%20respecting%20other%20ideas; Judith L. Pace and Wayne Journell, "Why Controversial Issues Must Still Be Taught in U.S. Classrooms," EdSource, last modified November 2, 2021, https://edsource.org/2021/why-controversial-issues-must-still-be-tau ght-in-u-s-classrooms/663103; "Hearing the Other Side of the Story," Teachers College Newsroom, last modified 2021, https://www.tc.columbia.edu/articles/2021/march/a-new-webinar-series-on-teaching-controversial-topics/.

8. I worry deeply that this "setting aside" of concepts such as racism conveys that I don't believe they are of significant importance to our citizens or to education. That is not the case and I hope my argument here will not be misconstrued in that way. I simply am trying to direct attention to the less emphasized role of learning about divisiveness and offering a way that we might better take up divisive concepts through inquiry.

9. H. James Garrett, Avner Segall, and Margaret S. Crocco, "Accommodating Emotion and Affect in Political Discussions in Classrooms," *The Social Studies* 111, no. 6 (2020): 320.

10. I want to be careful here also, for I am not meaning to convey that I agree with the concerns raised by policymakers who have authored these bills or even to suggest that we should adapt teaching practices to generally attend to the concerns they raise.

11. Anthony Izaguirre, "Florida Blocks High School African American Studies Class," Associated Press, last modified January 19, 2023, https://apnews.com/article/ron-desantis-florida-race-and-ethnicity-education-353417231de0a790c8e290479a5e52b8.

12. Giulia Heyward, "Critics Say Florida Aims to Rewrite History by Rejecting African American Studies," NPR, last modified January 27, 2023, https://www.npr.org/2023/ 01/27/1151725129/florida-advanced-placement-african-american-studies-backlash. Florida governor Ron DeSantis posted a tweet where he spoke about banning AP African American studies courses: Ron DeSantis (@GovRonDeSantis), "Education is about the pursuit of truth, not the imposition of ideology or the advancement of a political agenda," Twitter, January 23, 2023, https://twitter.com/GovRonDeSantis/status/161756444561 7553408.

13. "Relating to Education—Curriculum," Rhode Island HB 6070 (2021): Sec.1.a.10.i.

14. "Act Providing for Requirements Related to Racism or Sexism Trainings at, and Diversity and Inclusion Efforts by, Governmental Agencies and Entities, School Districts, and Public Postsecondary Educational Institutions," Iowa H.F. 802 (2021): Sec 2.1.a.8, https:// www.legis.iowa.gov/legislation/BillBook?ba=HF802&ga=89; "Prohibiting Public School Districts and Charter Schools from Teaching Certain Divisive Concepts," Oklahoma S.B. 803, 58th Legislature (2021): Sec.1.A.1.h, http://www.oklegislature.gov/BillInfo.aspx?Bill= sb803&Session=1900.

15. "Prohibit Teaching, Advocating, or Promoting Divisive Concepts," Ohio H.B. 327, 134th General Assembly (2021): Sec.3313.6027.A.1.b, A.3, https://www.legislature.ohio.gov/legi slation/134/hb327.

16. Joint Hearing on Education, Wisconsin State Assembly, 105th Wisconsin Legislature (2012) (statement of Chuck Wichgers, Wisconsin state representative of the 83rd Assembly District), https://docs.legis.wisconsin.gov/misc/lc/hearing_testimony_and_materials/2021/ ab411/ab0411_2021_08_11.pdf?fbclid=IwAR1-oDXiEI5wDyh4qA12HzVfajJh7aSpqGREF I5Cys4amg5Vc1OA-XMLXpg.

17. Ohio H.B. 327.

18. "Regards the Teaching of Certain Current Events, Race, and Sex," Ohio H.B. 322, 134th General Assembly (2021): Sec. 3313.6027.B.3, https://ohiohouse.gov/legislation/134/ hb322.

19. "The Civics Alliance: Open Letter and Curriculum Statement," National Association of Scholars, last modified March 22, 2021, https://www.nas.org/blogs/article/the-civics-allia nce-open-letter-and-curriculum-statement.

20. State and Local Government Committee Hearing, Ohio General Assembly, 134th General Assembly (2021) (sponsor testimony of Diane Grendell, state representative of Ohio's 76th House District), https://www.legislature.ohio.gov/legislation/134/hb327/committee.

21. Robin Barrow and Ronald Woods, *An Introduction to Philosophy of Education*, 5th ed. (New York: Routledge, 2022).

22. Ohio House State and Local Government Committee, Ohio General Assembly, 134th General Assembly (2021) (sponsor testimony of Don Jones, Ohio state representative for the 95th District).

23. Sponsor testimony of Don Jones.

24. Peter Greene, "The Conversation About Critical Race Theory in Schools Is Over," *Forbes*, last modified November 5, 2021, https://www.forbes.com/sites/petergreene/2021/11/05/ the-conversation-about-critical-race-theory-in-schools-is-over/?sh=7a087a66f049; Peter Greene, "Oklahoma and Florida Consider a More Aggressive Approach to Teacher Gag Laws," *Forbes*, last modified December 29, 2021, https://www.forbes.com/sites/petergre ene/2021/12/29/oklahoma-and-florida-consider-a-new-approach-to-teacher-gag-laws/ ?sh=79d297b3513f; Peter Greene, "Arizona GOP Hopes to Clamp Down on Teachers," *Forbes*, last modified May 6, 2021, https://www.forbes.com/sites/petergreene/2021/05/06/ arizona-gop-hopes-to-clamp-down-on-teachers/?sh=4763624c5aca; Peter Greene, "New Hampshire and Moms for Liberty Put Bounty on Teachers' Heads," *Forbes*, last modified November 12, 2021, https://www.forbes.com/sites/petergreene/2021/11/12/new-hampsh ire-and-moms-for-liberty-put-bounty-on-teachers-heads/?sh=69d46439a4bf.

25. Greene, "The Conversation About Critical Race Theory in Schools Is Over"; Greene, "Oklahoma and Florida Consider a More Aggressive Approach to Teacher Gag Laws"; Greene, "Arizona GOP Hopes to Clamp Down on Teachers"; Greene, "New Hampshire and Moms for Liberty Put Bounty on Teachers' Heads."

26. Diana Hess, *Controversy in the Classroom: The Democratic Power of Discussion* (New York: Routledge, 2009).

27. I'm not saying that all concepts listed in divisive concept legislation are open issues. This list is long, and some things on it may more appropriately be understood as settled.

28. Statement of Chuck Wichgers.

29. I draw here on a distinction that is common in the literature on controversial discussions in classrooms, most notably shaped by Diana Hess and Paula McAvoy. I recognize, however, that the depth of recent contestation over matters such as the 2020 U.S. election suggests that the distinction itself may be problematic or even no longer fully valid or useful. Perhaps part of what inquiry does is to expose that the distinction is not easily drawn, and yet inquiry also provides us a way for working through and even past it.

30. Again, I'm giving a more generous read here to the motivations behind some policymakers and backers of divisive concept legislation.

31. Veli-Mikko Kauppi and Johannes Drerup, "Discussion and Inquiry: A Deweyan Perspective on Teaching Controversial Issues," *Theory and Research in Education* 19, no. 3 (2021): 213–234, https://doi-org.uc.idm.oclc.org/10.1177/147787852110521.

32. Diana Hess and Paula McAvoy, *The Political Classroom: Evidence and Ethics in Democratic Education* (New York: Routledge, 2014); Emil Saetra, "Discussing Controversial Issues in

the Classroom: Elements of Good Practice," *Scandinavian Journal of Education Research* 65, no. 2 (2021): 345–357, https://doi-org.uc.idm.oclc.org/10.1080/00313831.2019.1705897.

33. Kei Kawashima-Ginsberg, "Do Discussion, Debate, and Simulations Boost NAEP Civics Performance?," Center for Information and Research on Civic Learning and Engagement, April 2013, https://circle.tufts.edu/sites/default/files/2020-01/discussion_debate_naep_2 013.pdf.

34. Michael Hand, "What Should We Teach as Controversial? A Defense of the Epistemic Criterion," *Education Theory* 58, no. 2 (2008): 213–228; Meira Levinson and Jacob Fay, *Democratic Discord in Schools* (Cambridge, MA: Harvard University Press, 2019); John Tillson, "When to Teach for Belief: A Tempered Defense of the Epistemic Criterion," *Educational Theory* 67, no. 2 (2017): 173–191, https://doi-org.uc.idm.oclc.org/10.1111/ edth.12241; Bryan Warnick and D. Spencer Smith, "The Controversy over Controversies: A Plea for Flexibility and for 'Soft-Directive' Teaching," *Educational Theory* 64, no. 3 (2014): 227–244, https://doi-org.uc.idm.oclc.org/10.1111/edth.12059; Jonathan Zimmerman and Emily Robertson, *The Case for Contention* (Chicago: University of Chicago Press, 2017).

35. Dana Goldstein, "Two States. Eight Textbooks. Two American Stories," *New York Times*, January 12, 2020, https://www.nytimes.com/interactive/2020/01/12/us/texas-vs-califor nia-history-textbooks.html.

36. I borrow this example from Barrett Smith and Sarah M. Stitzlein, "Classroom Conflict, 'Divisive Concepts,' and Educating for Democracy," in *Who's Afraid of Political Education: The Challenge to Teach Civic Competence and Democratic Participation*, ed. Henry Tam (Bristol, UK: Bristol University Press, 2023), 43.

37. To be clear, it is okay for some discussions to get heated and for emotions to play out in the classroom. My point here is only about how those instances may exacerbate problems of polarization and division. See my discussion of the value of emotions in civic reasoning in "Defining and Implementing Civic Reasoning and Discourse: Philosophical and Moral Foundations for Research and Practice," in *Educating for Civic Reasoning and Discourse*, ed. Carol D. Lee, Gregory White, and Dian Dong (Washington, DC: National Academy of Education, 2021), 23–52.

38. Paula McAvoy and G. E. McAvoy, "Can Debate and Deliberation Reduce Partisan Divisions? Evidence from a Study of High School Students," *Peabody Journal of Education* 96, no. 3 (2021): 275–284; David Schkade, Cass R. Sunstein, and Reid Hastie, "When Deliberation Produces Extremism," *Critical Review* 22, nos. 2–3 (2010): 227–252.

39. Kauppi and Drerup, "Discussion and Inquiry," 220.

40. Hess, *Controversy in the Classroom*; Hess and McAvoy, *The Political Classroom*; Zimmerman and Robertson, *The Case for Contention*; Stitzlein, "Defining and Implementing Civic Reasoning and Discourse."

41. John Dewey, "How We Think," in *John Dewey: The Later Works, 1925–1953*, ed. Jo Ann Boydston (Carbondale: Southern Illinois University Press, 2008), 8:329–330.

42. Anna Clark and Maria Grever, "Historical Consciousness: Conceptualizations and Educational Applications," in *The Wiley International Handbook of History Teaching and Learning*, ed. Scott Alan Metzger and Lauren McArthur Harris (Hoboken, NJ: Wiley-Blackwell, 2018), 177–120, https://doi-org.uc.idm.oclc.org/10.1002/9781119100812.ch7.

43. Keith Barton and Linda S. Levstik, "Why Don't More History Teachers Engage Students in Interpretation?," in *Social Studies Today: Research and Practice*, 2nd ed., ed. Walter C. Parker (New York: Routledge, 2015), 35–42; Chauncey Monte-Sano and Abby Reisman,

"Studying Historical Understanding," in *Handbook of Educational Psychology*, 3rd ed., ed. Lyn Corno and Eric M. Anderman (New York: Routledge, 2015), 281–294; Abby Reisman, "Reading Like a Historian: A Document-Based History Curriculum Intervention in Urban High Schools," *Cognition and Instruction* 30, no. 1 (2012): 86–112; Bruce VanSledright, "What Does It Mean to Think Historically . . . and How Do You Teach It?," in *Social Studies Today: Research and Practice*, 2nd ed., ed. Walter C. Parker (New York: Routledge, 2015), 138–146; Samuel S. Wineburg, *Historical Thinking and Other Unusual Acts: Charting the Future of Teaching the Past* (Philadelphia: Temple University Press, 2002).

44. VanSledright, "What Does It Mean to Think Historically."

45. McAvoy and McAvoy, "Can Debate and Deliberation Reduce Partisan Divisions?"

46. Bryan Warnick, Douglas Yacek, and Shannon Robinson, "Learning to Be Moved: The Modes of Democratic Responsiveness," *Philosophical Inquiry in Education* 25, no. 1 (2018): 31–46.

47. Douglas Yacek, "Should Anger Be Encouraged in the Classroom? Political Education, Closed-Mindedness, and Civic Epiphany," *Educational Theory* 69, no. 4 (2019): 421–437, https://doi-org.uc.idm.oclc.org/10.1111/edth.12378.

48. Study by Mirra and Garcia as cited in Joseph Kahne and Carlos E. Cortes, "Free Speech: Time for a Different Kind of Discussion," *Social Studies*, 87, no. 1 (2023): 17–18.

49. Eamonn Callan, "Education in Safe and Unsafe Spaces," *Philosophical Inquiry in Education* 24, no. 1 (2016): 64–78.

50. Judith Butler makes a similar case for how to best head off allegations of indoctrination by using critical inquiry in "A Dissenting View from the Humanities on the AAUP's Statement on Knowledge," AAUP, last modified spring 2020, https://www.aaup.org/article/dissenting-view-humanities-aaup%E2%80%99s-statement-knowledge.

51. Stanley Kurtz, "'Action Civics' Replaces Citizenship with Partisanship," The American Mind, last modified January 26, 2021, https://americanmind.org/memo/action-civics-replaces-citizenship-with-partisanship/.

52. Kathy Swan et al., *College, Career, and Civic Life (C3) Social Studies State Standards* (Silver Spring, MD: National Council for the Social Studies, 2013), https://www.socialstudies.org/standards/c3, 12.

53. Educating for American Democracy, *Educating for American Democracy: Excellence in History and Civics for All Learners* (n.p.: iCivics, 2021), 31.

54. Educating for American Democracy, *Educating for American Democracy*, 17.

55. Educating for American Democracy, *Educating for American Democracy*, 17.

56. Paula McAvoy, Diana Hess, and Kei Kawashima-Ginsberg, "The Pedagogical Challenge of Teaching Politics in Like-Minded Schools," in *Crosscultural Case Studies of Teaching Controversial Issues: Pathways and Challenges to Democratic Citizenship Education*, ed. Thomas Misco and Jan De Groof (Oisterwijk, Netherlands: Wolf, 2014), 253.

57. Iris M. Young, "Activist Challenges to Deliberative Democracy," *Political Theory* 29, no. 5 (2001): 670–690.

58. H. J. Garrett, "Why Does Fake News Work? On the Psychosocial Dynamics of Learning, Belief, and Citizenship," in *Unpacking Fake News: An Educator's Guide to Navigating the Media with Students*, ed. Wayne Journell (New York: Teachers College Press, 2019), 15–29; Patrick W. Kraft, Milton Lodge, and Charles S. Taber, "Why People 'Don't Trust the Evidence': Motivated Reasoning and Scientific Beliefs," *Annals of the American Academy of Political and Social Science* 658, no. 1 (2015): 121–133.

59. The work on critical media literacy coming out of the Stanford History Education Group is especially promising. See, for example, Sarah McGrew, Teresa Ortega, Joel Breakstone, and Sam Wineburg, "The Challenge That's Bigger than Fake News: Civic Reasoning in a Social Media Environment," *American Educator* 41, no. 3 (2017): 4–9.

60. Educating for American Democracy, *Educating for American Democracy*, 19; Erica Hodgin and Joseph Kahne, "Judging Credibility in Un-credible times: Three Educational Approaches for the Digital Age," in *Unpacking Fake News: An Educator's Guide to Navigating the Media with Students*, ed. Wayne Journell (New York: Teachers College Press, 2019), 92–108.

61. I thank Danny Foster for pointing this out to me.

62. This includes addressing assumptions of honesty within reports I authored for the National Academy of Education and UNESCO: Sarah M. Stitzlein, "Using Civic Participation and Civic Reasoning to Shape Our Future and Education," United Nations Educational, Scientific, and Cultural Organization Educational Futures, part of the International Commission on the Futures of Education chaired by the President of Ethiopia, 2020.

Bibliography

Abadi, Mark. "One of Trump's Favorite Phrases was Named the 2017 Word of the Year." *Business Insider*, January 8, 2018. https://www.businessinsider.com/word-of-the-year-2017-fake-news-2018-1.

Abowitz, Kathleen Knight. "Populism, legitimidad y escolarización estatal." *Teoría de la Educación: Revista Interuniversitaria* 35, no. 2 (2023): 37–55.

Adams, Paul. "Populism: A Possible Future for Democratic Education?" Presentation, International Network of Philosophers of Education, Copenhagen, Denmark, August 19, 2022.

Algoe, S., and Jonathan Haidt. "Witnessing Excellence in Action: The 'Other-Praising' Emotions of Elevation, Gratitude, and Admiration." *Journal of Positive Psychology* 4 (2009): 105–127.

Allen, Danielle S. *Talking to Strangers: Anxieties of Citizenship After* Brown v. Board of Education. Chicago: University of Chicago Press, 2004.

Allen, Ira. "The Hegelian Spirit of Jamesian Truth." In *New Perspectives on Realism*, edited by Luca Taddio, 31–58. Sesto San Giovanni, Italy: Mimesis International, 2017.

Anderson, James A. "Some Say Occupy Wall Street Did Nothing. It Changed Us More than We Think." *Time*, last modified November 15, 2021. https://time.com/6117696/occupy-wall-str eet-10-years-later/.

Austin, Sharon D. Wright. "Contemporary Black Populism and the Development of Multiracial Electoral Coalitions: The 2018 Stacey Abrams and Andrew Gillum Gubernatorial Campaigns." *Political Science Quarterly* 136, no. 3 (2021): 417–438.

Baehr, Jason. "Education for Intellectual Virtues: From Theory to Practice," in *Education and the Growth of Knowledge: Perspectives from Social and Virtue Epistemology*, edited by Ben Kotzee, 106–123. Malden, MA: Wiley, 2013. https://intellectualvirtues.org/guiding-princip les/core-practices/.

Baehr, Jason. "Intellectual Virtues and Truth, Understanding, and Wisdom." Unpublished draft, 2013. https://jasonbaehr.files.wordpress.com/2013/12/iv-and-tuw.pdf.

Baehr, Jason. *Deep in Thought: A Practical Guide to Teaching for Intellectual Virtues*. Cambridge, MA: Harvard Education Press, 2021.

Baehr, Jason. "Democracy, Information Technology, and Virtue Epistemology." In *Virtues, Democracy, and Online Media*, edited by Nancy Snow and Maria Silvia Vaccarrezza, 1–27. New York: Routledge, 2021.

Barrow, Robin, and Ronald Woods. *An Introduction to Philosophy of Education*, 5th ed. New York: Routledge, 2022.

Barton, Keith, and Linda S. Levstik. "Why Don't More History Teachers Engage Students in Interpretation?" In *Social Studies Today: Research and Practice*, 2nd ed., edited by Walter C. Parker, 35–42. New York: Routledge, 2015.

Barzilai, Sarit, and Clark A. Chinn. "A Review of Educational Responses to the 'Post-Truth' Condition: Four Lenses on 'Post-Truth' Problems." *Educational Psychologist* 55, no. 3 (2020): 107–119.

BBC News. "'Youthquake' Declared Word of the Year by Oxford Dictionaries." BBC, last modified December 15, 2017. https://www.bbc.com/news/uk-42361859.

Bellucci, Gabriele, and Soyoung Q. Park, "Honesty Biases Trustworthiness Impressions." *Journal of Experimental Psychology: General* 149, no. 8 (2020): 1567–1586.

Ben-Porath, Sigal. *Citizenship Under Fire: Democratic Education in Times of Conflict*. Princeton, NJ: Princeton University Press, 2006.

Bessant, Judith, and Analicia Mejia Mesinas, eds. *When Students Protest*. Lanham, MD: Rowman & Littlefield, 2021.

Bohman, James. "Democracy as Inquiry, Inquiry as Democratic: Pragmatism, Social Science, and the Cognitive Division of Labor." *American Journal of Political Science* 43, no. 2 (1999): 590–607.

Boler, Megan, and Elizabeth Davis. "The Affective Politics of the "Post-Truth" Era: Feeling Rules and Networked Subjectivity." *Emotion, Space and Society* 27 (2018): 75–85.

Brady, Henry E., and Thomas B. Kent. "Fifty Years of Declining Confidence and Increasing Polarization in Trust in American Institutions." *Daedalus* 151, no. 4 (2022): 43–66. https://doi.org/10.1162/daed_a_01943.

Brady, Jacqueline. "Introduction: Visions of New Student Activism." *Radical Teacher* 118 (2020): 1–7. https://doi.org/10.5195/rt.2020.868.

Brown, Etienne. "Civic Education in the Post-Truth Era: Intellectual Virtues and the Epistemic Threats of Social Media." In *Philosophical Perspectives on Moral and Civic Education: Shaping Citizens and Their Schools*, edited by Colin Macleod and Christine Tappolet, 45–67. New York: Routledge, 2019.

Brown, Matthew J. "The Concept of 'Situation' in John Dewey's Logic and Philosophy of Science." Presentation at the USCD History of Philosophy Roundtable, Winter 2017. https://www.matthewjbrown.net/professional/papers/situation-science.pdf.

Bump, Phillip. "Democrats Have Joined Republicans in Calling Their Opponents 'Enemies.'" *Washington Post*, August 1, 2022.

Butler, Judith. "A Dissenting View from the Humanities on the AAUP's Statement on Knowledge." AAUP, last modified spring 2020. https://www.aaup.org/article/dissenting-view-humanities-aaup%E2%80%99s-statement-knowledge.

Callan, Eamonn. "Education in Safe and Unsafe Spaces." *Philosophical Inquiry in Education* 24, no. 1 (2016): 64–78.

Carlson, Jim. "In-School Discussion About Activism Not Consistent, Research Shows." Penn State University, last modified June 21, 2021, https://www.psu.edu/news/research/story/school-discussion-about-activism-not-consistent-research-shows-0/.

Castro, Maria Martinez. "How Did the Watergate Scandal Popularize Conspiracy Theories?" *Curiosity Gaps* (blog), University of California, Davis, last modified June 3, 2022. https://www.ucdavis.edu/blog/curiosity/how-did-watergate-scandal-popularize-conspiracy-theories.

Center for Information and Research on Civic Learning and Engagement. "So Much for 'Slacktivism': Youth Translate Online Engagement to Offline Political Action." Tufts University, October 15, 2018. https://circle.tufts.edu/latest-research/so-much-slacktivism-youth-translate-online-engagement-offline-political-action.

Chen, Annie Y., Brendan Nyhan, Jason Reifler, Ronald E. Robertson, and Christo Wilson. "Exposure to Alternative and Extremist Content on YouTube." Anti-Defamation League, last modified May 3, 2022. https://www.adl.org/resources/report/exposure-alternative-extremist-content-youtube.

Cho, Alexander, Jasmine Byrne, and Zoe Pelter. "Digital Civic Engagement by Young People." UNICEF Office of Global Insight and Policy, February 2020.

Clark, Anna, and Maria Grever. "Historical Consciousness: Conceptualizations and Educational Applications." In *The Wiley International Handbook of History Teaching and Learning*, edited by Scott Alan Metzger and Lauren McArthur Harris, 177–220. Hoboken, NJ: Wiley-Blackwell, 2018. https://doi-org.uc.idm.oclc.org/10.1002/9781119100812.ch7.

"The Common Core State Standards: English Language Arts Standards—History/Social Studies." National Governors Association Center for Best Practices, Council of Chief State

School Officers, 2010. https://corestandards.org/wp-content/uploads/2023/09/ELA_Sta ndards1.pdf.

Culp, Julian. "Democratic Citizenship Education in Digitized Societies: A Habermasian Approach." *Educational Theory* 73, no. 2 (2023): 178–203.

Curato, Nicole, John S. Dryzek, Selen A. Ercan, Carolyn M. Hendriks, and Simon Niemeyer. "Twelve Key Findings in Deliberative Democracy Research." *Daedalus* 146, no. 3 (2017): 28–38.

Curren, Randall. "Populism and the Fate of Civic Friendship." In *Virtues in the Public Sphere*, edited by James Arthur, 92–107. Milton Park, UK: Routledge, 2018.

Damico, James S., and Mark C. Baildon. *How to Confront Climate Denial: Literacy, Social Studies, and Climate Change.* New York: Teachers College Press, 2022.

DeCesare, Tony. "The Lippmann-Dewey 'Debate' Revisited: The Problem of Knowledge and the Role of Experts in Modern Democratic Theory." *Philosophical Studies in Education* 43 (2012): 106–117.

DeCesare, Tony. "The Future Is Now: Rethinking the Role for Children in Democracy." *Philosophy of Education Society* 78, no. 3 (2022): 111–125.

Delgado, Richard, and Jean Stefancic. *Critical Race Theory: An Introduction.* New York: New York University Press, 2012.

Dennett, Daniel. "Postmodernism and Truth." In *Philosophy: The Quest for Truth*, 6th ed., edited by Louis Pojman, 233–239. Oxford: Oxford University Press, 2006.

DeSantis, Ron. *The Courage to Be Free.* New York: Broadside Books, 2023.

Dewey, John. "Creative Democracy: The Task Before Us." In *John Dewey: The Later Works, 1925–1953*, edited by Jo Ann Boydston, 14:224–230. Carbondale: Southern Illinois University Press, 2008.

Dewey, John. "Democracy and Education." In *John Dewey: The Middle Works, 1899–1924*, edited by Jo Ann Boydston, 9:282–283. Carbondale: Southern Illinois University Press, 2008.

Dewey, John. "Democracy Is Radical." In *John Dewey: The Later Works, 1925–1953*, edited by Jo Ann Boydston, 2:296–309. Carbondale: Southern Illinois University Press, 2008.

Dewey, John. "Education as Politics." In *John Dewey: The Middle Works, 1899–1924*, edited by Jo Ann Boydston, 13:329–344. Carbondale: Southern Illinois University Press.

Dewey, John. "How We Think." In *John Dewey: The Later Works, 1925–1953*, edited by Jo Ann Boydston, 8:329–330. Carbondale: Southern Illinois University Press, 2008.

Dewey, John. "Human Nature and Conduct." In *John Dewey: The Middle Works, 1899–1924*, edited by Jo Ann Boydston, 14:1–227. Carbondale: Southern Illinois University Press, 2008.

Dewey, John. "Logic: The Theory of Inquiry." In *John Dewey: The Later Works, 1925–1953*, edited by Jo Ann Boydston, 12:1–528. Carbondale: Southern Illinois University Press, 2008.

Dewey, John. "The Problem of Method." In *John Dewey: The Later Works, 1925–1953*, edited by Jo Ann Boydston, 2:365. Carbondale: Southern Illinois University Press, 2008.

Dewey, John. *The Public and Its Problems.* New York: Henry Holt, 1927.

Dewey, John. "The Quest for Certainty: A Study of the Relation of Knowledge to Action." In *John Dewey: The Later Works, 1925–1953*, edited by Jo Ann Boydston, 4:10–81. Carbondale: Southern Illinois University Press, 2008.

Dewey, John. *Reconstruction in Philosophy.* Boston, MA: Beacon Press, 1948.

Dewey, John. "Theory of Valuation." In *John Dewey: The Later Works, 1925–1953*, edited by Jo Ann Boydston, 4:189–252. Carbondale: Southern Illinois University Press, 2008.

Dishon, Gideon, and Sigal Ben-Porath, "Don't@ Me: Rethinking Digital Civility Online and in School." *Learning, Media and Technology* 43, no. 4 (2018): 434–450.

D'Olimpio, Laura. "Trust as a Virtue in Education." *Educational Philosophy and Theory* 50, no. 2 (2018): 193–202.

Douglas, Karen M., Joseph E. Uscinski, Robbie M. Sutton, Aleksandra Cichocka, Turkay Nefes, Chee Siang Ang, and Farzin Deravi, "Understanding Conspiracy Theories." *Political*

Psychology 40, no. S1 (2019): 3. https://onlinelibrary-wiley-com.uc.idm.oclc.org/doi/full/10.1111/pops.12568.

Dow, Philip E. "Developing Truth Seekers." In *Integrity, Honesty, and Truth Seeking*, edited by Christian B. Miller and Ryan West, 274–310. New York: Oxford University Press, 2020.

Dreisbach, Tom. "UCLA Student Charged in Capitol Riot Took Inspiration from Online Extremist." NPR, last modified March 15, 2021. https://www.npr.org/2021/03/15/971931742/ucla-student-charged-in-capitol-riot-took-inspiration-from-online-extremist.

Driver, Julia. "The Conflation of Moral and Epistemic Virtue." *Metaphilosophy* 34, no. 3 (2003): 367–383.

Educating for American Democracy. *Educating for American Democracy: Excellence in History and Civics for All Learners*. n.p.: iCivics, 2021. www.educatingforamericandemocracy.org.

Florido, Adrian. "Teachers Say Laws Banning Critical Race Theory Are Putting a Chill on Their Lessons." NPR, last modified May 28, 2021. https://www.npr.org/2021/05/28/1000537206/teachers-laws-banning-critical-race-theory-are-leading-to-self-censorship.

Frank, Thomas. *The People, No: A Brief History of Anti-Populism*. New York: Metropolitan Books, 2020.

Frankel, Tamar. *Trust and Honesty*. New York: Oxford University Press, 2006.

Frega, Roberto. *Pragmatism and the Wide View of Democracy*. Cham, Switzerland: Palgrave Macmillan, 2019.

Freking, Kevin. "Santos Steps Down from House Panels amid Ethics Issues." Associated Press, January 31, 2023. https://apnews.com/article/george-santos-congress-house-committees-6e46e2badad39fb190d38105a800236f.

Fritz, Janie Harden. "Honesty as Ethical Communicative Practice: A Framework for Analysis." In *Integrity, Honesty, and Truth Seeking*, edited by Christian B. Miller and Ryan West, 127–152. New York: Oxford University Press, 2020.

Fuerstein, Michael. "Epistemic Democracy Without Truth: The Deweyan Approach." *Raisons Politiques* 81, no. 1 (2021): 81–96.

Fuller, Steve. *Post-Truth: Knowledge as a Power Game*. Cambridge: Cambridge University Press, 2018.

Galston, William. *Anti-Pluralism: The Populist Threat to Liberal Democracy*. New Haven, CT: Yale University Press, 2018.

Galston, William. "Truth and Democracy: Theme and Variations." In *Truth and Democracy*, edited by Jeremy Elkins and Andrew Norris, 130–145. Philadelphia: University of Pennsylvania Press, 2012.

Garrett, H. James. "Why Does Fake News Work? On the Psychosocial Dynamics of Learning, Belief, and Citizenship." In *Unpacking Fake News: An Educator's Guide to Navigating the Media with Students*, edited by Wayne Journell, 15–29. New York: Teachers College Press, 2019.

Garrett, H. James, Avner Segall, and Margaret S. Crocco. "Accommodating Emotion and Affect in Political Discussions in Classrooms." *The Social Studies* 111, no. 6 (2020): 312–323.

Gawn, Glynis, and Robert Innes. "Do Lies Erode Trust?" *International Economic Review* 59, no. 1 (2018): 137–161.

Generation Citizen. "Democracy Doesn't Pause." Accessed February 8, 2023, https://www.generationcitizen.org/democracy-doesnt-pause/.

Gerlach, Philipp, Kinneret Teodorescu, and Ralph Hertwig. "The Truth About Lies: A Meta-Analysis of Dishonest Behavior." *Psychological Bulletin* 145, no. 1 (2019): 1–44.

Geurkink, Bram, Anrej Zaslove, Roderick Sluiter, and Kristof Jacobs. "Populist Attitudes, Political Trust, and External Political Efficacy: Old Wine in New Bottles?" *Political Studies* 68, no. 1 (2019): 250.

Gibson, Melissa. "From Deliberation to Counter-Narration: Toward a Critical Pedagogy for Democratic Citizenship." *Theory and Research in Social Education* 48, no. 3 (2020): 431–454.

Goldstein, Dana. "Two States. Eight Textbooks. Two American Stories." *New York Times*, January 12, 2020. https://www.nytimes.com/interactive/2020/01/12/us/texas-vs-california-history-textbooks.html.

Greene, Peter. "Arizona GOP Hopes to Clamp Down on Teachers." *Forbes*, last modified May 6, 2021. https://www.forbes.com/sites/petergreene/2021/05/06/arizona-gop-hopes-to-clamp-down-on-teachers/?sh=4763624c5aca.

Greene, Peter. "New Hampshire and Moms for Liberty Put Bounty on Teachers' Heads." *Forbes*, last modified November 12, 2021. https://www.forbes.com/sites/petergreene/2021/11/12/new-hampshire-and-moms-for-liberty-put-bounty-on-teachers-heads/?sh=69d46439a4bf.

Greene, Peter. "The Conversation About Critical Race Theory in Schools Is Over." *Forbes*, last modified November 5, 2021. https://www.forbes.com/sites/petergreene/2021/11/05/the-conversation-about-critical-race-theory-in-schools-is-over/?sh=7a087a66f049.

Greene, Peter. "Oklahoma and Florida Consider a More Aggressive Approach to Teacher Gag Laws." *Forbes*, last modified December 29, 2021. https://www.forbes.com/sites/petergreene/2021/12/29/oklahoma-and-florida-consider-a-new-approach-to-teacher-gag-laws/?sh=79d297b3513f.

Guerin, Emily. "Untangling Disinformation: She Was a Popular Yoga Guru. Then She Embraced QAnon Conspiracy Theories." NPR, last modified January 2, 2023. https://www.npr.org/2023/01/02/1146318331/yoga-guru-qanon-conspiracy-theories.

Hand, Michael. "What Should We Teach as Controversial? A Defense of the Epistemic Criterion." *Education Theory* 58, no. 2 (2008): 213–228.

Hannah-Jones, Nicole. "The 1619 Project." *New York Times*, last modified September 4, 2019. https://www.nytimes.com/interactive/2019/08/14/magazine/1619-america-slavery.html.

Hanson, Isabelle. "Illinois High School Students Will Learn Media Literacy Skills Next School Year." KFVS, last modified October 25, 2021. https://www.kfvs12.com/2021/10/25/illinois-high-school-students-will-learn-media-literacy-skills-next-school-year/.

Harris, Adam. "Conservative High Schoolers Want to 'Own the Libs.'" *The Atlantic*, last modified July 26, 2018. https://www.theatlantic.com/education/archive/2018/07/conservative-high-schoolers-are-ready-to-own-the-libs/566177/.

Heffer, Chris. *All Bullshit and Lies? Insincerity, Irresponsibility, and the Judgment of Untruthfulness.* New York: Oxford University Press, 2020.

Hess, Diana. *Controversy in the Classroom: The Democratic Power of Discussion.* New York: Routledge, 2009.

Hess, Diana, and Paula McAvoy. *The Political Classroom: Evidence and Ethics in Democratic Education.* New York: Routledge, 2014.

Heyward, Giulia. "Critics Say Florida Aims to Rewrite History by Rejecting African American Studies." NPR, last modified January 27, 2023. https://www.npr.org/2023/01/27/1151725129/florida-advanced-placement-african-american-studies-backlash.

Higley, John. "Elite Trust and the Populist Threat to Stable Democracy." *American Behavioral Scientist* 64, no. 9 (2020): 1211–1218.

Hodgin, Erica, and Joseph Kahne. "Judging Credibility in Un-credible Times: Three Educational Approaches for the Digital Age." In *Unpacking Fake News: An Educator's Guide to Navigating the Media with Students*, edited by Wayne Journell, 92–108. New York: Teachers College Press, 2019.

Horsthemke, Kai. "'#FactsMustFall'? Education in a Post-Truth, Post-Truthful World." *Ethics and Education* 12, no. 3 (2017): 273–288.

Ivie, Robert. "Democratic Dissent and the Trick of Rhetorical Critique." *Critical Methodologies* 5, no. 3 (2005): 276–293.

Ivie, Robert. "Enabling Democratic Dissent." *Quarterly Journal* 101, no. 1 (2015): 46–59.

Ivie, Robert. "A Democratic People's Dissent from War." *Javnost: The Public* 24, no. 3 (2017): 199–217.

Izaguirre, Anthony. "Florida Blocks High School African American Studies Class." Associated Press, last modified January 19, 2023. https://apnews.com/article/ron-desantis-florida-race-and-ethnicity-education-353417231de0a790c8e290479a5e52b8.

Jacobsen, Rebecca, Anne-Lise Halvorsen, Amanda Slaten Frasier, Adam Schmitt, Margaret Crocco, and Avner Segall. "Thinking Deeply, Thinking Emotionally: How High School Students Make Sense of Evidence." *Theory and Research in Social Education* 46, no. 2 (2018): 232–276.

James, William. "Lecture VI: Pragmatism's Conception of Truth." In *Pragmatism: A New Name for Some Old Ways of Thinking*. n.p.: Project Gutenberg, 2013 [1907].

James, William. *The Meaning of Truth.* Project Gutenberg, 2002. https://www.google.com/search?q=James%2C+William.+The+Meaning+of+Truth&oq=James%2C+William.+The+Meaning+of+Truth&gs_lcrp=EgZjaHJvbWUyBggAEEUYOTIICAEQABgWGB4yCAgCEAAYFhgeMggIAxAAGBYYHjINCAQQQABiGAxiABBiKBdIBBzY4NGowajmoAgCwAgE&sourceid=chrome&ie=UTF-8

Jones, Carolyn. "Media Literacy Would Be Required for California K-12 Students Under New Bill." EdSource, June 5, 2023. https://edsource.org/2023/media-literacy-would-be-required-for-all-california-students-under-new-bill/691667?.

Journell, Wayne, ed. *Teaching Social Studies in an Era of Divisiveness: The Challenges of Discussing Social Issues in a Non-Partisan Way.* Lanham, MD: Rowman & Littlefield, 2016.

Journell, Wayne, ed. *Unpacking Fake News: An Educator's Guide to Navigating the Media with Students.* New York: Teachers College Press, 2019.

Journell, Wayne, and Christopher H. Clark. "Political Memes and the Limits of Media Literacy." In *Unpacking Fake News: An Educator's Guide to Navigating the Media with Students*, edited by Wayne Journell, 109–125. New York: Teachers College Press, 2019.

Kahne, Joseph, Jacqueline Ullman, and Ellen Middaugh. "Digital Opportunities for Civic Education." In *Making Civics Count*, edited by David E. Campbell, Meira Levinson, and Frederick Hess, 207–228. Cambridge, MA: Harvard Education Press, 2012.

Kahne, Joseph, and Benjamin Bowyer, "Educating for Democracy in a Partisan Age: Confronting the Challenges of Motivated Reasoning and Misinformation." *American Educational Research Journal* 54, no. 1 (2016): 3–34.

Kakutani, Michiko. *The Death of Truth: Notes on Falsehood in the Age of Trump.* New York: Crown, 2018.

Kalpokas, Ignas. *A Political Theory of Post-Truth.* Cham, Switzerland: Palgrave Macmillan, 2019.

Kashdan, Todd. *The Art of Insubordination: How to Dissent and Defy Effectively.* New York: Avery, 2022.

Kauppi, Veli-Mikko, and Johannes Drerup. "Discussion and Inquiry: A Deweyan Perspective on Teaching Controversial Issues." *Theory and Research in Education* 19, no. 3 (2021): 213–234. https://doi-org.uc.idm.oclc.org/10.1177/147787852110521.

Kawashima-Ginsberg, Kei. "Do Discussion, Debate, and Simulations Boost NAEP Civics Performance?" Center for Information and Research on Civic Learning and Engagement, Tufts University, April 2013. https://circle.tufts.edu/sites/default/files/2020-01/discussion_debate_naep_2013.pdf.

Keegan, Patrick. "Critical Affective Civic Literacy: A Framework for Attending to Political Emotion in the Social Studies Classroom." *Journal of Social Studies Research* 45 (2021): 15–24.

Kingsberry, Janay. "Gen Z Is Influencing the Abortion Debate—from TikTok." *Washington Post*, last modified June 28, 2022. https://www.washingtonpost.com/nation/interactive/2022/gen-z-tiktok-abortion-debate/.

Koopman, Colin. *Pragmatism as Transition: Historicity and Hope in James, Dewey, and Rorty.* New York: Columbia University Press, 2009.

Kraft, Patrick W., Milton Lodge, and Charles S. Taber. "Why People 'Don't Trust the Evidence': Motivated Reasoning and Scientific Beliefs." *Annals of the American Academy of Political and Social Science* 658, no. 1 (2015): 121–133.

Kurtz, Stanley. "'Action Civics' Replaces Citizenship with Partisanship." *The American Mind*, last modified January 26, 2021. https://americanmind.org/memo/action-civics-replaces-citizenship-with-partisanship/.Laclau, Ernesto. *On Populist Reason*. New York: Verso, 2005.

Laden, Anthony Simon. *Reasoning: A Social Picture*. New York: Oxford University Press, 2012.

Laden, Anthony Simon. "Two Concepts of Civility." In *A Crisis of Civility? Political Discourse and Its Discontents*, edited by Robert G. Boatright, Timothy J. Shaffer, Sarah Sobieraj, and Dannagal Goldthwaite Young, 2–6. New York: Routledge, 2019.

Lapsley, Daniel, and Dominic Charloner. "Post-Truth and Science Identity: A Virtue-Based Approach to Science Education." *Educational Psychologist* 55, no. 3 (2020): 132–143.

LePage, Brooke. "These Are the States That Passed Laws Restricting the Teaching of Racial History." The 74, last modified September 3, 2021. https://www.the74million.org/article/these-are-the-states-that-passed-laws-restricting-the-teaching-of-racial-history/.

Levine, Peter. "Media Literacy for the 21st Century: A Response to the Need for Media Education in Democratic Education." *Democracy and Education* 23, no. 1 (2015): 1–3.

Levine, Peter. *What Should We Do? A Theory of Civic Life*. New York: Oxford University Press, 2022.

Levinson, Meira. *No Citizen Left Behind*. Cambridge, MA: Harvard University Press, 2012.

Levinson, Meira, and Jacob Fay. *Democratic Discord in Schools*. Cambridge, MA: Harvard University Press, 2019.

Lin, Cong, and Liz Jackson. "From Shared Fate to Shared Fates: An Approach for Civic Education." *Studies in Philosophy and Education* 38 (2019): 537–547.

Little, Olivia, and Abbie Richards. "TikTok's Algorithm Leads Users from Transphobic Videos to Far-Right Rabbit Holes." Media Matters, last modified October 5, 2021. https://www.mediamatters.org/tiktok/tiktoks-algorithm-leads-users-transphobic-videos-far-right-rabbit-holes#paragraph--section-heading--3421981.

Lovett, Frank. "Civic Virtue." In *The Encyclopedia of Political Thought*, edited by Mike Gibbons, 7–9. New York: Wiley, 2014.

Luckey, Eric. "Refining Dissent: Response to Sarah M. Stitzlein's 'Democratic Education in an Era of Town Hall Protests.'" *Theory and Research in Education* 20, no. 1 (2022): 119–124.

Lynch, Michael Patrick. "Teaching in the Time of Google." *Chronicle of Higher Education*, April 24, 2016. http://chronicle.com/article/Teaching-in-the-Time-of-Google/236180/.

Lynch, Michael Patrick. *Know-It-All Society: Truth and Arrogance in Political Culture*. New York: W. W. Norton, 2019.

Mann, Brian. "Santos Took Office One Month Ago and His New York District Says He's Got to Go." NPR, February 5, 2023. https://www.npr.org/2023/02/04/1153843337/george-santos-new-york-district.

Mårdh, Andreas, and Ásgeir Tryggvason. "Democratic Education in the Mode of Populism." *Studies in Philosophy and Education* 36, no. 6 (2017).

McAvoy, Paula, and Diana Hess. "Classroom Deliberation in an Era of Political Polarization." *Curriculum Inquiry* 53, no. 1 (2013): 14–47.

McAvoy, Paula, Diana Hess, and Kei Kawashima-Ginsberg. "The Pedagogical Challenge of Teaching Politics in Like-Minded Schools." In *Crosscultural Case Studies of Teaching Controversial Issues: Pathways and Challenges to Democratic Citizenship Education*, edited by Thomas Misco and Jan De Groof, 14–47. Oisterwijk, Netherlands: Wolf, 2014.

McAvoy, Paula, and Gregory E. McAvoy. "Can Debate and Deliberation Reduce Partisan Divisions? Evidence from a Study of High School Students." *Peabody Journal of Education* 96, no. 3 (2021): 275–284.

McCullough, Alan, Felton Morrell Jr., Bernard Thomas, Vicente Waugh, Nicholas Shubert, and Amy Donofrio. "The EVAC Movement Story: Why Youth Storytelling Is Powerful . . . and Why It's Dangerous." *Harvard Educational Review* 90, no. 2 (2020): 195–228.

McGrew, Sarah, Teresa Ortega, Joel Breakstone, and Sam Wineburg. "The Challenge That's Bigger than Fake News: Civic Reasoning in a Social Media Environment." *American Educator* 41, no. 3 (2017): 4–9.

McGrew, Sarah, and Virginia Byrne. "Who Is Behind This?: Preparing High School Students to Evaluate Online Content." *Journal of Research on Technology in Education* 53, no. 4 (2020): 457–475.

McLogan, Jennifer. "Rep. George Santos' Constituents Feel Left in Limbo as Congressman Faces New Allegations." CBS News, last modified January 30, 2023.

McNeill, Erin. *U.S. Media Literacy Policy Update 2021*. Watertown, MA: Media Literacy Now, 2022.

Middaugh, Ellen. "More than Just the Facts: Promoting Literacy in the Era of Outrage." *Peabody Journal of Education* 94, no. 1 (2019): 17–31.

Miller, Christian. *Honesty: The Philosophy and Psychology of a Neglected Virtue*. Oxford: Oxford University Press, 2021.

Miller, Christian. "The Virtue of Honesty Requires More than Just Telling the Truth." Aeon, December 13, 2021. https://psyche.co/ideas/more-than-just-truth-telling-honesty-is-a-virtue-to-cultivate.

Mirra, Nicole, and Antero Garcia. "Civic Participation Reimagined: Youth Interrogation and Innovation in the Multimodal Public Sphere." *Review of Research in Education* 41, no. 1 (2017): 136–158. https://doi.org/10.3102/0091732X17690121.

Misak, Cheryl. "Making Disagreement Matter: Pragmatism and Deliberative Democracy." *Journal of Speculative Philosophy* 18, no. 1 (2004): 9–22.

Misak, Cheryl. "Pragmatism on Solidarity, Bullshit, and other Deformities of Truth." *Midwest Studies in Philosophy* 32, no. 1 (2008): 111–121.

Monte-Sano, Chauncey, and Abby Reisman. "Studying Historical Understanding." In *Handbook of Educational Psychology,* 3rd ed., edited by Lyn Corno and Eric M. Anderman, 281–294. New York: Routledge, 2015.

Moore, Elena. "The First Gen Z Candidates Are Running for Congress—and Running Against Compromise." NPR, last modified July 6, 2022. https://www.npr.org/2022/07/06/1109193929/the-first-gen-z-candidates-are-running-for-congress-and-running-against-compromi.

Mouffe, Chantal. *Deliberative Democracy or Agonistic Pluralism*. Vienna: Institute for Advanced Studies, 2000.

Mouffe, Chantal. *On the Political*. New York: Routledge, 2005.

Mouffe, Chantal. *For a Left Populism*. New York: Verso, 2018.

Mudde, Cass, and Cristobal Kaltwasser. *Populism: A Very Short Introduction*. Oxford: Oxford University Press, 2017.

National Council for the Social Studies. "Position Statement: Powerful and Purposeful Teaching and Learning in Elementary School Social Studies." *Social Education* 73, no. 5 (2009): 252–254.

National Association of Scholars. "The Civics Alliance: Open Letter and Curriculum Statement." Last modified March 22, 2021. https://www.nas.org/blogs/article/the-civics-alliance-open-letter-and-curriculum-statement.

Naylor, Brian. "Read Trump's Jan. 6 Speech, a Key Part of Impeachment Trial." NPR, last modified February 10, 2021. https://www.npr.org/2021/02/10/966396848/read-trumps-jan-6-speech-a-key-part-of-impeachment-trial.

New Jersey Education Association. "Discussing Controversial Topics in the Classroom." Last modified February 28, 2021. https://www.njea.org/discussing-controversial-top

ics-in-the-classroom/#:~:text=Whenever%20a%20controversial%20topic%20is,appropriat ely%20while%20respecting%20other%20ideas.

Nguyen, C. Thi. "Escape the Echo Chamber." Aeon, April 9, 2018. https://aeon.co/essays/why-its-as-hard-to-escape-an-echo-chamber-as-it-is-to-flee-a-cult.

Nishiyama, Kei. "Democratic Education in the Fourth Generation of Deliberative Democracy." *Theory and Research in Education* 19, no. 2 (2021): 109–126.

Obama, Barack. "Why Obama Fears for Our Democracy." Interview by Jeffrey Goldberg. *The Atlantic*, last modified November 19, 2020. https://www.theatlantic.com/ideas/archive/2020/11/why-obama-fearsfor-our-democracy/617087/.

O'Brien, Karen, Elin Selboe, and Bronwyn M. Hayward. "Exploring Youth Activism on Climate Change." *Ecology and Society* 23, no. 3 (2018): 42–55.

Pace, Judith L., and Wayne Journell. "Why Controversial Issues Must Still Be Taught in U.S. Classrooms." EdSource, last modified November 2, 2021. https://edsource.org/2021/why-controversial-issues-must-still-be-taught-in-u-s-classrooms/663103.

Pedwell, Carolyn. *Revolutionary Routines: The Habits of Social Transformation*. Montreal: McGill-Queen's University Press, 2021.

Pelter, Zoë. "Pandemic Participation: Youth Activism Online in the COVID-19 Crisis." UNICEF Office of Global Insight and Policy, last modified April 14, 2020. https://www.uni cef.org/globalinsight/stories/pandemic-participation-youth-activism-online-covid-19-crisis.

Pennycook, Gordon, Ziv Epstein, Mohsen Mosely, Antonio Arechar, Dean Eckles, and David Rand. "Understanding and Reducing the Spread of Misinformation Online." In NA-Advances in Consumer Research, vol. 48, edited by Jennifer Argo, Tina M. Lowrey, and Hope Jensen Schau, 863–867. Duluth, MN: Association for Consumer Research, 2020.

Petrie, Margaret, Callum McGregor, and Jim Crowther. "Populism, Democracy and a Pedagogy of Renewal." *International Journal of Lifelong Education* 38, no. 5 (2019): 493.

Philanthropy for Active Civic Engagement. "Language Perceptions Project." April 19, 2019. http://www.pacefunders.org/wp-content/uploads/2019/05/PACE-Language-Perception-Project_May-16.pdf.

Pierre, Joseph M. "Mistrust and Misinformation: A Two-Component, Socio-Epistemic Model of Belief in Conspiracy Theories." *Journal of Social and Political Psychology* 8, no. 2 (2020): 617–641.

Porter, Steven L., and Jason Baehr. "Becoming Honest: Why We Lie and What Can Be Done About it." In *Integrity, Honesty, and Truth Seeking*, edited by Christian B. Miller and Ryan West, 182–206. New York: Oxford University Press, 2020.

Project Zero. "Digital Civics Toolkit." 2018. https://pz.harvard.edu/resources/digital-civics-toolkit.

Rahn, Wendy. *Populism in the US: The evolution of the Trump Constituency*. New York: Routledge, 2018.

Rathje, Steve, Jon Roozenbeek, Jay J. Van Bavel, and Sander van der Linden. "Accuracy and Social Motivations Shape Judgements of (Mis)information." *Nature Human Behaviour* 7 (2023): 892–903. https://www.nature.com/articles/s41562-023-01540-w.

Rauch, Jonathan. *The Constitution of Knowledge: A Defense of Truth*. Washington D.C.: Brookings Institution Press, 2021.

Reisman, Abby. "Reading Like a Historian: A Document-Based History Curriculum Intervention in Urban High Schools." *Cognition and Instruction* 30, no. 1 (2012): 86–112.

Ridley, David. *The Method of Democracy: John Dewey's Theory of Collective Intelligence*. Bern: Peter Lang, 2021.

Ritchart, Rob, Mark Church, et al. *The Power of Making Thinking Visible*. New York: Jossey-Bass, 2020.

Roberts, Robert C., and Ryan West. "The Virtue of Honesty: A Conceptual Exploration." In *Integrity, Honesty, and Truth Seeking*, edited by Christian B. Miller and Ryan West, 97–126. New York: Oxford University Press, 2020.

Rorty, Richard. "Is Truth a Goal of Enquiry?" *Philosophical Quarterly* 45, no. 180 (1995): 281–300.

Rosenfeld, Sophia. *Democracy and Truth: A Short History*. Philadelphia: University of Pennsylvania Press, 2018.

Ruitenberg, Claudia W. "Educating Political Adversaries: Chantal Mouffe and Radical Democratic Citizenship Education." *Studies in Philosophy and Education* 28, no. 3 (2009): 269–281.

Russell, Jacob Hale. "Post-Truth and the Rhetoric of 'Following the Science.'" *Critical Review: A Journal of Politics and Society*, August 2023, 122–147.

Saetra, Emil. "Discussing Controversial Issues in the Classroom: Elements of Good Practice." *Scandinavian Journal of Education Research* 65, no. 2 (2021): 345–357. https://doi-org.uc.idm.oclc.org/10.1080/00313831.2019.1705897.

Sandel, Michael, *Justice: A Reader*. New York: Oxford University Press, 2007.

Sant, Edda. *Political Education in Times of Populism: Towards a Radical Democratic Education*. London: Palgrave Macmillan, 2021.

Santarelli, Matteo, and Just Serrano-Zamora. "The Affective Side of Political Identities: Pragmatism, Populism and European Social Theory." In *Pragmatism and Social Philosophy*, edited by Michael Festl, 248–264. Milton Park, UK: Routledge, 2020.

Sawchuk, Stephen. "Student School Board Members Flex Their Civic Muscle in Supreme Court Free-Speech Case." *Education Week*, last modified April 7, 2021. https://www.edweek.org/policy-politics/student-school-board-members-flex-their-civic-muscle-in-supreme-court-free-speech-case/2021/04.

Schkade, David, Cass R. Sunstein, and Reid Hastie. "When Deliberation Produces Extremism." *Critical Review* 22, nos. 2–3 (2010): 227–252.

Schneider, Jack, Eric Soto-Shed, and Karalyn McGovern. "Teaching Students to Be Skilled Citizens." *Kappan* 104, no. 8 (2023): 47–51.

Schwartz, Sarah. "Map: Where Critical Race Theory Is Under Attack." *Education Week*, last modified February 3, 2023. https://www.edweek.org/policy-politics/map-where-critical-race-theory-is-under-attack/2021/06.

Schwörer, Jakob. *The Growth of Populism in the Political Mainstream: The Contagion Effect of Populist Messages on Mainstream Parties' Communication*. Cham, Switzerland: Springer, 2021.

Scullion, Richard, and Stuart Armon. "Democracy in a DeCivilizing Age: The Rise of Shameless Personal Truths." *International Journal of Media and Cultural Politics* 14, no. 3 (2018): 283–300.

Seemiller, Corey, and Meghan Grace. *Generation Z: A Century in the Making*. New York: Routledge, 2018.

Serrano-Zamora, Just. "What Kind of Epistemology Is Required for Democratic Renewal?" Open Conference on the Future of Deliberation: Exploring Political, Social, and Epistemic Control, University of Iceland EDDA Research Center, June 3, 2023.

Serrano-Zamora, Just, and Matteo Santarelli. "Experts and Citizens in the Times of COVID-19: A Deweyan Perspective." *Dewey Studies* 6, no. 1 (2022): 378–415.

Sim, Stuart. *A Call to Dissent: Defending Democracy Against Extremism and Populism*. Edinburgh: Edinburgh University Press, 2022.

Smith, Barrett, and Sarah M. Stitzlein. "Classroom Conflict, 'Divisive Concepts,' and Educating for Democracy." In *Who's Afraid of Political Education: The Challenge to Teach Civic Competence & Democratic Participation*, edited by Henry Tam, 35–49. Bristol, UK: Bristol University Press, 2023.

Stanford Encyclopedia of Philosophy. "Pragmatism." https://plato.stanford.edu/entries/pragmatism/.

Stern, Jeremy A., et al. *State of State Standards for Civics and U.S. History in 2021.* Washington DC: Thomas B. Fordham Institute, 2021. https://fordhaminstitute.org/national/research/state-state-standards-civics-and-us-history-2021.

Stitzlein, Sarah M. *American Public Education and the Responsibility of Its Citizens.* New York: Oxford University Press, 2017.

Stitzlein, Sarah M. *Breaking Bad Habits: Transforming Identity in Schools.* Lanham, MD: Rowman & Littlefield, 2008.

Stitzlein, Sarah M. "Children as Citizens." *Philosophy of Education Society* 78, no. 3 (2022): 126–133.

Stitzlein, Sarah M. "Defining and Implementing Civic Reasoning and Discourse: Philosophical and Moral Foundations for Research and Practice," In *Educating for Civic Reasoning and Discourse*, edited by Carol D. Lee, Gregory White, and Dian Dong, 23–52. Washington, DC: National Academy of Education, 2021. https://naeducation.org/educating-for-civic-reasoning-and-discourse/.

Stitzlein, Sarah M. "Democratic Education in an Era of Town Hall Protests." *Theory and Research in Education* 9, no. 4 (2011): 73–86.

Stitzlein, Sarah M. "Divisive Concepts in Classrooms: A Call to Inquiry." *Studies in Philosophy and Education* 41 (2022): 595–612.

Stitzlein, Sarah M. *Learning How to Hope: Reviving Democracy Through Our Schools and Civil Society.* New York: Oxford University Press, 2020.

Stitzlein, Sarah M. "Political Dissent and Citizenship Education During Times of Populism and Youth Activism." *Theory and Research in Education* 20, no. 3 (2022): 217–236.

Stitzlein, Sarah M. "Populist Challenges to Truth and Democracy met with Pragmatism Alternatives in Citizenship Education." *Educational Theory* 74, no. 5 (2024).

Stitzlein, Sarah M. *Teaching for Dissent: Citizenship Education and Political Activism.* New York: Routledge, 2014.

Stitzlein, Sarah M. "Teaching Honesty and Improving Democracy in the Post-Truth Era." *Educational Theory* 73, no. 1 (2023): 51–73.

Stitzlein, Sarah M. "Using Civic Participation and Civic Reasoning to Shape our Future and Education." United Nations Educational, Scientific, and Cultural Organization Educational Futures. Part of the International Commission on the Futures of Education chaired by the President of Ethiopia, 2020.

Swan, Kathy, et al. *College, Career, and Civic Life (C3) Social Studies State Standards.* Silver Spring, MD: National Council for the Social Studies, 2013. https://www.socialstudies.org/standards/c3.

Talisse, Robert. *Overdoing Democracy.* Oxford University Press, 2021.

Teachers College Newsroom. "Hearing the Other Side of the Story." Last modified 2021. https://www.tc.columbia.edu/articles/2021/march/a-new-webinar-series-on-teaching-controversial-topics/.

Temple-Raston, Dina. "A Tale of 2 Radicalizations." NPR, last modified March 15, 2021. https://www.npr.org/2021/03/15/972498203/a-tale-of-2-radicalizations.

Thoilliez, Bianca. "'Making Education Possible Again': Pragmatist Experiments for a Troubled and Down-to-Earth Pedagogy." *Educational Theory* 72, no. 4 (2022): 1–17.

Tillson, John. "When to Teach for Belief: A Tempered Defense of the Epistemic Criterion." *Educational Theory* 67, no. 2 (2017): 173–191. https://doi-org.uc.idm.oclc.org/10.1111/edth.12241.

Trump, Donald. Inaugural Address, January 20, 2017. https://www.govinfo.gov/content/pkg/CREC-2017-01-20/pdf/CREC-2017-01-20-pt1-PgS362-4.pdf.

"Trump Gives Remarks at White House History Conference at National Archives Museum in DC." *PBS NewsHour*, September 17, 2020. https://www.youtube.com/watch?v=Pd9j Q2KY4fs.

Tryggvason, Asgeir. "Democratic Education and Agonism: Exploring the Critique from Deliberative Theory." *Democracy and Education* 26, no. 1 (2018): 1–9.

Tully, James. *Public Philosophy in a New Key*, 2nd edition. Cambridge: Cambridge University Press, 2008.

Turner, Corey. "School Principals Say Culture Wars Made Last Year 'Rough as Hell.'" NPR, last modified December 1, 2022. https://www.npr.org/2022/12/01/1139685828/schools-democracy-misinformation-purple-state.

VanSledright, Bruce. "What Does It Mean to Think Historically . . . and How Do You Teach It?" In *Social Studies Today: Research and Practice*, 2nd ed., edited by Walter C. Parker, 138–146. New York: Routledge, 2015.

van Zoonen, Liesbet. "I-Pistemology: Changing Truth Claims in Popular and Political Culture." *European Journal of Communication* 27, no. 1 (2012): 56–67.

Waisbord, Silvio. "The Elective Affinity Between Post-Truth Communication and Populist Politics." *Communication Research and Practice* 4, no. 1 (2018): 17–34.

Warnick, Bryan, Douglas Yacek, and Shannon Robinson. "Learning to Be Moved: The Modes of Democratic Responsiveness." *Philosophical Inquiry in Education* 25, no. 1 (2018): 31–46.

Warnick, Bryan, and D. Spencer Smith. "The Controversy over Controversies: A Plea for Flexibility and for 'Soft-Directive' Teaching." *Educational Theory* 64, no. 3 (2014): 227–244. https://doi-org.uc.idm.oclc.org/10.1111/edth.12059.

Welch, Kirsten. "Misplaced Tolerance and Educating for Intellectual Humility." *Educational Theory* 71, no. 6 (2021): 681–702.

Westheimer, Joel, and Joseph Kahne. "What Kind of Citizen? The Politics of Educating for Democracy." *American Educational Research Journal* 41, no. 2 (2004): 237–269.

Westoff, Laura M. "The Popularization of Knowledge: John Dewey on Experts and American Democracy." *History of Education Quarterly* 35, no. 1 (1995): 34.

Williams, Bernard. *Truth & Truthfulness: An Essay in Genealogy*. Princeton, NJ: Princeton University Press, 2002.

Wineburg, Samuel S. *Historical Thinking and Other Unusual Acts: Charting the Future of Teaching the Past*. Philadelphia: Temple University Press, 2002.

Woodley, Deva. *Reckoning: Black Lives Matter and the Democratic Necessity of Social Movements*. Oxford: Oxford University Press, 2022.

Yacek, Douglas. "Should Anger Be Encouraged in the Classroom? Political Education, Closed-Mindedness, and Civic Epiphany." *Educational Theory* 69, no. 4 (2019): 421–437.

Yang, Seo Yoon. "I Arranged a Protest at My High School. The Reactionary Racist Attacks Changed Me." Daily Kos, last modified August 17, 2020. https://www.dailykos.com/stories/2020/8/17/1969290/-I-arranged-a-protest-at-my-high-school-The-reactionary-racist-attacks-changed-me.

Young, Iris Marion. *Justice and the Politics of Difference*. Princeton, NJ: Princeton University Press, 1991.

Young, Iris Marion. "Activist Challenges to Deliberative Democracy." *Political Theory* 29, no. 5 (2001): 670–690.

Youth in Front. "Understanding and Supporting Student-Led Activism." Accessed February 8, 2023. https://www.youthinfront.org/student/collection/744064-understanding-and-supporting-student-led-activism.

Zadrozny, Brandy. "'Carol's Journey': What Facebook Knew About How It Radicalized Users." NBC News, last modified October 26, 2021. https://www.nbcnews.com/tech/tech-news/facebook-knew-radicalized-users-rcna3581.

Zagzebski, Linda. *Exemplarist Moral Theory*. Oxford: Oxford University Press, 2017.

Zembylas, Michalinos. *Affect and the Rise of Right-Wing Populism: Pedagogies for the Renewal of Democratic Education*. Cambridge: Cambridge University Press, 2021. https://www.cambridge.org/core/books/affect-and-the-rise-of-rightwing-populism/226FA89E047395044B4B09EEA9E0324B

Zembylas, Michalinos. "The Affective Grounding of Post-Truth: Pedagogical Risks and Transformative Possibilities in Countering Post-Truth Claims." *Pedagogy, Culture and Society* 28, no. 1 (2020): 77–92.

Zembylas, Michalinos. "Dewey's Account of Habit Through the Lens of Affect Theory." *Educational Theory* 71, no. 6 (2021): 767–786.

Zembylas, Michalinos. "Interrogating the Affective Politics of White Victimhood and Resentment in Times of Demagoguery: The Risks for Civics Education." *Studies in Philosophy and Education* 40, no. 6 (2021): 579–594.

Zheng, Jiawen. "Motivated Open-Mindedness: Rectify Biased Perceptions in Preparation for Deliberation." *Communication and the Public* 1, no. 2 (2016): 193–210.

Zimmerman, Jonathan, and Emily Robertson. *The Case for Contention*. Chicago: University of Chicago Press, 2017.

Index

For the benefit of digital users, indexed terms that span two pages (e.g., 52–53) may, on occasion, appear on only one of those pages.

Tables, figures, and boxes are indicated by *t*, *f*, and *b* following the page number